Ronsard

PRINCE OF POETS

(((((((((((((((((((((((❋)))))))))))))))))))))))

Ronsard

PRINCE OF POETS

By

MORRIS BISHOP

(((((((((((((((((((((((❋)))))))))))))))))))))))

OXFORD UNIVERSITY PRESS

London   New York   Toronto

1940

Acknowledgments

OUR knowledge of Ronsard is in large part due to the work of Professor Paul Laumonier, of the University of Bordeaux. In his youth M. Laumonier consecrated himself to Ronsard's fame ; he has spent his life in that service, and his task is not yet done. To M. Laumonier's studies my obligation is too great for any adequate expression.

If any one should be persuaded by this book to read a more compendious life of Ronsard, he should begin with M. Pierre Champion's *Ronsard et son temps.* The reader will recognize, I fear, my own constant indebtedness to that magisterial work. I have availed myself also of the writings of many other modern *Ronsardisants,* especially Pierre de Nolhac, Jules Jusserand, Gustave Cohen, Henri Chamard, Joseph Vianey, Henri Longnon, and Jean Martellière.

In my quotations of Ronsard's poetry, I have modernized the spelling and punctuation, wherever I could do so without interfering with the laws of French prosody.

I would acknowledge especially the aid given me by Miss Annie Cameron (Mrs. G. B. Dunlop) in the search of Scottish archives, and by Mr. Gilbert M. Weeks. And I should like to recall the common labors of a Seminary in Cornell University, in 1937-8. These were the members of our *Brigade* : Arthur Bates, Katherine Benton, Jean Botsford, LeRoy Breunig, John Chamberlain, Helen Euler, Bernard Goldstein, Mary McCormack, Philip Nolan, Glen Shortliffe, Frank Untermyer, Charles Wahl, Charlotte Walker, and Edith Babiy.

Contents

Ronsard

PRINCE OF POETS

A Manor in the Vendômois

A HUNDRED miles southwest of Paris is the Vendômois. To journey there is to leave the calamitous present for a changeless land, where the seasons govern, where life seems only an attribute of the earth. It is a serene and ancient country, heedless of time. There man builds houses to outlast him for centuries, and makes songs that will outlast his houses. There the homesick spirit finds peace, which men's malevolence cannot trouble long.

From the old Roman city of Vendôme one descends the placid Loir, winding through a broad valley cut in a great plateau. The curves of the valley are soft and slow. Nature poses here, to display her voluptuous lines. One follows the Roman way to Montoire, crossing the pilgrim road to Saint Martin of Tours, trodden since the fifth century. The little Loir flows on, under the guard of crumbling towers, to its junction with the tinier Braye. Here is Couture, a huddle of plastered houses around a small stone church.

A mile to the south, where the valley steps up to the plateau, stands the manor of La Possonnière. It was of old the residence of the family of Ronsard. The house, like the family, ruled the forest and the tilth. The Ronsards were for centuries superintendents, fieffed sergeants, of the widespread woodland of Gastine. They

3

built their house with its back to the dark trees, and its face to the ploughed lands of their seigniory.

In the great bedroom of this house, during the night between Saturday and Sunday, September 10 and 11, 1524, the noble lady Jeanne Chaudrier, wife to the noble man Louis de Ronsard, lay in travail. She groaned upon her high canopied and curtained bed, awaiting the fulfilment of the mystery, consisting, like the Eucharist itself, in oblation, invocation, the miracle of life, thanksgiving, and ablution. The wavering light of beeswax tapers made grotesque her agony's grimaces. The sealed room was pungent with spices burning in a brazier. A cluster of women stood about the bed, whispering their reminiscences of many another child-bed. The husband was not present ; with the three children, he knelt in the little chapel across the courtyard, while the village priest prayed for a happy issue out of all afflictions.

The recurring pains of the woman on the bed fused to a single great pain which escaped in screams from her body. The midwife recognized the moment. She tossed to the floor the wolfskins on the bed, pulled back the white wool coverlet, and with her aides slipped the quaking woman to a sitting position in the obstetrical chair. So Pierre de Ronsard was born.

Scissors snipped. The midwife took the boy, and washed him in a tub of warm water. She worked his fingers and limbs, to chase any lingering evil humors. She rubbed him with salt and with honey, to dry and comfort his members. She laid him on a little bed of rose-leaves mashed with salt. She dipped her finger in honey, and cleaned therewith his palate and gums. She filled her mouth with the good wine of the Loir, and expelled a few drops into the baby's wailing mouth.

The rites of childbirth were completed. The father was admitted to see and to admire his son, before he should be bound in swaddling clothes, which keep the limbs straight and the head shaped properly.

On the day following his birth, the child was borne to the parish church of Couture for his christening. The procession left the road and turned across a field, the, short way to the church. And the lady who carried little Pierre stumbled and fell. 'When I was barely born,' he was wont to say, 'I almost saw myself ravished away by the Fates.' But he seems to have taken no injury. The family liked to recall the accident ; after his death it was embellished, to become a pretty legend. According to his adoring friend and biographer, he fell among flowers, which received him gently ; and a lady carrying a jug of rose-water sprang to his aid, and spilled the perfume on his head. 'And this was a presage of the sweet odors with which he was to fill all of France, by the flowers of his writings.' This is the story still soberly told in the village of Couture, where your peasant guide will point out to you the *pré Bouju,* and the very clump of roses where the day-old Ronsard fell.

The child survived the perils Nature sets for infancy, and the greater perils contrived by ignorance and country lore. Playing with his brother and sister, agape at his mother's knee, he learned the story of his house and the pride proper to its youngest member.

The family fondly cherished a romantic genealogy. It was asserted that a Balkan count, by name Ross-hart, had come to France in the fourteenth century, and had so well served Philippe de Valois that he was granted a fief in the Vendômois. But it is clear that the Ronsards, whose name is allied to *roncier,* bramble-bush, had dwelt for centuries in the land where we find them.

Perhaps they were descended from the Celtic, druidical tribe of the Carnutes, forest-men, bound by mystical ties to this region of the Loir. The Ronsards were gentry, possessing some small eminence by their hereditary post as superintendents of the forest. They were related to half the gentlefolk of the Vendômois.

Pierre's grandfather and father struggled to attain more eminence than they were born to, favor at court, and an increase of property. In 1494, when Pierre's father, Louis de Ronsard, was fifteen, he enrolled under Louis d'Orléans, the king's brother, and was assigned to the naval patrol off the Genoese coast. He fought on sea and land, and ate cats and rats at the siege of Novara. During the intervals of warfare he learned the usages of the courts. He returned from the Italian campaigns with the precious order of Saint Michael and the favor of Louis d'Orléans, who became King Louis XII. He gained also tangible profits, and as well a taste for the new Italian art and culture. In 1518 he was given the important post of steward to the baby Dauphin, son of King François I.

The boy Pierre saw little of his father during his formative years. For in 1526, when Pierre was two years old, the father was summoned to an urgent and ominous task. King François I had been taken prisoner by the Spanish at the battle of Pavia, and had bought his freedom only by surrendering his two sons as hostages in his place. Louis de Ronsard accompanied little François, eleven years old, and Henri, nine, into their Spanish durance. The unkind Emperor Charles V separated the royal children from all their train, even from their doctor and nurse. Their steward, Louis de Ronsard, was imprisoned in Medina del Campo and at Villalpando. When, after some time, he was permitted pen and ink, he employed his disconsolate leisure in writing poetry, and a rhymed treatise on heraldic devices.

In 1530 the children and their servitors were repatriated. Louis de Ronsard may have paused on the journey from Spain to see his home and his children, for the first time in four years.

Even after the return to France, there was little communication between father and son, for Louis followed the court until his death in 1544. But even an absent father can exert some influence. Louis was a man of artistic taste and poetic culture. The decoration of his house expressed his character, the new spirit of half-pagan enlightenment he had brought from Italy. He was himself a versifier, and a friend of certain professional verse-makers of his time. Pierre de Ronsard, in his old age, liked to recite examples of his father's art. But not a line of it remains for our judgment.

Louis de Ronsard's worldly success brought him a wife of higher standing and of greater wealth than a mere country squire could have pretended to. Jeanne Chaudrier came of one of the oldest and best-connected families of Poitou. She possessed the outright, headstrong humor of old and well-connected families. Her father died about 1498, leaving the motherless Jeanne and her child sister as heirs to his lands. Jeanne must have been sixteen or seventeen years old. Her uncle, seeing his opportunity, took possession of her fiefs. Jeanne's loud protests came to the ears of King Louis XII, who consigned her to the care of her grandmother, pending the outcome of the case. Jeanne trusted her grandmother no more than her uncle ; she chose her own warder, a certain Jacques de Fontbernier, seigneur de la Rivière. In disguise she escaped to her Jacques.

The two were clandestinely married, and lived happily together for the space of two months. The king then vindicated his flouted authority by summoning the bridegroom and forcing him to sign a renunciation of his marriage. The bride resumed her bedraggled snood of maidenhood. But not for long. When she won her suit and her lands, suitors pressed forward, attracted by her wealth and perhaps by her evidence of spirit. She married Guy des Roches, seigneur de la Basme. He gave her a son, and died. After a proper interval, she wed Louis de Ronsard, a step below her in rank, but a coming man, high in the king's favor. For her he built La Possonnière. (Unless, by a reversal of cause and effect, he chose her as a suitable mistress for his fine house a-building.) The marriage contract was signed on February 2, 1515. Though Jeanne was 33 or 34, she had still time to present her husband with seven children, of whom three died in infancy.

What sort of mother was she to the young poet ? Evidently she was bold and self-willed ; evidently she ruled well her house and her farms. But was she kind, loving, understanding, comforting ? There is a hint that Ronsard had no happy memories of her, or he chose not to think of her, for he, who loved to dwell upon his own affairs and those of his friends, never once, in all his works, mentions his mother.

She had, no doubt, little time for him. He was the youngest of the four surviving children. He was born when the mother was forty-two, and perhaps impatient of child-bearing. Claude, the first-born son, the heir, received as his due the fullness of her love and pride. In her husband's constant absences, she assumed the burden and the feudal duties of a large house and wide-spreading lands. Her days were filled with administration, with endless disputes with her vassals and her lords. Hide and scutage, seizin and fee occupied her thoughts, to the exclusion of the problems of child-rearing. Pierre grew up under the tutelage of nurses and governors, with the companionship of the two older brothers and the sister. With them he explored the little world of La Possonnière.

One entered the château from the village side, under the view of two towers, part of a medieval defensive system which served Louis de Ronsard as a quarry for his new buildings. The Middle Ages had based their architecture on fear, not on display. Even in the new Renaissance manor, fear showed its blind face. The outer wall of La Possonnière had few apertures or none at all; there was no need to tempt an enemy with a crossbow or a blazing torch. One passed into the interior court through a low, wide gate surmounted by a Gothic arch and by a single story with its rooms.

One stood then in a rectangular space, securely walled on four sides. The forbidding face of the exterior was not needed here. The builder could indulge his fancy, and make a home for happy people in security. On the north side rose the main building, the quarters of the Ronsard family. It was, and is today, a graceful and comely structure, ornamented with the Italian elegance Louis de Ronsard loved. Enormous windows, symbols of Renaissance enlightenment, open to the southern sun. The grace of the façade is marred, but the charm of incongruousness is enhanced, by a pentagonal medieval tower, out-topping the roof-line, and bearing, beneath its crown, a richly ornamented Renaissance window. The old tower peers abroad like an ancient bedizened patrician of Antonio Moro or Titian.

At the base of the tower opens a narrow door giving

access to the spiral staircase contained within. Over the door is an elaborately carved Italian lintel, with the inscribed dedication of the house : VOLVPTATI ET GRATIIS, to pleasure and the Graces. A shield, a part of the decoration, bears the arms of the Ronsards, three entwined fish called *rosses,* the English red-eye or rudd.

The high window in the tower has the inscription : DOMÎ OCUL. LONGE SPEC., for *Domini oculus longe speculatur,* the master's eye sees far. Between two of the windows of the façade is carved a wild rose bush, licked by flames, to signify *ronce ard,* the brambles burn, a punning derivation of the master's name. Elsewhere on the façade the eye catches the words : AVANT PARTIR, before we depart ; and RESPICE FINEM, look to the end ; and VERITAS FILIA TEMPORIS, truth the daughter of time ; and DNE CONCERVA ME, God save me. Here was matter for a child to spell and meditate upon.

The east side of the courtyard was formed by one of those natural, nearly perpendicular walls common in the Vendômois, where ancient streams have cut and quarried the soft tufa underlying all the region. In this yielding stone Louis, or some Ronsard before him, dug a series of eight caves. Each is marked by an appropriate motto. The first is surcharged, LA BVANDERIE BELLE, the pretty laundry ; the second, LA FOVRIERE, the hayloft, with two hay-bundles grossly carved ; the third, VVLCANO ET DILIGENTIAE, to Vulcan and diligence, with three kettles to make the meaning clear ; the fourth, VINA BARBARA, *vins ordinaires,* or possibly, wines from afar, superior wines ; the fifth, a jug and two glasses, and CVI DES VIDETO, look well to whom thou givest, an ungenerous motto for the storage-place of delicacies ; the sixth, CVSTODIA DAPVM, the food-cellar ; the seventh, mysteriously, SVSTINE ET ABSTINE, bear and forbear,

Epictetus's counsel, perhaps addressed ironically to prisoners whom the cavern quartered ; and the eighth, Tibi
Soli Gloria, to Thee alone the glory, the sign of a
chapel or oratory.

The south side of the court consisted of farm-build-
ings, which have now disappeared. In the southwest
angle stood a small chapel. The west side was closed by
a crenelated wall, with a continuous step along its top,
for communication or for defense.

Of the interior of the manor-house, not much has
survived an outrageous century, from about 1750 to
1850, when the building served as farmers' quarters.
There is the noble fireplace of the great hall, all carved
stone up to the lofty ceiling, and the masterpiece of
Louis de Ronsard's Italian sculptors. Viol and lute, the
attributes of poetry, enclose the main panel, which represents the burning wild rose bushes of the Ronsards.
Out of the flame emerges the family shield, and the con-
fident device : Non Falvnt Fvtvra Merentem, the future shall not fail the well-deserving. Above, a stone
banner sown with fleurs-de-lis, surrounding the shield
of France. And over all, the escutcheons of forty families allied to the master's line.

In the room which was apparently Louis de Ronsard's
office and study is another carven fireplace, with cupids,
stars, suns, heraldic beasts, viols, and lutes, and the device : Nyqvit Nymis, dog-Latin for the ancient rule,
nothing in excess.

So much remains ; enough to permit us, with a little
antiquarian goodwill, to restore the routine of a country day.

The stirring of the household woke the boy Pierre at
dawn. He lay in his truckle-bed and stared at the light-
ening gloom of his mother's high bedroom. He pon-

dered on the familiar patterns of the ostentatious bed, the *lit de parade*. He picked out the elaborate scroll-work of its oaken frame, the clumsy beasts portrayed on its tapestried curtains. There was nothing else in the room to hold his interest, only a table, a stool or two, and a great carved oaken chest.

A maidservant entered with a draught of white wine, to rouse the châtelaine to her day's duties. The noble lady pulled back her bed-curtains, and sat up, naked, tousle-headed, showing her remaining teeth in a yellow yawn.

Pierre crept from bed, slipped on his coarse linen shift, his small doublet and hose. He eased his night's surplus in the warm hearth. He cleaned his teeth with a capon's spur, and, if the need were urgent, washed his hands. He combed his hair back from the forehead, to send backward the humors, which descend by preference over the eyes and face. His toilet was completed.

If a priest, uncle Jean or another, was available, mass was celebrated in the manor chapel. Otherwise the household walked to the parish church of Couture. Their way took them through fields of wheat or stubble, rimmed by files of poplars, stripped of their lower branches and holding high their balls of mistletoe with slim fingers. On the slopes writhed the stumpy vines, clipped to the very blood. They came thus to the cottages of Couture, squatting like partridges at a field's edge. Thin smoke rose above the slate roofs mottled with brown. The lingering smell of night was disturbed by the prickling odor of *sarments,* close-bound vine-clippings, burning in the cottage hearths.

The château party entered the village church, with hardly a glance at its admirable early Gothic tower. Like any peasants, they dropped their sabots at the door, and scuffed down the aisle in slippers. From the seignioral seats directly before the altar, Pierre, shivering with the church's damp, quaking with his fast, watched the priest at his miracle. The surpliced back bowed and dipped, moved from side to side, sank to earth and rose again. Three steps to the left, one back. The grubby hands moved swiftly in the sacred business, took the stiff postures of Byzantine frescoes. The priest turned to face the worshippers, and Pierre bowed to the holy presence. The mutter of Latin ceased suddenly. At the sharp jingle of the sacring-bell Pierre crossed himself, in the fear of God.

Then home, between the high hawthorn hedges of the lane, or gayly across the fields to La Possonnière. The family sat at the long kitchen table to a light breakfast, designed to scour the stomach : a sheep's foot, or a bit of salt meat, with bread and a pot of white wine, diluted for the children's weakness.

The kitchen was the centre of manorial life. By the glow of its hearth all the activities of the day were warmed. Here the châtelaine met her farmers, vassals, and villeins, and here she did her business. Here the family took its meals, except on occasions of great show and festival. At the dinner hour, which fell about ten in the morning, all mannerly people repaired to the well, to wash their hands and to sharpen their knives on the curbing. They returned to the kitchen table, to admire the oozing roasts, the vegetables, well boiled with herbs to a common broth, the little plates of dainties and nubbins of garlic, the giant loaves of gray-brown bread from the field bakery. Dogs and chickens competed for the scraps among the rushes under the table, and kept the masters in high humor by their quarrels and frights and misadventures.

Country dinners were gay in regions of plenty. The worthy Noël du Fail, who lived through these good times and remembered them in grim years that followed, happily describes a trencherman at table. 'He would begin to laugh and salute the company on entering, saying, "God be in this house, and the monks at the devil's. Here's fine company ; God grant that a hundred years from now we may all strangle each other." After he had taken off his cloak and laid it on a chest, he would draw up to the table ; and whatever doughty eaters were present, there was none more deft than he, telling forever some tale, some modern instance, some fresh news invented on the spot, or the story of some lawsuit he was about to bring, which he would detail with such circumstances that it would redound much to his honor. And then he would say, "Give me some of this ; lend me that knife ; give me some wine to drink ; don't take that away, but serve without clearing away. God pardon such a one, for there is the bit that he liked best to eat. Of all fish except the tench, take a capon's wing. Madame, because you don't sleep well, would you like this chicken's foot ? Oh, the fine beef, I think it comes from Carhaix. Give me that pigeon, I will put it in stays. Another drop of that vinegar, my girl. Ha, the devil ! Those maidservants have let it spoil ! You aren't looking well, Madame. A little sharp sauce here wouldn't go badly. Who will put this on the spit again ? Hello, pretty hare, you are welcome, welcome. Faith, it's half raw ! Give it here, I will fix it in the style of the late Queen Gillette. What, sir, shall this remain untouched ? I am sure the first morsels make one crave more. Here, my boy, put this on the grill, and I'll marry you to my eldest daughter, with God's help ; and then give me to drink from that flagon. Gramercy, sir, I will

pledge you ; pour as if for yourself, and I will serve you
on your wedding-day. Here, my young friend, how much
could you eat of this before your ears would fall off ?
That bit wouldn't have escaped me fifteen years ago.
Oh, the good appetite, how it falls to ! 'Twould undo
the man who would tie bells to its chin, *vertu saint
Gris* ! I haven't a good tooth left. There are some who
won't eat between meals, or who eat more in the morning than after noon. I eat at all times, and feel the better
for it. Let us praise eating ; but I wouldn't give a rush
for all our eating, unless we drink. Take away that
water ; the wine is strong enough without it. In the
morning drink your wine pure, in the evening without
water. My friend, pick up that napkin ; give a churl a
napkin, he'll make stirrups of it. For fear I forget my
knife, give me to drink. I am drunk, my belly is
stretched like a corded drum, I should like to dance a
round. Pish ! If my children are proper men, they will
live ; after having adventured far, we have nothing but
the cost of it. Wine, or I'll ask for some ! After dessert,
to drink's no hurt. If woman knew an apple's worth,
she'd give one to no man on earth. Here, my good
friend, a drink for his sake and for her love. There,
sweet coz, if I have drunk to my lady yonder, she has
drunk to me. You won't die of a glass in the Breton
style. I won't leave this house with the thirst in me !" '

Commonly the Ronsard household was too busy to
welcome such ravenous guests and their time-devouring
gayety. Pierre's mother retired to her duties of manage-
ment, the children to their lessons or their play. They
had their wooden horses, which they trained to pace,
trot, rack, gallop, and amble. They played at the two
hundred and twenty-one games which Rabelais lists.
Like the genial Gargantua himself, they frollicked at

puffe, or let him speak that hath it, at the last couple
in hell, at trudgepig, at prickle me tickle me, at thrust
out the harlot, at trill madam, or grapple my Lady, at
hinch, pinch, and laugh not, at the quoits, at nine pins,
at tip and hurl, at hide and seek, or are you all hid, at
whip-top, at the soilie smutchie, at St. Cosme, I come
to adore thee, at swaggie, waggie, or shoggieshou, at the
dillie dillie darling, at blinde-man-buffe, at the fallen
bridges, at the morish dance, at bo-peep, at jog-breech,
or prick him forward.

The children roamed the fields and woods, picking
wild strawberries and the black cherries that come to
perfection at La Possonnière. They watched the brown
besmocked peasants at their innumerable labors. They
were allowed to sickle the wheat, to turn the hay, until
their small arms tired, and then, as gentry, they were
permitted to desist. They observed, with the intense
absorption of children, the vine-pruning, the sheep-
branding, the hog-gelding. When Pierre became a poet
he loved to recall such scenes, to picture the fields under
the midsummer heat, with a file of women balancing
on their heads wooden bowls for the workers' dinner,
and spinning thread from their distaffs as they walked.

The day drew on. After a massive supper the country-
men relaxed with bowling, wrestling, running and
jumping games, spear-throwing, stone-putting. The
women strolled two by two along the flowering river-
banks. So Ronsard remembered them, in the delicious
negligence of local fashion, wide-collared, bare-bosomed,
au tétin découvert. As dusk came down there was dancing on the village common, the furious leaping, hand-
clapping, finger-snapping dances of the country, such
dances as the Celtic fathers of these peasants had footed,
beneath the fathers of these oaks.

In the winter evenings, the children sat before the kitchen fire, while an elder told some long tale of witches and ogres, or of Tristan and the knights of le Roy Artus, a tale in which lingered still the cadence of forgotten verses. When some visitor of mark appeared, the salon, or *salle basse,* was opened, and ceremonial candles of beeswax and tallow lit, or even the precious lamp with its belly full of rape-seed oil. The guests sat on straw-bottomed stools, and admired the carving of the great fireplace, the tapestries lifting in the chill drafts, the staghorns hung for decoration, the crossbows, pikes, and muskets skewered on the walls for show, but prudently within reach of a hurried hand.

Then hasty prayers, and a scamper to bed, in the high windy chamber. And dreams of knightly prowess, of glittering armor, of the clang of battle. Dreams also of the great green forest of Gastine and of its misty inhabitants, half seen, half clutched.

The forest crowds against the southern wall of La Possonnière. Its secular oaks and ancient solitudes early wakened the boy's poetic imagination. Medieval wonder had peopled its shades with chimeras, unicorns, and a race of savage, hairy men, unredeemed by Christ. Little Pierre was already a child of the Renaissance. The figures he perceived, clad in the motley of sun-shafts and leaf-shadows, transforming themselves into slim white birches, were the dryads and fauns, the satyrs and sylvans, of classic tradition. In later years he would return forever to Gastine for solace and for inspiration, to his Gastine, 'mother of the demi-gods,' with her 'green mane,' her 'enverdured arms.' Trees are closer to man than anything in nature. Every forest dreamer understands readily enough the language of rustling leaves, and remembers their whispered messages.

> There, in my childhood land,
> How simply did I see
> The Muses' gentle band
> Come to companion me !

> *Et vous, riches campagnes,*
> *Où presque enfant je vis*
> *Les neuf Muses compagnes*
> *M'enseigner à l'envi.*

And when the heartless woodsmen had come, to lay waste his glades and murder his oaks :

> Farewell, Gastine, where Zephyr loved to quire,
> Where first I learned to tune the fumbling lyre,
> Where first I heard Apollo's firm-flung dart
> Ring in the tree, and echo in my heart ;
> Where first I saw Calliope divine,
> And vowed to love fore'er her sacred Nine.
> Her very hand with roses garlanded me,
> And with her very milk Euterpe fed me.

> *Adieu, vieille forêt, le jouet de Zéphyre,*
> *Où premier j'accordai les langues de ma lyre,*
> *Où premier j'entendis les flèches résonner*
> *D'Apollon, qui me vint tout le cœur étonner ;*
> *Où premier admirant la belle Calliope,*
> *Je devins amoureux de sa neuvaine trope,*
> *Quand sa main sur le front cent roses me jeta,*
> *Et de son propre lait Euterpe m'allaita.*

The Muses told him of his destiny, and in the trembling light of the forest consecrated him to poetry. So it seemed to him, when he was of an age to look back over his life. But as a boy he could not so interpret the tumultuous imaginations that possessed him when he walked or lay at length in old Gastine. The classic, and renaissance, woodfolk of whom he had read in his books greeted him and welcomed him to their home. An intolerable delight filled him, and an urge to utter his delight, to find a relief, a discharge for this oppressive beauty. He made songs, he wrote his first poems. He remembers :

> Not yet a dozen years had charged my little head,
> When in the secret caves by fear inhabited,
> And in the high dark woods, far from all human haunts,
> Careless, oblivious, I made my childish chaunts.
> And Echo answered me, the dryad leafy-clad,
> The satyr, faun, and Pan, napead, oread ;
> The hornèd aegipan among the antic crew
> Would leap a capering reel, as goats in frolic do.
> Fantastic fairy troops, my solitude espying,
> Would ring me in a dance, their undone dresses flying.

> *Je n'avais pas douze ans, qu'au profond des vallées,*
> *Dans les hautes forêts des hommes reculées,*
> *Dans les antres secrets de frayeur tout couverts,*
> *Sans avoir soin de rien je composais des vers ;*
> *Écho me répondait, et les simples Dryades,*
> *Faunes, Satyres, Pans, Napées, Oréades,*
> *Aigipans qui portaient des cornes sur le front*
> *Et qui ballant sautaient comme les chèvres font,*
> *Et les Nymphes suivant les fantastiques fées*
> *Autour de moi dansaient à cottes dégrafées.*

Never, throughout Ronsard's life, did the dryad and the faun desert him.

II

The Page of Princes

THE four Ronsard children learned their letters from a tutor, perhaps the scholarly incumbent of a near-by priory. At the age of nine, Pierre was removed from his instruction and sent to Paris to school, whether from his promise or the lack of it. His parents chose the best of academies, the Collège de Navarre, famous for its good Latin and for the aristocratic lineage of its student body. ('One meets such *nice* boys there ; so useful in later life.') Here Pierre began to learn courtly manners, and to unlearn his rustic habits. He made at least one useful friend, Charles de Guise, the future Cardinal de Lorraine, already stern and unsmiling, as he was through life. But Pierre was unhappy. He hated the school, the unending confinement, the stern discipline. The country boy was homesick for his woodlands and his liberty. His single term was 'utterly without profit,' as he confesses. His family withdrew him, determined to send no more good money after bad.

Back at La Possonnière, he resumed the life of the fields and woods. But with a difference ; his developing mind, his delight in classic story and Arcadian dream brought him a new friend. This was his uncle, Jean de Ronsard, an eminent churchman, canon of the cathedral of Le Mans, and vicar-general of his diocese. Like so many men of the cloth, he was a poet. Pierre watched him labor over his rhymes, far into the night, with a

mad but magnificent waste of candles and of oil. The
boy's gaping admiration, and his crude imitations,
touched the tuneful canon. The two were comrades.
They prowled the woods and fields together, the priest
lifting his cassock above the dew. They hunted the
aegipans and oreads, shy of the black uniform of hostile
Christ. The canon died in 1535, when Pierre was eleven.
To this youngest of his nephews and nieces he left his
large and varied library.

The happiest days in La Possonnière were those when
the father returned, on leave from his court duties.
When, with timorous pride, Pierre showed him his
clumsy verses, the father affected to scoff. Though he
had himself dallied with the muse, he knew that this
was no trade for a gentleman, for a Ronsard. 'Poor fool,'
he would say, as the son himself affectionately recalls,
'poor fool, you are wasting your time in your poetizing.
What can that glorious bard Apollo give you, but lyre,
lute, and plectrum, and a song that vanishes in the
wind like smoke ? What can the Muses, who own nothing, give you ? Unless a length of myrtle or ivy to crown
your head ? What can they do, but tempt you to a
spring's bank, or some ancient grotto, where you will
repose your addled head, and, gape-gazing, compose
verses which will give you the name of "good fool" in
proper company ? No, quit that barren trade, which has
never profited the best of its artisans. With that frenzy
which they call divine, their faithfulest friend till death
is still pale Hunger. That Homer you have so often in
your hands, whom in your sickly brain you picture as
a god, never had a penny. That Trojan fiddle of his,
and his muse, who they say had such a fine voice,
couldn't keep him fed, and he had to go begging his
wretched bread from door to door. Poor fool, quit that

mad sort of learning. Thumb me the law books, and
haunt the courts of justice. Try your golden tongue on
the judge, to some poor devil's cost. Let me see you
bellow and sweat for money before the high magistrates.
That's the way to rise to wealth, and see all hats come
off before you as you pass. Or else embrace the profitable trade of Hippocrates. Learn what nature can do in
our bodies, what she purposes and what she dodges. By
excellent skill in aiding others one arrives at riches. Or
else if bold and generous ardor heats your blood, and
if your heart can scorn the perils of this earth, take a
soldier's weapons in your gripe, and follow the wars ;
and with a fine wound opening your belly, die on a
powder-blackened rampart. By such noble means one
often gets rich, for to stout soldiers no good prince is
stingy.'

Such counsel, strained of its sarcasm, fell on willing
ears. Pierre's dreams abandoned the Muses, to hover
above the fields of glory. His father had fought beside
the Chevalier Bayard, and had seen bloody business on
land and sea. The tales he told were sufficient to stir the
boy to martial purpose, had they been necessary in an
age when valor was the virtue and the career of the
gentleman. He confesses :

My little heart was puffed with love of war's alarms,
I longed to show my mettle among the knights-at-arms.
My nature sought dispute, the brangle fierce and snarling ;
And peace was my despite, and war my only darling.

Car j'avais tout le cœur enflé d'aimer les armes,
Je voulais me braver au nombre des gendarmes,
Et de mon naturel je cherchais les débats,
Moins désireux de paix qu'amoureux des combats.

The father, content with such spirit, used all his favor
at court to set the boy on the right road. In the summer

of 1536 Pierre received an express from his father, with
a document inscribed with the best flourishes of the
royal scrivener. Pierre de Ronsard was ordered to join
the army of King François I in Provence, to serve as a
page in the royal household. He was not yet quite twelve
years old.

He travelled across France, through the Nivernais and
Burgundy to Lyon, and down the Rhône to Tournon.
There he overtook his new master, François de France,
the dauphin, heir to all the lands of France. There he
met and embraced his father, the dauphin's steward.

He was in the nick of time to see high tragedy. Three
days after Pierre's arrival, the dauphin, hot from a furious game of racquets, called insanely for a draught of
cold water. A new page, Montecuculli, as madly drew
him a cup from an icy well, an ominous well which one
may still see, from which the foolhardy may still drink.
The dauphin drained the cup, took to his bed, and in
three days died. Poison was inevitably presumed, and
the royal body publicly opened. The horrid sight of the
extraction of his master's heart and lungs remained forever in Pierre's memory. This was an early lesson in
mortality, and in the end of earthly pride. A lesson also
in the ways of fate. Had the dauphin called to Pierre to
draw the fatal draught, he would have suffered the lot
of Montecuculli, whose body was dismembered by four
horses, pulling north, east, south, and west, whose four
quarters were hung on the gates of Lyon, whose head
was impaled on a lance and set on the Rhône bridge.

Pierre was transferred to the service of the king's
third son, Charles, duc d'Orléans (who had abandoned
his quaint baptismal name of Abdenago, too grotesque
for a possible king of France). He saw the armed camp
at Avignon ; soon he returned with the court to Lyon.

And as the court moved up and down France, according to policy or whim, the boy learned the trade of the courtier.

The rules of politeness were innumerable and exact. The novice must learn to walk gracefully and without haste ; to salute with the back-thrust leg straight, the plumed hat dipping to a distance from the ground proportionate to the rank of the person addressed ; to keep the sword-scabbard from clattering and tripping ; to kiss a gift, on offering it, and on receiving one, to kiss the offering hand ; to shield the mouth when spitting on the floor ; not to scratch and fidget, but to nip a flea or louse without ostentation. The ritual of the table was elaborate and baffling for easygoing country gentry. One washed the hands with aromatic water, for fingerprints on a saltcellar or other vessel were known jokingly as the Arms of a Boor. One sat with the napkin on the left shoulder, one's bread to the left, one's goblet to the right. The hands should be constantly on the table, when not engaged. A child piped 'Benedicite,' and all responded 'Dominus.' The child then said a Latin grace for all the company. Every man dipped his own soup from a common bowl. Meat should be seized in its platter with three fingers, and should not be chased about with a plunging hand. It was the mark of a gourmand to possess three morsels, one with the mouth, one with the hand, and one with the eyes in the central dish. Gentlefolk chewed with the mouth half open, not in the ugly shut-mouth style of Germany. If one dropped one's bread on the floor, one should kiss it upon retrieving it. In drinking, one should take the cup with three fingers, raise it with one hand, and empty it at a draught. When a lady drank, it was permitted for a valet to hold a napkin under her chin. On concluding the meal, one should wipe the hands daintily on the table-cloth, and pick the teeth with a mastic thorn.

Pierre's education progressed, while the restless court journeyed about France. As the war in the south had died away, King François moved toward his beloved châteaux of the Loire, the great Loire with an *e*, thirty miles south of Ronsard's little Loir.

The royal train was between Lyon and Nevers in October 1536. A point of troopers led the way, followed by mounted gentlemen of the King's Guard. Then the royal party : King François, thrusting out his arrogant beard ; his queen, Eleanor of Austria ; his two sons. Two ambling palfreys followed in file, connected by a pair of long poles. The mid-point of the poles supported a litter, or travelling bed, surmounted by a canopied roof and side-curtains. In this swaying structure reclined the Princess Madeleine, a sickly girl who could not bear the saddle.

The soldiers in advance raised their hands to signal a halt. Another party was approaching at a gallop. The newcomers reined in and identified themselves. A handsome, red-haired knight, wearing the insignia of highest rank, detached himself, and rode forward to pay his homage to King François. It was another king, James the Fifth of Scotland. He kissed the hands of France and his queen, and turned to the litter. Madeleine of France smiled through the opened curtains, and fell in love with handsome Jamie, and he with her.

King James of Scotland was the darling of his country. He possessed the inestimable qualities of a popular ruler : good looks, a hearty, friendly air, a gift of gayety and laughter, a love of harum-scarum sport, and excellence in manly games. He was a poet, and is deemed the author of *The Gaberlunzie Man* and other celebrations of peasant jollity. To the ladies of his court he was irresistible. At least six noble bastards are recorded, several of them named James Stewart, to annoy genealogists. Ronsard was chiefly impressed by his long curly red-gold hair shining against the whiteness of his neck. In Scotland he was nicknamed the 'reid tod,' the red fox.

It was James's dream to marry a French princess, and he had come to France in hunt of a wife. If his love for Madeleine was instantaneous, his heart had been well prepared. But there were obstacles to the match. There was an inconvenient contract of espousal between King James and the daughter of the duc de Vendôme. The king had, however, visited Vendôme in disguise, and had found his affianced to be ugly and hunch-backed ; he would have none of her. There was also the hostility of Spain and England, fearful of the political consequences of a French-Scottish alliance. And there was the dissuasion of the physicians, who warned of the danger of transporting Madeleine to Scottish air ; she might prove too phthisical to make kings.

Love had its way, in spite of all. James would consider no substitute, and Madeleine vowed that she would have no other living man for her mate. François submitted, and at Blois, in November, the betrothal was signed, the thistle entwined with the lily, the red lion of Scotland somewhat fantastically crossed with the Valois salamander.

After the betrothal, James proceeded to Paris with his two future brothers-in-law, the new dauphin Henri and Charles d'Orléans. Ronsard, page of Charles d'Orléans, observed the frolics of royalty and applauded his master in the daily jousts in the court of the Louvre. No doubt he was present also at the procession of mer-

chants before King James, who was anxious to profit by
his stay in the centre of elegance. The Scottish treasurers
were later aghast at the bills for tapestries, costumes,
plumes, and jewels.

The wedding was celebrated on January 1, 1537, in
Notre-Dame-de-Paris, with a magnificence befitting the
mating of kingdoms. After the ceremony, a great banquet was held. King François paraded his wedding gifts :
horses, armor, cloth of gold, velvet, satin, tapestries,
jewels, and a dog named Basque. The Scots were in
those days reputed stingy ; to remove the reproach King
James served to the guests covered dishes containing, as
he announced, the fruits of Scotland. The covers were
lifted, and the dishes found to be filled with gold pieces.

The whole country of France was bidden to rejoice
with its monarch. Everywhere were joustings and tour-
naments and mimic sea-battles, and so much firing of
artillery, says the chronicler Pitscottie, that no man
might hear for the noise of them. And also plays and
feasts with pleasant sound of instruments of all kinds,
and also cunning conjurers having the art of nigromancy
to cause things to appear, which was as flying dragons
in the air shooting fire at either end, great rivers of
water running through the town and ships fighting
thereupon as it had been the bullering streams of the
sea, with shooting of guns like cracks of thunder.

One of the wedding gifts is our concern. Prince
Charles d'Orléans gave to his sister his page, Pierre de
Ronsard. No doubt Madeleine had taken a fancy to the
boy. She was only sixteen ; though a wife and a woman,
she was still a child, needing child companions as a relief from the bearded statesmen of her official day.

Now for the second time Pierre must transfer his
fidelity and affection. Indeed, it was easy for him to love

his mistress; her tired, white sweetness stirred tenderness in all who knew her.

King James and his bride lingered in France until
the spring. He professed a regard for his wife's health ;
he was loath, also, to leave the land of festival and return to his royal duties. But urgent summons from his
country at last moved him. Leave was taken, 'with great
bon aller drinking on every side,' says Pitscottie. The
Scottish party, followed by a long train of baggage, descended the Seine to the new port of Le Hâvre. They
boarded the waiting fleet, and were carried by a fair
wind in five days to Leith, the port of Edinburgh. It
was mid-May.

As the ships came to shore, Leith's bank was crowded
with courtiers in their velvet and commoners in plaids
and blue bonnets. The passengers disembarked in in-
verse order of rank. Finally King Jamie, with his new
queen on his arm, stepped on the soil of his realm.
Queen Madeleine had learned in her own courts the
trick of royal drama. When her foot touched Scottish
ground she 'bowed and inclined herself to the earth and
took the moulds thereof and kissed them, syne thanked
God that he had safely brought her with her husband
to their own country, giving him laud and glory there-
for.'

The procession wound up the hill to the sullen gray
towers of Holyroodhouse, the predecessor of the palace
we visit today. The new queen coughed in the shrewd
east wind ; her cheeks were flushed too bright. After the
reception she took to her bed. Encouraging news was
given to the people, and Scotland prepared a mighty
festival for the coronation, with processions, open-air
dramas, banquets, tourneys, fountains spouting wine.

But a consumption wasted the queen from day to day. The pages were bidden to walk softly.

Pierre, serving in her chamber, heard her lament. 'Alas ! I wished to be a queen !' she said. And, as he later told, 'she covered her sadness and the fire of her ambition with an ash of patience, as best she could.'

She died on July 7, 1537, 'painlessly, in her husband's arms, and under his kisses.' So Ronsard remembered. The excess of the king's grief impressed the young page, as it did all others. 'The king's privy and heavy moan that he made for her was greater nor all the lave,' says Pitscottie.

Within a year the boy Ronsard had twice seen death. And those who died so horribly were the son and daughter of his king, the great king of the French. He was learning, from the harshest and best of teachers, the ever astounding platitude of death.

All the court was put into mourning. It was, indeed, the first time that mourning black was used in Scotland. The Lord High Treasurer's accounts note the 20 ells of black fustian for the pages' doublets.

For a year the train of the deceased queen remained in Scotland. It was a curious group, ill assorted and troublesome, discontented, grumbling in the way of all exiles, French exiles most of any. There was the queen's governess, Mme de Montreuil, and eight ladies-in-waiting ; the queen's doctor, apothecary, and midwife ; her organist, trumpeters, drummers, and fifers ; her priest, her tailor, her cook ; and her female fool or jester, and her dwarf named Jeanne. And there were the nine pages.

The boy Ronsard was now thirteen. At that age one recovers quickly from grief. He looked about him with interest at the fenceless, treeless land of Scotland.

Though regretting his forests, he could scale with delight the crags of Arthur's Seat, and gaze far over land and sea, and plot the way to France. He could happily ride his small, shaggy Scottish pony over the stony heights, and down the ghylls to valleys with their tiny lochs and wide morasses. He saw on the moors no fat kine, like those of France, but small black cattle with a frisking, high-heeled gait. The rare sun shone with a milky light, unlike the broad beams upon the French homeland. He compared with the decent neatness of the Vendômois the abject Scottish villages, built of low stone-walled, sod-roofed hovels, with pigsties and middens at their door. Edinburgh itself, a city of some 20,000 souls, seemed poor enough after Paris, Lyon, and Rouen.

Holyrood and the Castle, already old and storied, were enchanting spots for an imaginative young mind. And at Linlithgow he climbed the dizzy donjon to Queen Margaret's Bower, where King James's mother had watched in vain for the return of her spouse, King James IV, from Flodden. Thence Pierre stared at the shadowy Grampians, and looked down at the blue loch at his feet, at the white swan leading his file of four fledglings, and the brown swan closing the file. He descended to the guard-room, where the soldiers listened humorously to the cries of the prisoners rising through the single vent from the dungeon below. And he fished for perch, pike, and eels from the royal eel-ark on the loch.

No doubt the best of his days were spent in the hunt, for King James loved to harry the deer through his glens, and to halt in peasant crofts for a refreshment of milk and oatcake. No doubt also he played those sturdy games in which he was later to excel : running, wrestling, swimming, racquets, pall-mall or croquet, football. No doubt he accompanied King James, in dour pursuit of the royal golf-ball over the links of Saint Andrews. In those faraway, gusty matches, the boy poet was, belike, the caddy of that dim king.

There were other excitements. He must have seen the burning of the Lady of Glamis for a poisoning plot, only ten days after the death of Queen Madeleine. He saw the Mayday frolic of Robin Hood and Little John, with its northern drunkenness and riot. He learned to strum the Scotch rebec, with its long neck and carved animal's head. And there were the small events of the French household, which loomed larger than state affairs in the boy's concern. One of his comrades broke his leg. We find in the Lord High Treasurer's accounts : 'Item, for ane cord to the chyld that brak his leg, to turn him in his bed with, xii d.' And 'ane reid bonet' to the said page, to console him. There were the measurings for new garments. The Lord High Treasurer seems to have been liberal, with doublets of white Milan fustian, and of yellow, gray, and red velvet, bonnets to match, and hose, both red and French gray. There were incessant complaints of the food ; the Frenchmen critically analyzed the cooking, as Frenchmen will.

As for the education of Pierre's spirit, it has been supposed that he knew Sir David Lindsay, the Scottish poet. There is no proof of this, and no great likelihood that the eminent bard would have noticed the stripling page. But it is certainly probable that in the endless northern nights, while the sea-wind soughed round Holyrood, the boy read Vergil and the poets he had already conned in the forest of Gastine. And it is likely that among his friends, French and Scottish, there were some to encourage him in his taste for letters.

When King James's grief for the death of Madeleine was somewhat assuaged, he began the search for a new mate. Lifelong fidelity is the privilege of the commoner. A king must have his queen, and a queen's first duty is to breed royal heirs. His choice fell on Marie, daughter of Claude of Guise and of the great princely house of Lorraine. He took her from under the nose of his uncle, Henry VIII of England, who, being recently relieved of Jane Seymour, proposed that Marie should next submit to his deadly embraces.

The wedding was celebrated by proxy in Notre-Dame-de-Paris, in May 1538. The bride immediately took ship for Scotland, and landed in Fifeshire, early in June. The nuptial ceremony was repeated in the cathedral of Saint Andrews, the bridegroom now taking his own part. Scotland was wild with joy ; the country could at last enact those pomps of which it had been balked a year before. It was probably pleased that its king had espoused a queen whose initial was M ; the festal banners prepared for Madeleine would still do. As the new queen entered the abbey of Saint Andrews, a great cloud came out of the heavens above the gate, and opened instantly ; and there appeared a fair lady most like an angel, having the keys of Scotland in her hands. Marie played her rôle in queenly style, and won the hearts of her country. She was indeed 'a werey beutifull lady,' as one chronicler attests ; and another terms her 'a lustie princess, a pleisand forme and fair, of honest maneris, sueit and plesand, of countenance verie cumlie.'

Pierre de Ronsard was present at these festivities, and no doubt had a chance to remark that he had known the queen's brother Charles at school. But the train of Queen Madeleine, 'the auld Queen,' was kept in the background, out of regard for the new queen's sensi-

bilities. After the ceremonies, James and Marie set forth
for a tour of their kingdom, while the retainers of 'the
auld Queen' returned to Edinburgh. At the end of July
Mme de Montreuil, her ladies and servants, departed
for France, by way of England. In the troop was 'a page
called Wandonoy,' evidently Pierre de Ronsard, Vendômois. He was equipped with a new cloak of Spanish
frieze, a French riding hat with tippet, new riding-boots
and shoon.

The party rode by easy stages, ladies' stages, past the
peel-towers of the border, over the stony Cheviots,
where fat starlings ride on the backs of fat sheep, and
through green summer England. The only memory pre-
served in Ronsard's poems is that of the white swans of
the Thames. Arriving in London, the party was met by
a high and inquisitive official of the English court. He
reported to King Henry that Mme de Montreuil complained of the poor food and poor company of Scotland. He took the ladies, and perhaps the pages, to visit
the king's castles of Westminster and Hampton Court.
They were feasted by the Lord Mayor of London. In
early September they continued to Rochester and Can-
terbury, where Mme de Montreuil refused to kiss the
head of Saint Thomas à Becket. ('Ah ça, non, mais des
fois !' I hear her cry to the grinning mummy.) Thence
to Dover, where King Henry met them, with his great
joviality. He gave to Mme de Montreuil and another
lady diamonds worth 300 crowns each ; to the remainder
paternoster beads and medals, worth thirty crowns
apiece, whereat they grumbled much. By mid-September
they were back in Paris.

Pierre returned to the service of Charles d'Orléans.
He embraced his father, who found him mightily grown
after his year abroad. He had great tales to tell his fellow

pages, of wild hunts and barbarous frolics among the
kilted men of the north. His companions did their best
to shame him with the advantage of their year's training in courtly civility.

He remained at court for only three months. Claude
d'Humières, sieur de Lassigny, departed on a mission to
the northland on Christmas Eve of the same year. He
took Pierre as his page. His route led through Flanders ;
the boy saw the yuletide festivals of Valenciennes. In
Zeeland the two took ship for Scotland.

This was no happy journey on a tranquil sea. A three-
day tempest brought the bark within an ace of destruction on the English coast. It was such a storm as Erasmus
remembered, when the Alps seemed, by comparison to
the waves, warts. When the vessel struggled into Queens-
ferry (on January 22, 1539), it sank at its moorings,
while the baggage floated on the tide.

Lassigny and his page proceeded to Linlithgow Castle
for the interview with King James. Pierre greeted his
friends among the courtiers and certainly his friends of
the stables, the grooms and hawkers. After six weeks the
courier and his young companion returned to France.

The fourteen-year-old boy was now too tall and sturdy
to have the look of a page. The changed voice, the
manly airs, hinted that he was no longer of an age for
intimate attendance on court ladies. Charles d'Orléans
graduated him from the page's status, with the ritual
present of thirty crowns. And Charles, who was busy
making for himself a personal party at court, arranged
for the boy's immediate education and future fidelity.
He had Pierre appointed to the Royal Stables, a sort of
cadet school for young gentlemen of promise.

The Royal Stables were 'the seminary of all good and
virtuous exercises,' such as music, dancing, gymnastics,

and manners. But mostly the life of the scholars revolved around the horses, great-hearted chargers bred to carry armored knights, light fettlesome coursers shaped for speed. They were named for eminent nobles ; a mule, even, was christened Chateaubriant, for the king's current mistress. The art of equitation had reached a high level ; the *haute école* of France was the admiration of Europe. Interminable weary hours were spent training the horses to feats and postures. Thus Hobère, the famous mount of Henri II, was taught to kneel in salute to his master. Pierre learned all the tricks of horsemanship, and of *voltige,* or spectacular horseback gymnastics. He learned also the cavalier's swagger, his way of walking bow-legged, as if reft from the better half of his body. He learned to love the stable-smell of straw, horse-sweat and manure, that sweet nostalgic perfume to all men who have lived with horses in their youth.

The mind, too, did not lie entirely fallow. There were some among the cadets who were touched by the circumambient humanism. Here and there, in saddle-bags and lockers, was a rubbed copy of Vergil or Horace, faintly redolent with the smell of horses.

In this stable-school Pierre remained for a year. Evidently his former master and patron, Charles d'Orléans, kept his eye on the boy. What he saw persuaded him that the young Ronsard might be trained to important tasks in the service of France and in the special service of Charles d'Orléans.

'I have very often heard,' said the Cardinal du Perron at the time of Ronsard's death, 'from those who knew him in his youth, that never had nature formed a frame of better composition, or better proportioned than was his. His face was beautiful and marvellously agreeable, his form and stature entirely august and martial, so that

it seemed that nature had put all her study and industry
in preparing a place to worthily receive that excellent
soul full of glory and light, of which the body's beauties
were to be as if the splendor and the effulgence. Monsieur d'Orléans, who saw the flower of this budding
virtue, and the prospect which this young man was beginning to give of himself, determined to leave him in
repose as little as might be, and rather to give him the
practice and conversation of foreign nations, to make
him some day fit for employment in those fine charges
to which his instinct and nature seemed to summon
him.'

Therefore, in May, 1540, Pierre de Ronsard, being
in his sixteenth year, was attached to a mission to Germany, under the leadership of Lazare de Baïf.

This eminent diplomat was no less eminent as a
scholar. When ambassador to Venice he had learned
Greek and had shared in the classical enthusiasms of
that new Athens. A distant relative of the Ronsards, he
had surely received the boy in his Paris home. There
Pierre made his first acquaintance of his lifelong friend,
the ambassador's natural son, Jean-Antoine de Baïf. But
Jean-Antoine was now only eight ; during the German
expedition he was left in Paris, to study his Greek under
the celebrated scholar Jacques Toussaint.

The mission was bound for a princely Diet in the
Rhenish city of Spires, or Speyer. The pest in Spires
caused the Diet's transfer to Haguenau, near Strasbourg.
Baïf's secret instructions were to win the Protestant
princes to the interests of France. But privately he was
lukewarm toward the German Reformation, and preferred the company of German hellenists and latinists
to that of Rhenish Junkers. In Haguenau he remained

till August, happily discussing philology and philosophy, while politics took its own course.

We are invited by Ronsard's biographers to see him discussing with the German doctors in Latin, and to perceive in the Haguenau visit the implanting of humanistic seeds. The supposition is a bold one. Pierre was not yet sixteen; his haphazard Latin must have been pitiable to the German pundits, and the beery, black-gowned pundits themselves must have seemed dull fellows to the boy, fresh from court elegances. Perhaps he caught something from the scholars, perhaps a momentary interest in the Reformed doctrines, an interest soon disavowed.

The result of his visit was, in fact, a disaster which altered, and seemed for a time to destroy, all his career. He fell grievously ill; and when he recovered he was partly deaf, and destined to remain so for life.

What was his illness? A contemporary biographer blames the German wines, which the French soberly alleged to be mixed with sulphur. More recent writers point to the fatigues of travel and the horrid fare of the German inns, with which the diplomat alternated excessive banquets. A modern physician suggests an acute arthritis. Or else Pierre simply picked up an infection, scarlet fever, typhoid fever, or the pest of Spires. 'The pest,' indeed, was a generic name for all sorts of epidemics.

At any rate, the way to a diplomatic career was closed, for the virtue of a diplomat is to hear whispers. And the hope of glory in arms was ended, for Mars will have none but perfect bodies for his sacrifices. Pierre returned to the dear ambition of his earlier days. He would be a poet; he would even be the prince of poets.

For such an end his adolescent years were no bad

preparation. He had missed, to be sure, the rigorous training of the schools. In exchange, he had seen some of the world's rulers at their manly trade. He had seen life in its glory, and death. He had seen ambition, and ambition betrayed. And he had seen nature in her infinite variety, her storms at sea, her mountains, her northern snows. He returned to the Vendômois, with a new appreciation for its gentle, moderate, voluptuous forms. He had gained for his homeland a deeper and more poignant love :

> I was not yet fifteen, when woods and hills and springs
> And brooks delighted me more than the courts of kings ;
> And the black forest-aisles with lofty foliage vaulted,
> The crumbling cliffs of Loir, by pecking birds assaulted,
> A valley, or a cave obscured in mystery,
> A horrid wilderness — 'twas these that tempted me
> Who only lived to glimpse the glimmering rigadoon
> Of kirtled nymphs and fays, flying beneath the moon.

> *Je n'avais pas quinze ans, que les monts et les bois*
> *Et les eaux me plaisaient plus que la cour des rois,*
> *Et les noires forêts en feuillages voûtées,*
> *Et du bec des oiseaux les roches picotées ;*
> *Une vallée, un antre en horreur obscurci,*
> *Un désert effroyable était tout mon souci,*
> *Afin de voir au soir les Nymphes et les Fées*
> *Danser dessous la lune, en cotte par les prés.*

III

The Muses' Prentice

PIERRE DE RONSARD was nearly sixteen when, half sick and half deaf, he returned to La Possonnière for rest and recovery. He could have chosen a better asylum. The little river Loir, idling through its broad valley, bred malaria in its backwaters. It was not Euterpe, alas, but the anopheles mosquito that lay in wait within these bosky coverts.

When the recurrent tertian fever left him at rest, he found life in the manor-house dreary enough. His father was absent on his everlasting court duties. The eldest brother Claude was married, and occupied with his own lands and his own children. The second brother Charles was in the Church, well endowed with fat benefices in the distant bishopric of Laval. His sister Louise was married. Pierre was alone in the solitary house with his mother, the mother of whom he has never spoken.

Between fever and ague he could perambulate his dear countryside. But the cold rains of winter set his teeth chattering and chilled him to the heart. Summer mocked him with its radiance, for with summer and its venomous insects came a redoubling of his illness. Country diversions, putting a prize on vigor, rebuffed him ; the broad village gayeties sickened him. At sixteen, at seventeen, to be so wasted, weary, so in love with solitude !

His tired thoughts turned forever inward. Exasper-

ated by deafness and weakness, he brooded on his missed
vocation, on the failure of his dreams of fame. For him
no honorable bloodshed in his prince's service, no diplomatic haggling for his country's advantage. For him
only the resources and consolations of the condemned
man, sentenced for life to the prison of the deaf.

Within those walls there are, indeed, solaces. Ronsard
could look coldly on his old ambition and perceive its
essential folly :

> Of all the animals on earth's unhappy shores,
> Man is the wretchedest, for on himself he wars ;
> A single trumpery thought is all his spirit's spur :
> To serve his fellow-man as executioner.

> *De tous les animaux qui vivent sur la terre,*
> *L'homme est le plus chétif, car il se fait la guerre*
> *Lui-mêmes à lui-même, et n'a dans son cerveau*
> *Autre plus grand désir que d'être son bourreau.*

War was once the game of heroes ; gunpowder has
made it a coward's trade :

> In acrid powder-smoke the heroes pass away ;
> Achilles, Ajax, Hector, if they revived today,
> Would perish at the hand of some obscure poltroon,
> Training his arquebus, his distant musketoon.

> *Par lui comme jadis on ne voit plus d'Hectors,*
> *D'Achilles, ni d'Ajax, hé Dieu ! car les plus forts*
> *Sont aujourd'hui tués d'un poltron en cachette*
> *A coups de harquebuse, ou à coups de mousquette.*

The consolation was poor enough, for the loss of all
his dreams of valor. Yet at sixteen and seventeen one
must dream of something. The prisoner must have some
secret country where he may gloriously rule. The secret
country sometimes captures its monarch ; the prisoner
transports himself so completely to the world of his im-

agination that he cannot return to the world of others. He is 'stir-simple,' in the argot of the jails.

Ronsard's dreams dealt mostly with poetry, his old love, never entirely forgotten in his far journeys. By poetry, by the Muses' aid, he might attain to fame and outwit malevolent fate. By poetry he might tell men the sweetness of his dreams, and make of his Vendômois a sacred spot, like the Sabine farm of Horace, like the Sirmio of Catullus.

His first effort was to imitate his masters in their own tongue. He soon realized that his knowledge of Latin was too uncertain for his purpose. When he thought of his teachers in the Collège de Navarre, conversing in Ciceronian periods, he was inclined to despair. In his clumsy Latin verses the rules of grammar warred with the rules of prosody, and sense received grievous wounds in the battle.

He turned, willy-nilly, to the vulgar tongue. His Paris masters, and some of his Paris companions, would have scorned such a yielding to popular taste. The Baïfs and their circle regarded French poetry as mere street-balladry, its cultivation treason to the new humanism. But Ronsard was now far from their influence. More compelling to him was the example of his own father and his father's old-fashioned friends, who wrote their stilted verses in the style of the previous century. And they wrote in French.

Ronsard sought his favorite retreats : the glades of Gastine, the murmuring banks of the Loir. There, in the praise of his own country, he wrote his first adult poems.

> Here, where the hillsides rise,
> The sacred wood, Gastine,
> Lifts proudly to the skies
> Her head of painted green ;

On t'other slope the vine
  Enverdures all the view ;
The promise of her wine
  Yields nothing to Anjou.

The broadly basking Loir
  Among the fields dispersed,
Brings water from afar
  To slake the valley's thirst,

Rendering rich the earth
  She touches as she fares,
Depositing the worth
  Of the brown boon she bears.

   .   .   .   .

And though my destiny
  May bid me soon depart,
This patch of earth shall be
  Still laughing in my heart.

And when the Fate shall snip
  My thread, obedient,
My shade shall board the ship
  For the long banishment ;

Then may the rain that plashes
  On Vendômois descend,
Weeping, upon the ashes
  Of him who was her friend.

Sur l'un Gastine sainte,
  Mère des demi-dieux,
Sa tête de verd peinte
  Envoie jusque aux cieux,

Et sur l'autre prend vie
  Maint beau cep, dont le vin
Porte bien peu d'envie
  Au vignoble angevin.

Le Loir tard à la fuite,
  En soi s'ébanoyant,
D'eau lentement conduite
  Tes champs va tournoyant,

Rendant bon et fertile
Le pays traversé
Par l'humeur qui distille
Du gras limon versé.

. . . .

Bref, quelque part que j'erre,
Tant le ciel me soit doux,
Ce petit coin de terre
Me rira par sus tous.

Là je veux que la Parque
Tranche mon fatal fil,
Et m'envoie en la barque
De perdurable exil.

Là te faudra répandre
Ruisseaux de pleurs, parmi
La vaine et froide cendre
De Ronsard ton ami.

He revisited the retreats of his familiar country, with the books he loved in hand. He dreamed in the caverns which pit the hillsides, where of old the Celts hid from the Romans, where giant serpents once lay in wait, to issue forth and capture travellers. In such a cave he listened long to the muttering spring which was supposed, on occasion, to speak oracles in French. He wandered deep into Gastine forest, 'talking with a book.' He celebrated, in imitation of Horace at the *fons Bandusiae,* a spring known as the fontaine Bellerie. Lying at full length by her tinkling waters, he listened to the rhythmic beat of the flails on the threshing-floor. He greeted the thirsty herdsmen and the cattle weary from the plow. He vowed to Bellerie the sacrifice of a suckling kid, with horns just budding from its forehead. He would make Bellerie the princess of all springs, and would commemorate the pierced rock, whence the water spurted hoarsely, and laughed and pattered on its way.

'Thus ever may the white moon see at midnight, near thy repair, the agile nymphs lead the ball. But O Fountain, I long to cease dreaming that I drink from thee, in summer, when fever brings grim-featured Death to be my company.'

Today the fountain's nymphs have vanished, the willows all are dead, and the poor thin spring of Bellerie serves as a field laundry.

With fever, with youth's melancholy, and with classic precedent, his thoughts ran much on death. He chose the place for his burial : the tiny 'green isle' near Couture, where the little Loir is met by the littler Braye, where the water-drabbled tresses of the willows signify sorrow, and the hurrying waters time flowing to eternity. He prayed that a tree should be his monument in place of marble, that ivy might grow from his bones, to spread high and cast a shade for pious visitors.

For three years, from 1540 to 1543, Ronsard continued in this weeping, shaking, brooding fit. In the last year his father gave him, evidently, a good talking-to. I can faintly hear the paternal voice, shouting above his son's deafness.

'What do you think to do with your life, my son ?'

'Why — I might be a poet. Like Clément Marot, like Mellin de Saint-Gelais —'

'Tush and fiddlesticks ! Where is jolly Clément Marot ? Singing psalms for his supper to the heretics of Geneva !' He crossed himself. 'And Saint-Gelais ? Bootlicking at court, writing everlasting wedding-songs for a grudged handful of crowns, rhyming praises of ancient harridans who have to pay for their praise ! Poetry is a gentleman's amusement, like fencing. It is not his business.'

'Need I do anything? May I not simply remain at home?'

'Listen, my son. Your brother Claude will receive, as my eldest son, La Possonnière. I have already bled myself to set aside a proper dowry for your sister. The remainder of our family wealth is divided into six equal parts. Four of these parts go to Claude, to enable him to support his position with dignity. Of the two remaining parts, one goes to Charles, and one to you. It is not sufficient to maintain you. I am sorry.'

'What can I do?'

'I will tell you what you can do and what you will do. You will become a tonsured clerk.'

'A priest? I have no liking for the cloth.'

'Never fear! You will be no village priest, rising early for the mass, confessing the yokels, absolving their dismal sins. All you need is the tonsure; just two minutes with a razor. A little healthy ventilation for the scalp, corbleu! Then you will be a holy clerk, qualified to receive the revenue from the Church's properties. It will go hard if, with my influence, I cannot get for you a couple of good benefices!'

'But there is a certain vow for a clerk in orders. . . .'

'Why, true, there is a little promise you must make. Never to marry. But jour de Dieu, what chance have you to marry, with your beggarly income? And why should you marry? From what I hear about the village girls, they don't ask you for a spousal ring! Hey? My dear fellow, the vow of celibacy is an inestimable thing, well worth a thousand crowns, they say at court. If a wench comes blubbering to you with a tale of letting out her petticoat, you can merely sigh and say: "What would you? Holy Church is my only bride!"'

Pierre surrendered. It was not, indeed, a matter for argument.

Early in March 1543 the father was summoned to the episcopal city of Le Mans, thirty miles away, to attend the funeral of the great Guillaume du Bellay, seigneur de Langeay. He called immediately on his distant kinsman, René du Bellay, Bishop of Le Mans, and persuaded him to tonsure in person the young Pierre.

Pierre received an urgent message, and hastened to Le Mans. He was in time to see the imposing obsequies of Guillaume du Bellay. Louis de Ronsard held one corner of the mortuary cloth that covered the coffin. In the audience was Dr. François Rabelais, inconsolably mourning his dead master.

The day after this ceremony, the Ronsards were convoked to the episcopal palace. Bishop René du Bellay led the guests to his chapel, and donned his vestments and mitre. Pierre knelt before the altar, in a cassock, with a folded surplice over his left arm, a lighted candle in his right hand. He may have smiled at the antiphonal : *Tu es, Domine, qui restitues haereditatem mihi.* He did not smile, as the Bishop took the sacrificial scissors and clipped four locks, from the brow, the crown, and above the ears. The symbolic vanity of the body fell into a bowl held by an acolyte. The Bishop took Pierre's surplice, unfolded it, and dropped it over his head. He was a consecrated member of God's holy church.

A little later he wrote a poem in which he offered his hair as a tribute to Phoebus, the hairy god. Maidens, he says, have begged one of his locks in vain, for Phoebus will have no shared offering. In his Renaissance imagination, Phoebus and Jehovah were strangely blent.

In the Bishop's palace he made the acquaintance, by

chance or design, of the episcopal secretary, Jacques
Peletier. This young man, in his twenty-seventh year,
was already reputed a poet, and a scholar in jurispru-
dence, geometry, medicine, and all humane learning.
His imagination peopled the bishopric with the gods of
Greece. 'Peletier, whose mind is full of Muses, gods,
nymphs, and all their snares,' says Ronsard.

To him the fresh-tonsured youth made his poetic confession. He pulled from his new cassock a packet of imitations of Horace, in Latin. Peletier cried out in horror.
What folly, to strive to rival the ancients in their own
tongue ! Understand better the true principle of imitation : try to do in our language what the masters have
done in theirs. Have none of this neo-Latin verse, which
can at best be only a moon-like reflection of the ancient
sun. And have none of the traditional French poetry, its
bloodless, witless exercises in antiquated forms. Take
the great thoughts of Greece and Rome, and their great
forms, ode, epode, elegy, and naturalize them in our
French idiom !

The adjurations fell on willing ears. In a great surge
of common feeling, Ronsard and Peletier swore friendship in a single purpose. Ronsard abandoned his efforts
to outdo the Romans in their language. But he recognized that to rival them in his own he must fit himself
to understand all their doctrine, and feel all their
beauty. He must know his Latin better, and chiefly
he must learn Greek.

The father, meanwhile, was making provision for
Pierre's future. The succession of events is here obscure.
But it would seem that in this year 1543 Pierre, his
health somewhat restored, returned to Paris, to begin
the campaign for a church living. Provisionally, he was
attached to the household of the dauphin Henri, and

was given quarters in his stable-school, in the old palace of Les Tournelles.

Here Pierre felt himself ill at ease. His shaved poll and his churchly purpose were perfect themes for the mockery of his companions, fledgling courtiers. The jokes could be triply barbed by utterance in such a tone that the deaf youth could suspect their tenor without full comprehension. By way of compensation, he threw himself violently into sports. His contemporary biographer, Claude Binet (a very untrustworthy biographer, it is true), tells us that he was much esteemed by the dauphin. 'And in fact the [future] king played no games in which Ronsard was not called to his side. For instance, the king having made up a team to play football on the Pré aux Clercs, where he would often take his pleasure, as this is one of the finest exercises for fortifying and suppling youth, he wouldn't have a game without Ronsard. The king and his team were dressed in white uniforms, and Monsieur de Laval, captain of the opposing side, in red. There Ronsard, who played on the king's side, did so well that His Majesty would say publicly that he had been the cause of winning the prize of victory.'

But when the games were over, Ronsard sank into despondency. He was out of place in this world of muffled clash and clamor. To escape, he would cross the river to the home of Lazare de Baïf, a princely mansion adorned with Greek mottoes which frightened superstitious passers-by. There he would gossip at ease with young Jean-Antoine de Baïf. Though the boy was only about twelve, he was a prodigy of learning. Latin, and especially Greek, were as familiar to him as French. His achievements were due to the insistence of his father, the eminent humanist, and especially to the instruction

of his tutors, Jacques Toussaint and his successor, Jean
Dorat.

On June 6, 1544, Louis de Ronsard died suddenly,
while serving his prince. Pierre mourned him sincerely.
Early in 1545 his mother died, and no doubt she too
was mourned. But in the first moment of his freedom
from parental control, Pierre absented himself from the
court, so far as he was able, and put himself to school to
Jean Dorat and to the Greeks.

IV

The School of the Greeks

JEAN DORAT had the qualities of a supreme teacher : mental and physical vigor, broad, exact knowledge, apostolic fervor, intolerance, and a large dose of fanaticism. He was a Limousin of common birth ; his Boeotian name of Dinemandy, Dine-in-the-morning, he had changed to the Attic Dorat. His rugged, rustic face betrayed his peasant obstinacy. He had a simple, readily communicable faith. All his ideas congregated around a single one : that wisdom was possessed only by the great ancients, and mostly by the Greeks, and that any non-classical study was a waste of a man's time.

He taught with fury, pouring his own passion into his pupils' minds. His partial deafness rendered him immune from interruption. He demanded an accurate, copious knowledge of the holy classic tongues. It was his device to teach Greek in Latin, and Latin in Greek. When the students attained linguistic ease, they launched into the study of Homer. Dorat examined the text, proposing brilliant emendations, translating extempore into lyric Latin. He revealed deep allegories, mystical meanings in the old adventure story. Odysseus is man, in lifelong pursuit of true wisdom, Penelope, and of happiness, Ithaca.

The pupils, Baïf, Ronsard, and young François de Carnavalet from the Royal Stables, listened transfixed. Dorat's faith flowed into them, and they thirstily drank.

If Ronsard had loved the Greek gods and heroes as a boy, he loved them the more when he could hear their praises in the very words of their poets. His own vocation became clearer : to bring Hellenic wisdom and beauty to France, to teach the deities French.

He was not yet entirely free to follow his bent. Still under a sort of feudal bondage to the dauphin, Henri, he was obliged to follow his master. Some part of his time was spent in travel, whether with the court or on special missions.

On these journeys he had two encounters decisive in his life.

In April 1545 the court was at Blois. The local gentry greeted the royal retinue with all due honor and festivity. The visiting courtiers were received in the sumptuous Château of Blois. In one of the high rooms a girl of fifteen, with gold-brown hair, was singing a *branle de Bourgogne* and plucking an accompaniment on the lute. It was a dance-tune, in which voice and instrument were heard now separately, now together. The music rang in Ronsard's heart. The song done, he pressed forward to be presented. The singer's name was Cassandre Salviati ; she was the daughter of a wealthy Italian banker domesticated in France.

He was soon separated from her by other urgent young courtiers. That evening he found his way again to her side, and spoke and heard words that fixed themselves in his memory.

Next day the court left Blois. There were other duties, other meetings with lovely girls. Yet somehow her beautiful name was not forgotten, nor did the image fade of her, bending over her lute, nor were the strains of the *branle de Bourgogne* muted. The goddesses of whom he read, Aphrodite, Hebe, Psyche, seemed to wear in his imagination the features of Cassandre. It was a shock to him to learn, in the following year, that she had married M. de Pray, a country gentleman of the Vendômois.

The other meeting was equally momentous. In 1547 (evidently) Ronsard was returning from Poitiers to Paris on some mission to us unknown. He dismounted for the night in a wayside inn. The host informed him that another young gentleman was honoring his poor hostelry, Joachim du Bellay, a junior member of the great house of Du Bellay, nephew of the seigneur de Langeay whose funeral Ronsard had attended. He was returning from his studies in the University of Poitiers to his home in Anjou.

The two young men scraped acquaintance, for the Ronsards were distant kin to the Du Bellays. An immediate sympathy drew them together. Joachim, like Pierre, was slightly deaf ; his disability resulted from an illness which had darkened his lonely, orphaned childhood. Over the friendly wine each made happy confession of his tastes, griefs, detestations, and purposes. Soon each was hunting in his doublet for verses composed during the long days on horseback. And miraculously it appeared that each scorned the fusty, inanimate poetry of the established versifiers, and each dreamed of a new and glorious art modelled on that of the shining Greeks. Through all that night the two discovered new affinities. Each had found his dearest friend. That friendship, indeed, was hardly marred till poor melancholy Joachim died, in 1560, at the age of thirty-seven.

The year 1547 was an important one for Ronsard. In that year King François died, and Ronsard's protector, the dauphin, became Henri II of France. (Ronsard's former master, Charles d'Orléans, the third son of François I, had died in 1545, in fine Valois style. A guest in a country house, he was barred from the best apartment, with the excuse that a victim of the pest had just died therein. 'The pest has never killed a son of France !' he cried, and entering, slashed the mattress to bits with his sword. The pest enveloped him in a feathery cloud, and killed the son of France.) At Henri's accession to the throne, Ronsard was relieved, probably at his own request, of all duties toward his master, and of his chance of royal rewards.

In this year Ronsard received the degree of Master of Arts of the University of Paris.

In this year he saw, for the first time, one of his poems in print. It is a pleasant bagatelle, in the manner of Clément Marot, entitled *Des beautés qu'il voudrait en s'amie*. The perfections of his ideal mistress are scrupulously detailed, from her black eyes and dark complexion to her slender legs. She must know Petrarch and the *Roman de la Rose*. She must be coy, but coyly she must yield. This is not the Cassandre of his dreams. Perhaps the poem was written before he met Cassandre, or perhaps the image of Cassandre did not demand the exclusive fidelity of his imagination. He sent the poem to his friend Jacques Peletier. Peletier wrote a reply, and published the pair in his first poetic collection. The little volume includes also the first printed verses of Joachim du Bellay.

It was in 1547, finally, that Jean Dorat was appointed director of the Collège de Coqueret, in Paris. Ronsard, his new friend Joachim du Bellay, and his old friend Jean-Antoine de Baïf, whose father had just died, went to live and study at Coqueret, in the Hellenic glory cast by their beloved teacher.

The Collège de Coqueret was one of many privately conducted schools which belonged, in a loose way, to

the University of Paris. The chief duty of the University
was the examination of the students and the awarding
of its degrees. In addition, it had a vague supervision
over all the educational enterprises on the left bank of
the Seine. Among these the ambitious student would
make his choice, much as he chooses an Oxford college
today. Between 16,000 and 20,000 young men were enrolled at this period. The average cost of an education
was a little over 100 livres a year. For the penniless student there were, however, innumerable scholarships and
foundations, and opportunity for self-help as a college
servant.

As is usual, the student had the kind of college life he
could pay for. Existence was very tolerable at a gentleman's school like the Collège de Navarre. At the charity
institute of Montaigu, Erasmus's alma mater, learning
was bought by suffering. A mouthful of vegetables,
cooked without butter, a roll, and an egg or half a her-
ring made a meal, and every other day was fast-day. The
vermin of Montaigu were proverbial ; Rabelais refers to
lice as 'Montaigu hawks.' In fact, in all the schools the
students were forbidden, for decency's sake, to touch
their heads while in the refectory.

The time-table of a school day began with the rising
bell at four. A student proctor made the tour of the
dormitories, woke the sluggards, and lit the candles.
The youths dressed drowsily, tying their long hose to
their doublets with laces, slipping on their black belted
gowns. They descended to the courtyard to make water
against the wall. After prayers and summary devotions,
lectures began at five. At six, mass. Then the first meal,
a single roll warm from the oven. From seven to eight,
repose. From eight to ten, lectures, the main class of the
morning. From ten to eleven, discussion and argumen-

tation, the students, in pairs or in groups, examining one another. At eleven, dinner, accompanied by a reading from the Bible or the Lives of the Saints, 'to deprive the devil of the advantage of finding minds unoccupied.' The chaplain said the Benedicite and the Grace, with a pious exhortation, and the principal made his announcements. From noon to two o'clock, review of lessons and various labors. From two to three, recreation. From three to five, lectures. From five to six, discussion and argumentation. At six, supper. At half-past, examination on the day's work. At seven-thirty, complines. Lights out at eight in winter, at nine in summer.

The classrooms were damp, and in winter icy cold. Deep straw on the floor gave a faint illusion of warmth. The only furniture was the master's lectern and the students' benches. The masters lectured to their hearts' content ; the students wrote on *scriptoria* balanced on their knees. These were folding boxes, containing paper, pens, a ruler, a horn inkwell, a penknife, and other scholastic necessities.

The professors were treated with the utmost deference. When one passed through the schoolyard, all the pupils stopped, uncovered, and bowed low. When he entered a classroom, they applauded, stamped on the floor, pounded the benches, and cried 'Vivat !'

The students were constantly supervised. An *explorator* kept order while the lecturer was busy. An *architriclin,* or student proctor, presided at each table in the refectory, wearing a napkin round his neck as symbol of authority. During the meals he corrected newcomers : *'Poculum a dextris ! Ad laevam panis !* Your cup to the right ! Your bread to the left !' If a lout failed to lower his eyes when drinking the proctor would hiss : *'Bibere intortis oculis illiberale est !'* Or if he did not cut his

meat in small bits : *'Carnem minutim in quadra disse-
care !'*

The punishments were as severe as the discipline. The
professors carried a ferule into class, for corrections on
the spur of the moment. If a student was caught lying,
swearing, or speaking French, *vae natibus,* woe to the
buttocks ! An old engraving shows a naked youth bound
to a pillar, the schoolmaster furiously beating him with
a rod, while the other pupils watch trembling. If, as
sometimes happened, a student died under the lash, the
educators consoled the parents by affirming that he had
better die than lead a wicked existence through the
weakness of his masters.

But at Coqueret it is evident that this grim discipline
was much relaxed. Ronsard and others were already
grown men, who had seen the world and its civility. In
student slang, they were *galoches,* or goloshes, prudent
elder fellows who wore wood pattens in bad weather.
(*'Turba galochiferum ferratis passibus ibat,'* said a
mocking poet.) These men would not have submitted
for years to a harsh scholastic routine. And Dorat himself had no need of enforcing attention by terror. He
was his pupils' companion ; they loved him and held his
every word as precious. 'How happy I was to suck the
savory milk of thy fecund breast !' wrote Ronsard, in
verses which recall the tribute of Rabelais to Erasmus :
'I called thee my father, but I should rather term thee
mother . . . Thou hast fed me with thy divine doctrine
from thy most chaste teats.'

The doctrine of the new masters seemed indeed divine to the new pupils. Their doctrine was Humanism.
Humanism is one of those floating, changing, plasmatic
words which are hard to fix, hard to define. One of the
best of the innumerable summaries is that of Gustave

Cohen. It was the faith of the humanists that one must live in beauty, and that art is a part of life. The flesh and its works are not to be condemned ; love and joy, attributes of life, are divine like life itself. Nature is virtuous, and a good guide. The intellectual life is possible outside the rules of established religion. Man is capable of attaining dignity, and he is worthy of man's study.

The humanists found their sanctions and philosophy in the classic past, and by a natural return, they found in the classic past a refuge for their own ideals and imaginations. They were hostile to the lingering Middle Age, its works, art, architecture, poetry, and scholastic philosophy. They turned for immediate support to Italy, where the Renaissance had long since won its cause.

In France, too, the Renaissance had won, at least at court and among the enlightened. Medieval forms of art and thought had yielded to the older pagan forms. When Henri II was made king, in 1547, the pageantry at Blois was not of saints and God's favor ; naked courtesans, representing heathen goddesses, reclined on oxen, and two elephants with trumpeters in their howdahs figured the glories of this world. On the king's entry into Paris he was offered a banquet in the Bishop's Palace by the Cardinal du Bellay. The dining-hall was decorated with gods and goddesses, painted with complete exactness, and with scenes of youths playing the games of venerable antiquity. The body was honored with Greek delight, not hidden with medieval shamefastness. Nudity was a vogue. Great ladies, Diane de Poitiers, Queen Catherine de Médicis herself, posed, regally naked, for painters and sculptors.

The return to antiquity was marked by a particular cult for ancient Greece, its language, poetry, and philos-

ophy. Those who could do so corresponded by preference in Greek, and attempted to add to Greek poetic
literature. Promising girls were put to Greek in their
childhood. At literary parties the guests came disguised
as gods, nymphs, and heroes. Greek was in style ; Greek
was the mode. A few fanatics were converted even to the
pagan faith. A Greek named Demetrios sacrificed a bull
to Jupiter, in Rome's Coliseum, to conjure away the
pest that raged in 1552.

To the Renaissance mind, Greek represented joy in
wisdom. It was a happy contrast to medieval theology,
which made of wisdom the knowledge of man's corrup-
tion on earth and doom in death. Joy in life, joy in
labor, were required of the humanist. Ronsard gives us
this specific testimony, in the introduction to his first
collection of verse : 'Although youth is always distracted
from every studious occupation, on account of the vol-
untary pleasures which possess it, yet from childhood I
have always esteemed the study of literature the happy
felicity of my life, without which one must despair of
ever attaining to the summit of perfect content.' And
fourteen years later : 'In sum, poetry is full of all honest
liberty, and, to say true, is a frolic trade. . . . Would
you know why I work at it so gayly ? Because such a
pastime is agreeable to me.' And he tells the aspiring
poet that since the Muses will not lodge in a soul unless
it be good, holy, and virtuous, he must be of good character, not malicious, nor sulky, nor woeful.

It was a happy time, before men lost faith in ancient
wisdom, before men doubted their own. With what magnificence Ronsard tells his page, in a sonnet, to guard
his door for three days, while he reads the Iliad from
end to end ! 'Permit not even the chambermaid to enter
to make my bed, nor admit a god descending from

heaven on purpose to visit me. Afterwards we shall make merry for a week. And yet — if a messenger come from Cassandre, then break all my rules, bid him enter incontinent.'

Among the adepts of happy erudition in the Collège de Coqueret the leader was Pierre de Ronsard. His person was prepossessing, his presence compelling, though fever had thinned his powerful frame, bleared his sharp eye, and turned his hair prematurely gray. Like many of his mates, he wore a close-clipped brown beard. Beard and short hair had been in fashion since young François I had got a torch on his head in a playful assault on the house of his cousins, and had grown a beard in compensation for the permanent searing of his scalp.

Ronsard shared a room with Jean-Antoine de Baïf. On their door a fellow student, Nicolas Denisot, had painted an allegory of Time with wingèd feet, with long locks clouding his eyes, and bearing a keen knife in his right hand. The room was the scene of glorious labors. Ronsard would sit over his books till two in the morning, and would then wake Baïf, who would take the warmed cushioned chair and read till morning his Greek poets, by the unquenched candle.

The young men were insatiate. One day Dorat read to Ronsard the *Prometheus* of Aeschylus from end to end, without a pause. 'Why, Master,' cried the pupil, 'have you hidden from me so long these riches?' Ronsard translated Aristophanes' *Plutus,* and the scholars produced it on their little school stage. It was the first comedy, in the ancient and modern (not medieval) sense, to be acted in France.

Dorat and his band were not rebuffed by the knottiest writers. They loved difficulty, indeed, and prized, equally with the great authors, the laborious Cal-

limachus, the bombastic Nicander, the pedantic Lyco-
phron, the intolerable Tzetzes. In their universal admiration one may perceive a certain gormandizer's lack
of taste, and a certain pleasure in puzzle-solving.

In this fanatic school of Coqueret Ronsard became a
scholar. He was known, later, as one of the first Hellenists of France. When a new professor of Greek was to be
appointed to the supreme Collège de France, Ronsard
was one of the committee that examined the candidate's
proficiency.

It would be strange if these enthusiasts of poetry did
not themselves woo the Muse. In the quiet evenings,
where a lone candle lit the chill cubicle, the young men
felt the shudder of poetic possession. Ronsard filled his
drawer with imitations of the classics, and with simpler,
sweeter lyrics, songs of love and memory. And with
rough notes for an epic poem of twenty-four books, a
glorious Iliad for France !

Splendid excess marked these minds and these days.
'Nothing in moderation' might have served for the
young men's device. As extreme as their study was their
revulsion from study. Ronsard celebrated anti-scholar-
ship in words which are, to be sure, authorized by
Horace and Anacreon :

> All my mind is murk and muddied ;
> Too persistently I've studied
> Arátus's *Phenomena.*
> Let us make in common a
> Journey to the meadows ! Gods !
> What a fool is he who lauds
> Those who, bent above a book,
> Have no care to live and look !
>
> What is study worth, unless
> To grieve the flesh in weariness,

And to furnish trist and care
For the spirit which shall fare
Or this evening or this morn
Down to Orcus' land forlorn?
Overweening Orcus can
Never pardon any man !

.   .   .   .   .

Now I'm in the humor, I'll
Drink and roundly drink awhile,
Lest the stealthy malady
Spring upon me suddenly,
Saying, as she darks the sun :
'Die, my hearty ! Drinking's done !'

J'ai l'esprit tout ennuyé
D'avoir trop étudié
Les Phœnomènes d'Arate ;
Il est temps que je m'ébatte
Et que j'aille aux champs jouer.
Bons Dieux ! Qui voudrait louer
Ceux qui collés sur un livre
N'ont jamais souci de vivre ?

Que nous sert d'étudier,
Sinon de nous ennuyer
Et soin dessus soin accroître
A nous qui serons peut-être
Ou ce matin, ou ce soir,
Victime de l'Orque noir,
De l'Orque qui ne pardonne,
Tant il est fier, à personne !

.   .   .   .   .

Ores que je suis dispos,
Je veux boire sans repos,
De peur que la maladie
Un de ces jours ne me die,
Me happant à l'imprévu :
Meurs, galant, c'est assez bu.

Fine weather tempted the scholars from their toil,
during the ritual freedoms of Thursday and Saturday

afternoons, and at other, unauthorized hours. On the
playing fields of the Pré-aux-Clercs, thousands of Paris
students met for their games. The athletic Ronsard,
football-lover, here showed his prowess. He probably
took part in the great riot of 1548, when the students
protested against encroachments on their playground
by thoroughly wrecking the intrusive buildings.

There were other diversions, evening diversions.

The French have always been lenient toward young
men's sins of the flesh. And the young men of Coqueret
had some reason to be lenient toward their master.
Dorat was married in December, 1548, immediately
after the birth of his daughter Marguerite. He was conducted to the altar by the ecclesiastical judge deputed to
settle suits for seduction and breach of promise. Marriage was his only punishment ; the authorities did not
seem to regard the improper sequence of parenthood
and wedlock as a disqualification for an educator. Marguerite, incidentally, lisped in Greek, and became a
most excellent Hellenist.

The master was still the master; in his pupils' revels
as in their toil. When the scholars, tired of study, sought
the ease of some dark, vaulted *cabaret,* Dorat led the
way and took the seat of honor. In his fine voice he sang
in Greek, Latin, and French, accompanying himself on
the fourteen-stringed lute. And if he noticed a pupil
toying with one of the ready doxies of the Latin Quarter, he was not severe. There had been hetæræ at the
Greek symposia, and lubricity had its justifications in
the best authors.

When the weather was fine and warm, the whole
school would declare a holiday and set off for the country. The youths were welcome at the Meudon estate of
Ronsard's former classmate at Navarre, the Cardinal de

Lorraine. Here they idled under the woods, and on the terraced slopes. Here, just possibly, they met the titular curé of Meudon, François Rabelais. Only just possibly, for Rabelais most likely never resided in his cure.

Sometimes they made short excursions to Gentilly or Vanves, names now familiar to tourists as the destinations of autobuses, destinations which the tourists never remain to see. Sometimes the scholars made the twenty-mile trip to Médan, beside the Seine, to visit Jean Brinon, Conseiller au Parlement. The château is today the home of Maurice Maeterlinck. Here they swam, and hunted, and trapped birds, or merely listened to their music. They recorded the sedge-warbler's song in musical notation, and determined his words to be 'toro, tret, fuis, huy, tret.' The country day would end with Greek epigrams and French sonnets, and the toasting of mistresses, present or ideal.

Unlettered spectators, ignorant of Hellenic precedent, looked sometimes sourly on these classic gayeties. There was one picnic that caused a long scandal. It was in 1552. The comrade Étienne Jodelle had just produced his *Cléopâtre captive,* the first French tragedy in the style of the ancients, the first forerunner of Corneille and Racine. *Cléopâtre* was acted before King Henri by the author and his friends. Soon after the triumph, the gay brigade arranged a country festival in celebration. A broad cloth was spread on the grass beside the little Bièvre. Many toasts and healths were drained by 'the holy, learned company.' Near by, a herd of goats gazed and wondered. Several of the merry-makers recalled that Bacchus's goat was of old the prize of the tragic bard. They seized the father of the marvelling flock, crowned him with a chaplet of flowers, set a coquettish bouquet above his ear, dyed his beard with wine, and presented

him to Jodelle. Very proud was that goat at his honor,
says Ronsard, proud even when Jodelle plucked for sacrifice hairs from his beard with one hand, holding aloft
a cup to Bacchus with the other. Ronsard then bestrode
the goat, like a courser of the Royal Stables. And all
together shouted interminably the old Greek cry of
Dionysiac frenzy : 'Iach, iach, evohe ; evohe, iach, iach !'

A ring of goatherds and country children stood about,
grinning. There was also the sour curé of Gentilly, who
grinned not. 'Pagans !' he muttered. 'What are these students coming to ! Absolute pagans !' His story, much repeated and magnified, spread the bruit that Ronsard
and his friends had publicly, and with every sign of serious devotion, sacrificed a goat to Bacchus. The story was
to return and plague Ronsard, years later.

Of another of the school's jolly outings Ronsard has
left us a detailed record. It was in July 1549. According to the ancient customs and usages of the Latin
Quarter, the students had paid their fees, and the principal, Dorat, had responded to their courtesy by giving
them a banquet. The pupils, still following tradition,
returned courtesy for courtesy for courtesy by inviting
their master to a country picnic.

It was still night when the town-dwelling pupils gathered before the Collège de Coqueret and waked the in-
ternes with an *aubade,* a dawn-song, accompanied with
the squalling of country pipes and the strumming of a
guitar. Heedless of sleepers' spite, the serenaders joined
hands in a stamping country dance. At last Abel, the
college porter, opened the doors. He distributed to each
his burden of wine in leather bottles, of hams, pasties,
gingerbread, black-puddings, saveloys, chitterlings, and
sausage of every size and shape. The procession wended
its way southward, through the rue Saint Jacques, the

highway of the Latin Quarter. At the present Boulevard de Port-Royal they came to the Paris walls and passed through the narrow gate, under the eye of lounging soldiers. They breasted the current of early market-wagons, then turned off along a byroad, beside meadows descending to a willowed stream. They sang a long antiphonal chorus, authorized by Vergil's words, *alternis contendere versibus.*

Ronsard marched with two large bottles slung on his back, and with an enormous two-handled loving-cup in his hands. He took the census of his companions. There was Dorat, Du Bellay, Baïf ; and Urvoy, carrying a bottle of white wine, wrapped in ivy, swinging from a stick over his shoulders ; and Peccate, taking comic surreptitious draughts from Urvoy's bottle, and receiving in punishment the bottle full in his face ; and Nicolas Denisot, known by his anagram of Le Conte d'Alcinois, pursing his lips and talking to himself. Denisot found by the wayside a great ass, untended. He slipped the beast's halter and, affectionately scratching his ears and neck, tempted him to join the band. The ass was loaded with bottles and garlanded with flowers. The porter, Abel, retrieved the fallen bottles and the posies which the bewildered animal twitched off with troubled ears.

> Abel pats the ass's jaw,
>   Pries his maw
> Open with a shout of 'Brother !'
> Thrusts courageous fingers there ;
>   Then they bare
> Mocking teeth at one another.
>
> *Ores cet Abel le touche,*
>   *Or la bouche*
> *Il lui ouvre, ore dedans*
> *Met ses doits, puis les retire,*

Et pour rire
Ils se rechignent des dents.

Ronsard resumes his enumeration. Here is Harteloyre, whose glory mounts swift to heaven ; and sober Latan, today playing the fool ; and Des Mireurs, the medical student, watching for dangerous excess with an eye already professional ; and Ligneri, the incomparable lute-player ; and Capel, who can see no good in the vulgar mob, as the vulgar mob sees none in Capel.

'Io, Io !' they cry, with the old bacchante shout of Greece. Aurora is leaving her husband's arms, and holding high her torch. The procession comes to its bourn, a grassy mead in Arcueil, beside the stripling Bièvre. High overhead stand the broken arches of the Roman aqueduct which once carried country water across the valley and down to the Baths of Julian in Paris. The dew is still heavy on the grass.

> How the willows, how the sedges,
>   How the hedges
> Feel the humid chill anew !
> How the dayspring seems to brush
>   Meadows lush
> With the silver of the dew !
>
> Io O the smoky look
>   Of the brook,
> Where the shaft of Phoebus passes !
> Io O the sombre shade
>   Of the glade,
> Carpeted with woven grasses !
>
> Now the Dawn, the saffron-gowned,
>   Rosy-crowned,
> Flowers in the sky bestrows.
> Dawn the earth below imbrues
>   With her dews,
> And the tears of human woes.

Iô comme ces saulaies
  Et ces haies
Sentent l'humide fraîcheur,
Et ces herbes, et ces plaines,
  Toutes pleines
De rousoyante blancheur !

Que ces rives écumeuses
  Sont fumeuses,
Au premier trait de Phébus !
Et ces fontainières prées,
  Diaprées
De mille tapis herbus !

Voici l'Aube safranée,
  Qui jà née
Couvre d'œillets et de fleurs
Le ciel, qui le jour desserre,
  Et la terre
De rosées et de pleurs.

The classic band is moved to classically propitiate the
Dawn, for assurance of fair weather. A cock, day-lover,
day-singer, is pinned in the Dawn's honor to a willow
tree, and the goddess adjured in suitable words in her
own Greek tongue. And Bacchus too receives his honor,
songs and shouts of 'evohe !' and libations till the sun
seems double. The poetic frenzy, *furor poeticus,* moves
all tongues to incoherent praise. But the chants are interrupted by a flight of butterflies. Bacchus is forgotten,
as his worshippers seek to prison the bright insects with
their hats. Dorat promises a hymn of his own making
for the pupil who shall take the loveliest butterfly.
Ronsard pursues the queen of all the flight, but trips
over a vine and falls flat. He is consoled by the recollection of Telephus, King of Lysia, who was wounded by
Achilles' lance after Bacchus had caused him to trip

over a vine-stump. (Or did Ronsard trip only to pro-
claim the recollection of Telephus ?) Berger, the buf-
foon of the school, stirs an enormous dust, and returns
with the trophy judged the finest. It is pinned to a willow, with an inscription : 'I, fleetfoot Berger, humbly
hang to the goatfoot gods these captured spoils, taken
by me at the age of fifty years.'

After the heat of the chase, the frolickers strip off
their clothes and bathe in the placid Bièvre. Urvoy
raises a laugh by flinging himself fully dressed into the
pool and swimming frog-like under the water. Ronsard
unceasingly apostrophizes thigh-born Bacchus and his
company of dryads, naiads, satyrs, and horn-browed
fauns.

Now the cooking-fires are dying, and cloths are spread
on the grass. In the midst of the feast the classic parallels
are not forgotten. When hunger is sated, the wine, sweet
Anjou dew, is drawn from the pool, where it has basked,
cooling.

> I adjure you, let the glass
>   Gayly pass
> Round the circle once again ;
> In the liquor bright and brown
>   Let us drown
> The worm's gnawing in the brain.
>
> Drink, my bawcocks ; lift the cup
>   Bravely up,
> And avow your happy fetters !
> Your fair conqueror proclaim ;
>   Of her name
> Drink to all the lucky letters !
>
> Nine times in Cassandra's praise
>   Shall I raise

High the cup, to pledge her fame ;
Nine times voiding it of wine,
   For the nine
Darling letters of her name !

Let us drink, and sing of love,
   Heedless of
Felon Care's malignant tooth !
Age, that pickpurse envious,
   Follows us,
Crowding on the heels of youth.

Je veux que la tasse pleine
   Se promène
Tout autour, de poing en poing,
Et veux qu'au fond d'elle on plonge
   Ce qui ronge
Nos cerveaux d'un traître soin.

Ores, amis ! qu'on n'oublie
   De l'amie
Le nom, qui vos cœurs lia ;
Qu'on vide autant cette coupe,
   Chère troupe,
Que de lettres il y a.

Neuf fois au nom de Cassandre
   Je vais prendre
Neuf fois du vin au flacon,
Afin de neuf fois le boire
   En mémoire
Des neuf lettres de son nom.

Iô ! qu'on boive, qu'on chante,
   Qu'on enchante
La dent des soucis félons !
La vieillesse larronnesse
   Jà nous presse
Le derrière des talons.

The fumes of the wine, he vowed, made drunk even
a gaping frog by the streamside.

But ho ! Dorat takes his lute in hand, and in his mellow voice intones a Latin chant. He celebrates the stream and its deities, and all he utters is divine, divine. No honey can be so sweet as the nectar of his verses. When we hear him, our spirits seem to be ravished away, and we walk in the underworld with the soul of Theban Pindar.

The good day at length draws down. The brown star Vesper pins over the skies a dusky veil. O black coursers, leave us our light, that we may hear a little longer the delicious words of Dorat, stirring our hearts, prickling our flesh. But the stars disdain our prayer, and their twinkling chases day beneath the distant waves. Jealous stars, you are not worthy to hear that perfect chant, fit only for the gods' pleasure !

> Now the sombre-skirted Night
> > Has bedight
> The ridges in her darkling dress.
> Therefore let our gallant group
> > Homeward troop,
> Nearly drunk with happiness.

> Not till life's undoing can
> > Wretched man
> Know complete felicity.
> In the gayest hour of gladness
> > Still is sadness
> Mingled shyly, secretly.

> *Donque, puisque la nuit sombre*
> > *Pleine d'ombre*
> *Vient les montagnes saisir,*
> *Retournons, troupe gentille,*
> > *Dans la ville*
> *Demi-saoulés de plaisir.*

Jamais l'homme, tant qu'il meure,
  Ne demeure
Fortuné parfaitement :
Toujours avec la liesse
  La tristesse
Se mêle parfaitement.

V

'O Muse, ma douce folie . . .'

IF you had asked a Frenchman of 1550 about the state
of French poetry, he would have put on an apologetic
face. It is no great shakes, he would have said ; the
Frenchman is not a poet, like the Italian. Old-fashioned
folks, to be sure, still quote the *rhétoriqueurs* ; and of
course there are the court poets, like Clément Marot
and Saint-Gelais, who have done some charming things,
delicious.

The school of *rhétoriqueurs* had its centre in Burgundy. While Burgundian artists performed amazing
feats of dexterity with stone, to make their flamboyant
Gothic, the poets twined and fitted words in flamboyant
verse. They loved difficulty ; their Muse was a contor-
tionist. They took the hard fixed forms of the Middle
Age, the ballade, rondeau, chant royal, and invented
new and harder forms, the double virelay, the *ballade
baladant,* the *ballade fratrisée,* the *riqueraque,* the
baguenaude. They wrote poems with one syllable to a
line, and others which had one meaning if read in the
ordinary way, and an opposite meaning if one read the
first half of each line, and then returned to read the
second halves. A *rhétoriqueur,* Meschinot, wrote an
eight-line stanza which was announced to have thirty-
two different meanings ; and a modern *rhétoriqueur* has
proved that Meschinot's stanza can in fact be read in 255

different ways, all ridiculous. My own favorite is a poem
of Jean Marot's which begins :

riant	fuz		nagueres
En			pris
T	D'une	O	affectée
V	tile	S	
espoir	haittée		
Que	vent		
	j'ay		

Which must be interpreted :

> En *sous*riant fuz nagueres *sur*pris
> D'une *sub*tile *entre* TOVS affectée,
> Que *sous* espoir j'ay *souvent sou*haittée

Meaning, in short, was subordinated to mechanism,
art to a marvellous craftsmanship.

These poetic carvers of ships in bottles were known
as *rimeurs,* and in rhyme they performed extraordinary
feats of dexterity. They invented a dozen novelties, such
as the internal rhyme :

> *Que feray je de ma laidure dure ?*
> *M'ardure dure et ma foiblesse blesse ;*
> *Mon corps s'encline a corrompure pure :*
> *Mercure cure et n'y procure cure ;*
> *Morsure sure a moy l'adresse dresse ;*
> *Richesse cesse, et trop m'oppresse presse.*

They pushed the rhyme forward from the line's beginning and back from its end till rhyme almost met in the
middle :

> *Quant cessera maultemps ? Incontinent*
> *Qu'en cepz sera desir incontinent,*
> *Desir entends cueur de vain et lasche homme,*
> *Desirant temps qu'heure vienne, et la chomme . . .*

Delaisse aller ces propos, et que j'oye
De les saller pour un temps quelque joye.

We have done better, to be sure, in our own time. The paragon of all French rhyme is the sonnet which Jean Goudezki sent to Alphonse Allais, in the 1890's, inviting him to a country party. Each line reproduces totally the sound of its mate :

Je t'attends samedi, car, Alphonse Allais, car
A l'ombre, à Vaux, l'on gèle. Arrive! Oh! la campagne!
Allons, bravo! longer la rive au lac, en pagne.
Jette à temps, ça me dit, carafons à l'écart.
Laisse aussi sombrer tes déboires, et dépêche!
Là, très puissant, un homme l'est tôt : l'art nourrit
L'attrait ; (puis, sens!) une omelette au lard nous rit,
Lait, saucisse, ombre et thé, des poires et des pêches ;

Et, le verre à la main — t'es-tu décidé? Roule!
Elle verra, là, mainte étude s'y déroule,
Ta muse étudiera les bêtes ou les gens.
Comme aux dieux devisant, Hébé (c'est ma compagne)
Commode, yeux de vice hantés, baissés, m'accompagne,
Amusé, tu diras, 'L'Hébé te soûle, eh, Jean!' 1

The craft of the *rhétoriqueurs* persists today, but it has fallen into the hands of ingenious light versifiers, artisans of the whimsy. Our tricksters in prosody ask acclaim only for their ingenuity, while the *rhétoriqueurs* thought themselves poets in deadly earnest.

To the *rhétoriqueurs* succeeded Jean Marot's son Clément, witty, graceful, an artist in language. In him much of the old rhetoric persisted ; his efforts to tap the great treasury of classic art were timid and ill informed. Ronsard admired him, and with reason, for so we admire him today. There was also Mellin de Saint-Gelais,

1 This is dragged in, the critic will say. In fact, for fifteen years I have been trying to drag it in.

the perfect court poet, ready with a huitain or a rondeau an hour after every palace contretemps. Professing poetry as an elegance, he made of it a livelihood. Though he brought, from an Italian education, new models, Petrarch and his successors, he earned only scorn from the young men of Coqueret. To them he represented the degradation of poetry to servile use.

There were other poets, especially the curious Platonists of Lyon. These wrote long, obscure, mystical dissertations on love purified to incomprehensibility. To this school Ronsard and his group were not hostile, but found its work merely uninteresting, a divagation from the course of true art.

Gradually the idea took shape that poetry, once the most illustrious form of man's spiritual expression, might again be something better than a courtly diversion. Jacques Peletier, Ronsard's friend, called for the imitation of the ancients in his introduction to a translation of Horace's *Ars Poetica* in 1544. Peletier was a frequenter of the Collège de Coqueret, and perhaps gave the creed to the young school.

To Coqueret's dismay, the first manifesto came from without its walls. In 1548 Thomas Sebillet published an *Art Poétique,* largely a collection of rules drawn from Clément Marot's example and from that of the *rhétoriqueurs.* But in some ways his views were radical. He took his definition of poetry from Plato's *Timaeus* : it is a divine inspiration. 'What is called art in verse is only the bare bark of poetry, which artificially covers its natural voice and its soul, naturally divine.' He proposed the introduction into French of several ancient forms, notably the ode of Pindar and Horace.

Coqueret found its faith half stated, which is worse than to have it mis-stated. Joachim du Bellay was deputed to utter the true doctrine of the group. In 1549, an important date in French literary history, he published his *Défense et Illustration de la langue française*.

The book falls into two parts, a defense and an illustration. The author defends the French language against its humanistic detractors, proves that it is capable of expressing great thoughts in noble form. He illustrates his case by an art of writing. We must, he says, establish the new French poetry upon the ancient forms, not upon the current forms inherited from the French Middle Age. We must create a poetic language and a poetic style, different from the language and style of prose.

Though the words were those of Du Bellay, they echo the prompting voice of Ronsard. He was the leader, the chief, the dominator of the school. To him all submitted and paid tribute. His *Brigade*, he called them. Some time later he renamed them the *Pléiade*, after the seven Greek poets who likened themselves to the stars. The composition of his pleiad varied from year to year, as poets fell out of favor and others took their place. There were usually, in fact, more than seven.

Du Bellay was first into print with his *Défense et Illustration*, which was closely followed by his *Olive*, a sonnet sequence imitated from Petrarch. In the same volume with *Olive* appeared thirteen Odes, clumsily imitated from Vergil and Horace. Ronsard knew it was high time for him to publish the poems which had been accumulating in his drawer, the poems he was wont to declaim in school, to appreciative cries of 'Io ! Evohe ! Iach, iach !'

In the early part of 1550 the twenty-five-year-old poet gave to the world his first volume, *Les quatre premiers livres des Odes de Pierre de Ronsard, Vendômois*. It consisted of 94 odes 'measured to the lyre,' and fourteen irregular pieces.

It was a brave book, and a startling one. It heaped an enormous, indiscriminate scorn upon all previous French poets, swine troubling poesy's clear waters. The book demanded liberty for the writer : 'your trade will not be slave to that art useless to the Muses.' In the matter of metrics, it broke every cherished rule. Its language seemed bizarre and shocking, for Ronsard coined new words, adopted Vendômois peasant idioms that pleased his ear, and turned many a Greek vocable insolently into French. Even the spelling was strange, following a new system of orthography. All the traditional forms of French verse disappeared, and were replaced by the classic ode. This was designed to be sung, to the accompaniment of the lyre, for, said Ronsard, 'the lyre alone can and should animate poetry and give it the just weight of its gravity.'

The book was noteworthy for its new conception, or its revival of an ancient conception, of the poet's dignity.

The poet's duty is enjoined upon him. He is more than man ; as Plato has said, he is bound to the gods by the links of a mysterious chain. Godhead inhabits him (thus Ovid) ; he is warmed by the divine unease. And Ronsard proclaimed that the man who honors not the poets as the prophets of the gods, contemns the gods in odious pride.

The poet is chosen and foretold from long aforetime. The favor of the Muses is bestowed as inscrutably as the grace of Jehovah upon his saints.

Ronsard knew himself to be of the elect. 'Assuredly before I was born thou hadst commanded me to sing thee,' he tells Calliope. And 'sacred Euterpe took me, a mortal, to be companion of the gods. . . .'

For with the water of her springs has she
Baptizèd me her priested votary,
Taught me the honor of her Grecian home,
And the long lore of venerable Rome.

Car elle m'a de l'eau de ses fontaines
Pour prêtre sien baptisé de sa main,
Me faisant part du haut honneur d'Athènes,
Et du savoir de l'antique Romain.

A Daimon comes by night to teach the bard in happy dreams. Only inspiration makes the singer ; those rhymers who have learned their trade by toil and tricks produce mis-shapen songs, they are crows spitefully croaking from the shadows against the sunny eagles. Plato has said that all good poets compose because they are inspired and possessed, under the power of music and metre, like Bacchic maidens who draw milk and honey from the rivers when they are under the influence of Dionysus, but not when they are in their right minds. 'For the poet is a light and winged and holy thing, and there is no invention in him until he has been inspired and is out of his senses, and the mind is no longer in him ; when he has not attained to this state, he is powerless and is unable to utter his oracles.' God takes away the minds of poets, and uses them as his ministers ; He Himself is the speaker, and through the poets converses with us.

O Muse, ma douce folie ! Ronsard knew well this sweet madness. For months, he confesses, he could not write a line, not at the command of a prince or at the dear entreaty of a lady. He gaped in vain, awaiting the poetic fury. But when, angry, ardent, shaking, the frenzy came, his whole body trembled under the oppression of deity. Poetry flowed through him like a released spring flood. He was a prophet, knowing the future, knowing

the secrets of nature and of heaven, the virtue of plants
and stones. He was himself a god. 'With fury I am
troubled ; my hair with horror stands. My soul is filled
with ardor, my breast is palsied, my voice can hardly
issue thence. A deity possesses me ; flee, people, leave
me. The goddess comes ; I feel her entering into me.
Happy is he whom she holds, and happy he who looks
upon her in her temple, where I see her now !'

The possession lasted a day, or two, or three. Then
pen and paper dropped from his hand, and from heaven
he fell crashing to earth. His body seemed paralyzed and
dead, his head sick. He was loathsome to himself. He
wakened horribly to the world of men.

His mystic moments were infinitely precious. They
proved his own vocation, and proved just the vaulting
claims of the ancients for the poet and his worth. A
man who could be rapt to the side of the gods was made
of another clay from common humanity. He deserved
the adoration of gross earthy creatures. Proudly, Ronsard demanded worship from his fellows, immortality
from the future. 'Up, then, Fame, charge upon thy
broad shoulder my name which attempts the skies, and
cover it with thy targe, for fear of envy's shaft.' 'Forever, forever, deathless ever, shall I wing my way
through the universe.' 'Death takes him not wholly un-
consoled whose spirit is fortified by the song that Ronsard sang.'

It was a noble arrogance. Pindar and Horace had
spoken thus defiantly before him, and it was his duty to
perpetuate their defiance, and by arrogance to uphold
not only his own fame, but the fame of all poets, of the
Poet.

There were, to be sure, quiet hours when, in privacy,
he cast off his public mantle of pride. After all his

boasts, he says to a friend that perhaps his labors may bring to him a little praise, for ten years or twenty. It is still true that Calliope lets the best singers of her troop die of hunger.

To illustrate his new conception of the poet and his work, Ronsard cast the first thirteen of his poems in Pindaric form.

Pindar is the darling of Hellenists, ancient and modern. The non-Hellenist, reading him in translation, marvels more at the Hellenists than at Pindar. These interminable adulations of the victor in the mule-chariot race, in the boxing-match with leaded gloves, these endless cross-references to the private life of the gods, these fantastic and ridiculous similes, stir the reader to a frenzy that is not poetic. But he is wonderful in the Greek, say the Hellenists. And he is so difficult, so adorably difficult ! Half the time you have no idea what he means !

Ronsard took Pindar as his master, and imitated him boldly and without shame. He had no scruples on the score of originality. According to his doctrine, to recast in French the thought of the godlike Greeks was the poet's noblest task. Originality is a vain purpose. If a thought has never been thought or never uttered, it is not worth uttering now. Let our aim be to choose the greatest thoughts, with a Grecian guarantee, and speak them again, in the sweetest accents of our tongue. The poet's labor should be put on form, not substance, for the poetic substance must be forever the same.

In his imitation, Ronsard encountered plenty of difficulties. For the athletes of Olympia, he substituted contemporary kings, nobles, and scholars, and the antique bays sat grotesquely on their brows. The Grecian myths, which Pindar's hearers knew and half believed,

dwindled to strange, obscure pedantries. The gods of
Olympus became wan changelings, pitiable, like their
naked statues cowering under northern rains. But the
poet grimly defied ridiculousness ; what Pindar said
must be beautiful, no matter if fools shall laugh. Ronsard heaps up incomprehensible epithets. His Jupiter,
appearing in the guise of a swan before Leda, informs
her that she will lay two eggs, one containing Castor,
the other Pollux. His book opens with the most cou-
rageous of similes : 'As one who takes a cup, his dearest
treasure, and pours forth to his troop the wine laughing within the gold, so do I pour the dew with which
my tongue is besprent upon the race of the Valois, and
slake with that sweet nectar the greatest king, in arms
and in laws.' King Henri may well have shuddered.

Tiresome as are these first odes to the modern reader
(I mean to me), they have a certain archaic charm, the
wistful formality of Greek vase-painting. They possess
as well a genuine importance in the history of French
poetry. For the first time the poet ventured to treat
great subjects of great meaning. He dealt with war,
peace, death, and love, and uttered his high thoughts in
majestic symbols. He demanded the right to speak the
emotion of the whole nation. Not many poets of our
day are so bold.

Nor, in his arrogance, was Ronsard satisfied to be the
Pindar of France. He dreamed an overweening dream.
He dared to conceive an epic poem of twenty-four
books, which should be to France what the Iliad was to
Greece, the Aeneid to Rome. And he, Ronsard, would
make a trinity with Homer and with Vergil !

For his theme he chose the medieval legend of Francus, son of Hector and Andromache, miraculously pre-
served from the sack of Troy and from the knowledge

of all the Greek poets and historians. Francus passed to Gaul, married the daughter of King Remus of Reims, and fathered the realm of France. As nothing at all was known of Francus, the legend-maker would have a free hand with him. Ronsard struggled helplessly with the epic style, and relieved his bafflement by talking much of his project. Coqueret was agog, to live familiarly with Homer in the making. Du Bellay announced the poem darkly in his *Défense et Illustration,* and Baïf proclaimed, in Greek, that the *Franciade* would surpass the Iliad. In long dormitory discussions and on country walks its form was debated, incidents suggested, and the amazement of the public happily forecast.

But nothing of this appeared in the poet's first volume. His collection consists largely of Pindaric odes, palinodes, epipalinodes. Fortunately, however, he chose to give bulk to his book by including many verses of a simpler sort, in which he released the surcharge of his passionate heart. In a dozen poems he remembers sweetly the scenes, the sounds, the warm earthy smell of his homeland, the forest of Gastine, the fontaine Bellerie, the meandering Loir. And in the collection are more than a dozen love poems, still resonant with a faraway beauty. Sincere or not, they have that perfection of form, that rightness of vowel and consonant, that turns simple songs into poetry. Such is the gift of Herrick (Ronsard's imitator), of Shelley, of Housman. Such was Ronsard's gift : the communication of emotion by a simple thought contained in a perfect design. Nothing could be more bare than his poem to Cupid, to punish cruel Jeanne. The opening is imitated from Horace, to be sure :

> The day drives out the night,
> And the night, sombre,

      Drives out the day, alight
        On evening umber.

The autumn follows summer ;
    The wind's blast
Yields to its overcomer,
    And storm is past.

Nevertheless the pain
    By love begot
Is resolute to remain ;
    It mends not.

Le jour pousse la nuit,
    Et la nuit sombre
Pousse le jour qui luit
    D'une obscure ombre.

L'automne suit l'été,
    Et l'âpre rage
Des vents n'a point été
    Après l'orage.

Mais le mal nonobstant
    D'amour dolente
Demeure en moi constant
    Et ne s'alente.

Who was his pitiless Jeanne? And his Madeleine, his Marguerite, his Rose, of the lovely *Des roses plantées près d'un blé* ? We do not know, and it does not matter much, as probably it did not matter much nor long to Ronsard. He was a soldier of Venus, proud of his conquests under her standard.

But the name of Cassandre is something else. This is the name that haunted his book, and haunted all his youth.

(((VI)))

Cassandre

PINDAR and Horace did not totally occupy the young men of Coqueret. There were hours when the flogged mind would not soar with poetry's sublimest coursers. There were hours when the rebel body strained for release, demanding its own pleasures, rejecting the consolations of philosophy. In such moments the spirit could somewhat cheat the flesh with the loving lewdness of Ovid and Catullus, with the voluptuous *Basia* of Johannes Secundus, with the *Erotopaignion,* or 'Love's Toy,' of Angerianus. And when the young men's thoughts turned to purer love, when they dreamt of lifelong devotion, of sacrifice, of the beautiful pity of a broken heart, they solaced themselves with the lovely words of Petrarch. Glorious Petrarch, faithful throughout his life to the vision of his Laura ! Petrarch with his melodious sighs, recording his sweet, interminable sorrow as an example to all future lovers !

Coqueret was a nest of Petrarchs, each with his Laura. Du Bellay had his Olive, Baïf his Francine, Magny his Castianire, Tahureau his Admirée, Pontus de Tyard, a churchman, his platonic Pasithée. The names were chosen for their mellifluousness, and no doubt represented often no living original. Ronsard required his subjects to worship his Cassandre, the noblest name of all. His companions supposed that she was no more than a high-sounding word. And most modern scholars, jeal-

84

ous of poets in love, have supposed the same. Only about forty years ago was she securely identified.

Needing an ideal mistress, Ronsard inevitably returned in fancy to that April day in the château of Blois, when he had seen the dark girl bending over her lute, singing the *branle de Bourgogne*. The sonorous syllables of her name fitted well in rhyme, and permitted erudite comparisons with the first Cassandra, daughter of Priam and Hecuba, and the sombre prophetess of Greece, who scorned the love of Apollo. Pronouncing the name endlessly in solitude, fitting it into tuneful plaints, the poet gave to it more magic than of itself it possessed. The magic he created worked upon its creator. Thus enchanters are ensorcelled by the demon-lemans they make, thus poets fall in love with themselves. The vision of Cassandre dwelt with Ronsard, high, pure, and vague. She was all virtue. He worshipped her, serene, as the symbol of heavenly beauty.

> If my releasèd spirit could but fly,
>   I'd gladly burn the bark of me entire,
>   Like great Alcmena's son, who came in fire
>   To take his seat among the gods on high.
> My rebel, craving spirit would deny
>   Its weight of flesh, and find its pure desire.
>   It gathers fuel for its own funeral pyre,
>   To kindle with the kindling of your eye.
> O holy brazier, chastely lovely flame,
>   Burn utterly away this carnal frame,
>   Let the soiled earthly garment be forsaken,
> And free and clean and naked let me soar
>   Beyond the highest heaven, there to adore
>   That other Beauty whence your own was taken.

> *Je veux brûler pour m'envoler aux cieux*
>   *Tout l'imparfait de cette écorce humaine,*
>   *M'éternisant, comme le fils d'Alcmène,*
>   *Qui tout en feu s'assit entre les dieux.*

Jà mon esprit chatouillé de son mieux,
Dedans ma chair, rebelle se promène,
Et jà le bois de sa victime amène
Pour s'enflammer aux rayons de tes yeux.
O saint brasier, ô feu chastement beau,
Las, brûle-moi d'un si chaste flambeau
Qu'abandonnant ma dépouille connue,
Net, libre, et nu, je vole d'un plein saut
Outre le ciel, pour adorer là-haut
L'autre beauté dont la tienne est venue.

Like Petrarch, he wandered sighing in the woodland reaches, speaking his beloved's name, and hearing the birds gladly chorus it in reply. He longed to be a brook, endlessly murmuring 'Cassandre — Cassandre.' He was alone with his love amid the city's throngs. Like Petrarch, still, he vowed to her a lifetime of hopeless tears, and like him, saw nothing amiss in dalliance which touched the sense but not the soul. Nor, like Petrarch, did he feel any conflict between profane love and the sacred character of the tonsured clerk.

In the beginning, Ronsard's passion was literary. His books were still his dearest love, his fine library in Greek, Latin, Italian, Spanish, French. 'I love them,' he wrote to a friend, 'more than my companions, more than you, more than myself.' But as love has made most of our books, so books can create love.

In the summer of 1551 Ronsard returned to La Possonnière for a long vacation. Paris irked him in the bright season ; he felt the need of earth underfoot and flowers in his hand. And as he walked one day in the meadows he met Cassandre. There was nothing miraculous in the meeting. Her château of Pray stood only twenty miles from La Possonnière, and the gentry of the region, all more or less related, paid each other long visits.

Like a flower, says Ronsard, Cassandre was sitting among the flowers. She wore a simple country dress, sweetly dishevelled with her walk. She had removed her bright colored hat, and toyed with it in her lap. 'From that day forth my mind was sick.'

His surprise was perhaps less than he alleges. Perhaps he knew of her presence in his neighborhood or he sought her in her own, his mind delightedly anticipating its own sickness. However that be, he was struck by the change in the matron from the girl of fourteen, ghostly in his memory. Her beauty disconcerted him by its mere discordance with his cherished fancy. This was no earthly representation of heavenly beauty ; this was the beauty of our world, which our world suffices, and which is sufficient for it. Ronsard fell in love a second time, but with another Cassandre.

His heart filled with sweet turmoil, he returned to La Possonnière. He had other meetings with Cassandre, in the manors and châteaux of the Loir, and used his prestige as a poet and scholar to allure Cassandre and to impress her husband, Jean de Peigné, seigneur de Pray. When he felt the time to be ripe, he importuned his brother Claude and Anne, his sister-in-law, to invite the châtelains of Pray to La Possonnière for a visit. Claude and Anne, whether blind or conniving, fell in with Pierre's proposal. Cassandre came with her waiting-women to the Ronsard manor. Perhaps her husband accompanied her ; the poet forbears to mention him. If he was present, he spent his days hunting and carousing with Claude, leaving Pierre and Cassandre to their womanish diversions.

Together they walked in the fields along the Loir, accompanied by her yapping spaniel, jealous of Ronsard, of whom Ronsard was jealous. Cassandre loved

flowers, loved to pick an armful in the fields, and meditate on their beauty and their evanescence. Ronsard
pointed the lesson of her mood, in one of his most remembered songs, *Mignonne, allons voir si la rose* . . .
(It is the theme that Herrick imitated endlessly, the
song that Wagner set his music to.)

Mignonne, we'll seek the rose
That we have watched unclose
This morning to the sun ;
We'll see if she display
The color that gleamed so gay,
Now that day is done.

Alas, Mignonne, alas !
See, strown upon the grass,
The crumpled crimson gown !
O Nature, mother of woe,
That bringeth beauty low,
Before the night come down !

And so, Mignonne, be wise ;
Seize on the hour that flies,
The hour that beauty blows.
And gather youth, dear maid,
Ere age shall come, to fade
Your beauty, like the rose.

Mignonne, allons voir si la rose
Qui ce matin avait déclose
Sa robe de pourpre au soleil,
A point perdu, cette vêprée,
Les plis de sa robe pourprée
Et son teint au vôtre pareil.

Las ! voyez comme en peu d'espace,
Mignonne, elle a dessus la place,
Las, las ! ses beautés laissé choir ;
O vraiment marâtre Nature,
Puis qu'une telle fleur ne dure
Que du matin jusques au soir !

Donc, si vous me croyez, mignonne,
Tandis que votre âge fleuronne
En sa plus verte nouveauté,
Cueillez, cueillez votre jeunesse :
Comme à cette fleur, la vieillesse
Fera ternir votre beauté.

There were country sports : a game of prisoner's base, wherein Cassandre ironically put Pierre in the hostile camp ; and great stag-hunts and boar-hunts in the woods of Gastine. A forest bramble tore the white arm of Cassandre ; her dear blood fell upon a flower, which the poet christened the Cassandrette. Pierre himself was scratched, in a fencing bout. Cassandre banished all his hurt, by herself dressing his wound with the simples whose virtue she knew. And when his eyes pained him, it was Cassandre who made for him a lotion of herbs. Her little gifts of flowers and confitures filled him with rapture and hope.

The two drifted in a skiff upon the Loir, Cassandre with her hair tucked under a boyish cap. They watched the birds pecking at the soft crumbling walls of the river valley. They halted by meadows to pick the flowers Cassandre loved. Pierre showed her the haunts of his own dreams, the mossy, green-lipped, gaping caverns, the lush *île verte* he had chosen for his burial place. Cassandre fell readily into long, silent reveries, and Ronsard, at the oars, watched her bowed head, her fingers trailing in the stream, and inwardly made passionate avowals which he feared to utter.

He read to her the poems he had written for her during the night vigils, such poems as this, in memory of her music :

More precious than the gold of all the west
  Is her bright brow where tyrant Love abides ;

Fairer that cheek wherein the rose resides
Than all the opulent purple Tyre possessed.
There is no beauty like her equal breast
That swims in secret, rises and subsides
With the heart's hidden Cytherean tides,
Lifting her bodice in a soft unrest.
Just as the spirit of Jove was filled with cheer,
When a Muse strummed her measures to his ear,
So by Cassandra's music am I raptured,
When, on the lute her fingers flying free,
She sings again the branle of Burgundy,
The song she sang, the day that I was captured.

Plus mille fois que nul or terrien
J'aime ce front où mon tyran se joue,
Et le vermeil de cette belle joue
Qui fait honteux le pourpre Tyrien.
Toutes beautés à mes yeux ne sont rien
Au prix du sein qui lentement secoue
Son gorgerin, sous qui pair à pair noue
Le branle égal d'un flot Cythérien.
Ni plus ni moins que Jupiter est aise,
Quand de son luth quelque Muse l'apaise,
Ainsi je suis de ses chansons épris,
Lorsqu'à son luth ses doigts elle embesogne,
Et qu'elle dit le branle de Bourgogne,
Qu'elle disait, le jour que je fus pris.

The poet looked up eagerly from his script. Cassandre smiled, and told him that his song was pretty, flattering him with the transparent flattery she would give a vain child. And Pierre was wounded, thinking of the ecstatic applause, the minute appreciation of details, that his sonnet would have received from the disciples of Coqueret. He hinted that Cassandre might properly recall her dreaming thoughts, and relish with him his beautiful words and subtle ideas. He burst forth with praise of art, with his claim upon posterity's admiration, with a promise to render Cassandre's name immortal. But in her mind's world poetry was not a serious matter. She smiled, with a woman's superior understanding of realities. Even, she mocked at his high pretensions. 'Silly boy !' she said. 'All your fine talk will never make me love you ! And as for posterity, surely you aren't serious !' As she spoke, a clap of thunder on the right proved Heaven's subscription to her words.

She did not love him. She loved more her own fidelity, and her own melancholy mood. Pierre perceived her sometimes, her eyes downcast, her lips moving in some secret discourse. He longed to speak to her, and dared not. He put on a tragic face for her to see, and she did not see it. He was angry in his pride, but his anger could not persist. He came to love her the more for her abstraction in a private world of dream.

The idle outings on the Loir brought mishap to Cassandre. The jealous naiads of the stream sent a winged evil against their rival. Cassandre fell ill with a fever. Pierre was chased from his room, and Cassandre was installed in his bed, in his very bed. He watched the course of her illness, shook with her chills and fever, and wrote poetry. Nicolas Denisot, his painter friend from Coqueret, came for a visit. The two wandered in the fields, gathering flowers for the sickroom, especially the poppy, sacred to sleep. For Cassandre tossed wakeful on her bed. Pierre wrote a prayer to sleep, kind sleep, father, care-loosener, life-giver, oblivious son of night and Lethe, nurse of men and gods, whose hovering wing sprinkles dew upon the brain, who shuts our eyes to sorrow. 'O sleep, O great Daimon, O serviceable peace of all our souls, accept these poppies, this incense, this manna, and shade with thy dark wing the eyes, the temples, and the brow of Cassandre sick ; and with deep slumber soothe her ill !'

Denisot made for Pierre a portrait of Cassandre, as Simone Martini had painted Laura for Petrarch. The poet directed the artist to paint her hair the color of cedar-wood, bound in a coif of black crepe, to show her eyebrows ebony black, her cheek a rose swimming on milk, or a blushing pink kissing a lily, her neck long and slender, her apple breasts subtly veined. When the painting was done, Pierre fled to the caves of Loir-side, and to the thickest tangles of Gastine, and drew forth the portrait, and sighed, like Petrarch, and like him wrote his woe.

She recovered. With her convalescence Pierre's courtship became more pressing. He was no longer content with sighs. Trembling and fearful, yet importunate, he avowed his desire. Cassandre, in her weakness following fever, burst into tears. Pierre refused to understand her grief. In a few days he was more pressing, more explicit. Now Cassandre, sure of herself, laughed at him, and at his protests of suffering and sure death. There is no better way to infuriate a poet-lover.

> . . . *Et quand je te veux dire*
> *Quelle est ma mort, tu ne t'en fais que rire,*
> *Et de mon mal tu as le cœur joyeux.*

In vain he read to her his sweet songs of despair. In vain he adjured her to seize the day, to profit by the fast-fleeing hours of youth. For the brevity of youth and beauty tortured him. He could hardly write a dozen lines without returning to his theme of flying time, and urgent age, and death which comes incontinent, and Mercury with his rod, waiting to lead us to the obscure valley and the cold odious kingdom.

One day, on waking, Cassandre found at her door a sheaf of fresh-culled roses, bound with a sonnet :

The roses that your waking eyes will see
   Were chosen in the meadows' bright parade ;
   Had I not plucked them in the advancing shade,
   The morrow would have sealed their destiny.
Let this an evident example be
   That beauty's heart is haggard and decayed,
   That all youth's comeliness will dry and fade,
   And, like the roses, perish suddenly.
Ah, time is flying, Lady, time is flying —
   No, it's not time ; 'tis we who fly away,
   And soon beneath the gravestone we'll be lying.
And all that love of which we talk today,
   When we are dead, no one will know nor guess.
   So love me now, in all your loveliness.

Je vous envoie un bouquet que ma main
   Vient de trier de ces fleurs épanies ;
   Qui ne les eût à ce vêpre cueillies,
   Chutes à terre elles fussent demain.
Cela vous soit un exemple certain
   Que vos beautés, bien qu'elles soient fleuries,
   En peu de temps cherront toutes flétries
   Et comme fleurs périront tout soudain.
Le temps s'en va, le temps s'en va, ma Dame,
   Las ! le temps non, mais nous nous en allons
   Et tôt serons étendus sous la lame ;
Et des amours desquelles nous parlons,
   Quand serons morts, n'en sera plus nouvelle :
   Pour ce aimez-moi, cependant qu'êtes belle.

Ronsard wrote of true love, or all the words of poets
are lies. It was born, indeed, of artifice and the desire
for experience. But out of the desire of love came forth
love. The assumed attitude became the natural posture ;
the words worked upon the utterer and became his
faith. Thus we repeat creeds as much to make our doctrine as to testify to it.

His pain was real, though its origin was in a curiosity
about pain. It was the more acute for having its share

of wounded self-esteem. For Cassandre would not love him. Her air showed that she thought the prince of poets a foolish boy, according to her understanding of men. When he besought her to seize her brief youth, her cool smile hinted that her deafish, gray-haired suitor was attempting to seize his own youth, already beyond his reach.

He begged her for kisses, to ease his thoughts, and rarely his importunings obtained that gift, from pity only. Though there was no yielding in the quick kiss, and a taste of bitterness in it, he vowed that it made him happier than the total embrace of a goddess.

There was a wild moment when his hand ventured too intimate a caress, and his lips made a too specific demand. Her anger was her reply. She summoned her waiting-women, and as soon as was seemly departed to her home. Her freezing manner gave Pierre no chance to gain her pardon by his eloquent repentance, or her pity by his woe. At the hour of leave-taking, he chose to run and hide. She looked for him in vain, and tossed her head, and left La Possonnière without an adieu.

To the woods again ; to the thickets and sun-spotted glades of Gastine, and to the reedy banks of Loir, holy with the memory of Cassandre's passage. Grief filled the poet's heart, grief for Cassandre's absence, and for her departure in anger. It was grief of love unrequited, of desire rebuffed, of devotion misprized.

Such sorrows mingle well with wounded pride. The poet examined his broken heart with interest, and then with some complaisance. Petrarch and all noble poets of love had suffered just so. It was the fate of great spirits to suffer, because consummated love is somehow gross, and perfect love is rather to be found in the perfect fidelity of suffering. Pierre drew forth the tablets

from his doublet pocket, and made melodious notes of
his despair :

> Sky, air, and winds, and naked hills and plains,
>   Tapestried woodland halls, and green morass,
>   And river-shores, and pools of sombre glass,
>   And viny slopes, and shivering gold champaigns,
> And moss-mouthed caverns' shadowy domains,
>   And buds and blossoms and dew-glimmering grass,
>   Gastine, and serpent Loir, and you, alas,
>   My melancholy songs, my weary strains :
> Since, when she went away, my angry stir
>   Of grief could find no parting word for her
>   Who, near or far, keeps me in misery,
> I beg you, air and sky and winds and mounts,
>   Forest and river, meadows, flowers, and founts,
>   And fields and caves, bid her farewell for me.

> *Ciel, air et vents, plains et monts découverts,*
>   *Tertres fourchus et forêts verdoyantes,*
>   *Rivages tors et sources ondoyantes,*
>   *Taillis rasés et vous, bocages verts,*
> *Antres moussus à demi-front ouverts,*
>   *Prés, boutons, fleurs et herbes rousoyantes,*
>   *Coteaux vineux et plages blondoyantes,*
>   *Gastine, Loir, et vous mes tristes vers !*
> *Puisqu'au partir, rongé de soin et d'ire,*
>   *A ce bel œil adieu je n'ai su dire,*
>   *Qui près et loin me détient en émoi,*
> *Je vous suppli', ciel, air, vents, monts et plaines,*
>   *Taillis, forêts, rivages et fontaines,*
>   / *Antres, prés, fleurs, dites-le-lui pour moi.*

As poets do, he found her docile image a better companion than her recalcitrant self had been. With sweet
terror at his own doom, he described, in terms of the
Roman de la Rose, how he had danced with False Danger in love's orchard, to the tune of Lady Ease my Pain ;
the drum was mad pleasure, the flute, error, the rebec,

vain desire ; and the five steps of the dance were the
perdition of his soul. He vowed to make an annual sacrifice at the spot where he had uttered his fatal declaration. (He fails to make any later reference to this holy
vow.) To charm away the poison in his heart, he called
for ink and paper, 'that future races may judge of the
pain I suffer in my love.'

Certainly many of the sonnets to Cassandre were
written, not by the Loir, but in Paris. In the quiet room
at Coqueret he could picture poignantly enough the
familiar country scenes, with the distraught poet in the
foreground. He had also his books at hand, for the veri-
fication of classical reference. And he had at hand his
friends, to applaud the daily drawing of his heart's
blood. And, finally, he had aids for one of his dearest
projects, the alliance of poetry and music.

The poet, he said, is first of all a singer, and poetry
should always be accompanied by music. The poet
should sing his words as he composes, though his voice
be poor. His own voice, Ronsard confesses, was not
good. He who hears the sweet concord of instruments
or of natural voices and does not rejoice and shiver in
ravishment from head to foot, as if transported out of
himself, has a twisted, vicious, depraved spirit. (Where
have we heard this, in words of our own great poet ?)
The divine furies of music, poetry, and painting do not
come to perfection by steady steps, but by sudden bursts,
by fiery lightnings. The music of the spheres, Plato tells
us, moves all this vast universe. Some few poets can, by
godlike inspiration, hear for a moment and record
these supernal strains. The lesson is that the poet should
make music as well as words.

But Ronsard had had no proper training in music.
He strummed upon his fine guitar, decorated with

mythologies, and bearing the initials of Cassandre entwined with his own. His random tunes were, he knew,
unfit accompaniment for his words. He turned, therefore, to the best musicians of his time for aid. He joined
the band of young enthusiasts who met in the shop of
Claude Goudimel, composer and music publisher, at
the sign of the Silver Griffin, in the rue Saint-Jean-de-
Latran. From Goudimel, Clément Jannequin, and
Marc-Antoine de Muret he obtained ten arrangements,
to which all his love-sonnets could be sung. (When, in
our time, a musical antiquarian had their music publicly chanted, it was found that the skillful polyphony
masked and muffled Ronsard's words, without adding a
beauty agreeable to the modern ear.)

Music, ink, and paper consoled the poet's stricken
heart. Eagerly he counted, from day to day, the number of publishable outcries of his woe. At length he had
assembled enough to make a book. He made his nego-
tiations with the Widow Maurice de la Porte, at the
sign of St. Claude in the Clos Bruneau. Followed the
happy task of proof-reading, the recitation of his own
poems from damp-smelling print, the intoxicating discovery of the elusive perfect word at the uttermost
moment, and the glad clanking of the presses, manu-
facturing immortality. In October 1552 appeared *Les
Amours de P. de Ronsard, Vendômois,* containing 183
sonnets, a *chanson,* and an *amourette.* In an appendix
were included the musical settings contributed by his
friends.

Nearly all the poems tell of Ronsard's long vain suffering for Cassandre. But there are several which can
by no means fit in that record of chaste love. Written in
memory of frank sensual delight, they celebrate the
hour of satisfaction. They were penned, surely, for some

Egeria with the habit of ready surrender. And Ronsard, tender toward his own, could not resist the temptation of a book in press. Regardless of their disharmony, as of Cassandre's anger, he inserted them in his *canzoniere* of pure love. A bard with a poem in pocket must read it or die.

At the beginning of his book he placed a portrait of himself and one of Cassandre, face to face. Ronsard is shown in strong profile, with sharp aquiline nose, receding lower lip, and a short, curling, coquettish beard. He wears a kind of toga, clasped on the shoulder with a brooch ; on his head is a wreath of laurel. Cassandre regards him with a sulky air. The artist, or the engraver, has lamentably failed to render the beauty of which Ronsard tells. The face is coarse and heavy. The opulent bared breasts suggest that the portrait is wholly imaginary, for the poet testified :

> *Las ! car jamais tant de faveur je n'eus*
> *Que d'avoir vu ses beaux tétins à nu.*

The book did very well. The public accepted the Petrarchan artifice as the necessary frame of the new poetry, and took pleasure in some grotesque conceits, outdoing Italian grotesquerie. None objected even to the statement that one of Cassandre's eyes was armed with a spark, while the other poured a lake down her cheek. The contemporaries admired the baroque decoration, which today we find artificial and absurd. But they felt, as we feel, the simple poignancy of emotion which animated his work, and which escapes from it still, in the accents of lyric beauty.

Ronsard's renown spread beyond the schools and the literary clubs to the reading people of the court and the city. His Coqueret title of 'Prince of Poets' became almost official ; indeed, there was none to dispute it with him.

The name of Cassandre was everywhere on the lips of the cultured and in the hearts of sighing lovers. Her celebrity overshadowed that of Laura, and well-nigh eclipsed the Olives and Pasithées of rival bards. A dance was called the *Cassandre* in her honor, a high dance, a kind of gaillarde, in which the man flutters round and round his coy partner. The beautiful name became a popular symbol for the woman vainly beloved, and common folk, who knew not the name of Ronsard, made songs about his darling.

Few in Paris could identify the real Cassandre, and those few, in time, forgot. And Cassandre, in her far country house, knew little and cared less about her Paris fame. Melancholy, dreaming over her flowers, falling into long fits of thoughtless abstraction, she let the years slip by.

Ronsard was too busy with other loves and with his professional career to keep her much in mind. But sometimes, in dreaming hours, his thoughts would return to the long fruitless woe in the fields of the Loir. The old grief would return, banishing his satisfaction in the celebrity grief had brought him. And he sorrowed for the ardent young man he had been, that he was no more. When he was thirty-five he wrote for Cassandre a brooding elegy, concluding :

> But as for me, I think my youth was dead
> In serving you. I seem to see it spread,
> Impaled upon these pages I have writ.
> I see my error ; I've no grief for it.
> Error has brought me wisdom, to esteem
> Life as a wind, and folly, and a dream.

Or quant à moi je pense avoir perdue
En te servant ma jeunesse épandue
De ça, de là, dedans ce livre ici.
Je vois ma faute et la prends à merci,
Comme celui qui sait que notre vie
N'est rien que vent, que songe et que folie.

Some years later he saw her again. It was in 1569 ; the poet was forty-five, a sobered and understanding man, who had learned something of joy and sorrow, and how they befool us until they have passed beyond our reach. Cassandre was nearly forty, a serene matron with a grown daughter. The poet wrote :

Absence, oblivion, the crowding haste
Of all my harried days have not effaced
The love with which my youthful heart was sore,
When I was made Cassandra's servitor.
Cassandra ! Dearer to me than my eyes,
My blood, my life ! It was my enterprise
To praise you only, always, and to choose
You the eternal subject of my muse.

.   .   .   .   .   .

If time which tumbles walls and fortress-towers
Has reft away that little youth of ours,
Cassandra, it's no matter ; all I see
Is the first far-away look you gave to me,
The childish grace by which I was possessed.
I feel the old wound open in my breast.

.   .   .   .   .   .

And if I were a great king anywhere,
I'd set a column in the public square
To token love, where all the piteous
Would kiss the pillar, and remember us.

L'absence, ni l'oubli, ni la course du jour
N'ont effacé le nom, les grâces ni l'amour
Qu'au cœur je m'imprimai dès ma jeunesse tendre,
Fait nouveau serviteur de toi, belle Cassandre !
Qui me fus autrefois plus chère que mes yeux,

Que mon sang, que ma vie, et que seule en tous lieux
Pour sujet éternel ma Muse avait choisie,
Afin de te chanter par longue poésie.

. . . . . .

Et si l'âge, qui rompt et murs et forteresses,
En coulant a perdu un peu de nos jeunesses,
Cassandre, c'est tout un ; car je n'ai pas égard
A ce qui est présent, mais au premier regard,
Au trait qui me navra de ta grâce enfantine,
Qu'encore tout sanglant je sens en la poitrine.

. . . . . .

Et si j'étais un roi qui toute chose ordonne,
Je mettrais en la place une haute colonne
Pour remerque d'amour, où tous ceux qui viendraient,
En baisant le pilier, de nous se souviendraient.

Cassandre's age was unhappy. She lived long, after the death of Ronsard and that of her husband and her single daughter. Her estate, badly administered, fell into many difficulties. She died about 1606.

Her destiny was entangled with poets. Her niece was courted by the warrior bard of Protestantism, Agrippa d'Aubigné. Her daughter married Guillaume de Musset, seigneur de la Lude. And her distant descendant, in the direct line, was Alfred de Musset, that most tragical poet of love.

(((VII)))

Roses and Wine

THE Paris world in which Ronsard moved was no friend
to doleful fidelity. Though the sins of the flesh have
remained, probably, constant throughout time, in the
Middle Ages they were committed under religion's menace, defiantly, with Satan under the bed and damnation
buzzing like a gnat. The high Renaissance forgot hell
and took its pleasure in the open sun. The amorous
pastime was no one's secret. Ronsard's epithalamia for
royal marriages describe the business of the wedding
night with details that embarrass the modern reader
more than they did the princely participants. Not only
poets, but the common folk, and even the clergy, let
their imaginations run free over the charms of the royal
mate. Thus the free-spoken Père Valladier celebrated in
a sermon the arrival in France of Marie de Médicis, in
1600, to wed Henry IV. He divided her person into
three stories. The top story, the face, he compares to
stars, precious stones, and flowers. The second story he
likens to 'two crystalline fountains of milk, two maga-
zines of manna, two sources of ambrosia, two fountains
of nectar, two sugar-canes, two pots of honey, two plants
of balm, two faces of the inward clock, two bastions and
ramparts of the heart.' For his description of the lower
story, he has recourse to the audacious phrasing of the
Song of Solomon, IV, 12, 15.

Love, the light love of velleity and inclination, was

102

the occupation of the jolly court of Brantôme's *Dames galantes*. Even the scholars played the game in their own way, according to the precedents of Greek and Latin literature. Book in hand they sinned, following the texts of ancient bawdry.

There were texts enough, in the voluptuous Alexandrians, in Catullus, Horace, Ovid. The modern Latin poets, Pontanus, Joannes Secundus and plenty of others, had written imitations which improved on the originals in specificity. And in the vulgar tongue the poets, Villon, Marot, Mellin de Saint-Gelais and many more had retold the old tales of French *gauloiserie,* the same tales that are reprinted today in grubby volumes entitled *Le Compartiment des hommes seuls,* or *Histoires de commis-voyageurs.*

Ronsard, exhausted by his long fidelity to Cassandre, found himself in the mood to relish the frank ribaldry of the bawdy bards. With Ronsard, admiration meant imitation. In 1553 appeared his *Livret de folastries,* offerings, mostly, to shameless Priapus. Modern times sternly reprobate them, while frequently reprinting them. They are, at least, excellent of their abject sort. That grace of language which was typically Ronsard's adorns, if it does not purify, his subjects. How sweetly his tale of the sturdy lust of Jaquet and Robine concludes :

> *O bienheureuses amourettes,*
> *O amourettes doucelettes,*
> *O couple d'amants bienheureux,*
> *Ensemble aimés et amoureux,*
> *O Robine bien fortunée*
> *De s'être au bon Jaquet donnée,*
> *O bon Jaquet bien fortuné*
> *De s'être à Robine donné,*

O doucelettes amourettes,
O amourettes doucelettes!

Few of his contemporaries took the licentious poems
ill. 'One can reprove them only laughing,' said a critic.
His friends objected mostly that these trivialities were
unworthy of the prince of poets, and capable of hinder-
ing his advancement at court. Such considerations led
him to omit the most obscene of the *folastries* from later
collected editions of his work.

The poems make clear, at least, that his mind was
dwelling fondly on easy joys, without pledges, consequences, and regrets. In this mood he paid a long visit
to the Vendômois, in the summer of 1554. It was a
happy stay. 'I died with pleasure,' he says, 'seeing in the
groves the trees enlaced with wandering ivy, and the
vines crawling far among the hawthorn and the wild
roses. I died with pleasure, hearing the sweet language
of the tufted larks, and the cuckoos, and the gurgling
ring-doves billing beak to beak on a beech-tree's top,
and watching the marriages of the turtle-doves. I died
with pleasure, seeing the stags step daintily out of the
woods at dawn, and seeing the lark quivering in the
sky. I died with pleasure ; but now I die of care, as I
see not the bright eyes of one I long to hold solitary in
my arms for an hour, in this quiet grove.'

He revisited his sacred spring of Bellerie, and heard
the hoarse babble of its water emerging from the rock.
He saw his darling caves, vine-curtained, mossy-walled,
and listened to the wind which 'moos forever in the low
caverns,' *qui meugle toujours dans les cavernes basses.*
He had a horrifying experience one night, on his way
to a love-tryst beyond the Loir. A skeleton on a great
black horse accosted him, and held out a hand of bone

to lift him to the pillion. He was aware of a demon hunt, running the ghost of a usurer. He drew his sword, and slashed at the night air until the apparitions fled.

Most of his companions were by no means ghosts. There was a certain Jeanne, and a certain Marguerite. Perhaps there were other roguish girls, with 'lizard tongues,' familiar with the lee of hedges. At any rate, the poet did not see Cassandre, and he spent no time bemoaning her. His friend Marc-Antoine de Muret, scholar, musician, and libertine, wrote in his commentary on the *Amours* of Cassandre : 'Poets are not always so impassioned or so constant in love as they make themselves out to be. And although they say to the first girl they can approach that heaven and earth would sooner perish than they would love another, still, when they find a shoe that fits their foot, it is their nature not to make it a matter of conscience.' This is the cynic's view. A more thorough-going cynic may, on the other hand, believe that the poet is not telling the exact truth when he boasts of his innumerable light loves and of his surrender to earthy joys.

Ronsard's days were certainly not devoted to the mere revel of the senses. He was tiring himself daily in active physical sports, hunting, fishing, swimming, fencing, wrestling, tennis. He was combating love with exercise, according to the modern prescription. (True, he says, 'the more I exercise, the more love springs in me.') And he was working tirelessly.

He had brought with him the just-published edition of the Greek poems of Anacreon (or of pseudo-Anacreon, if any one cares), revealed to the modern world by his friend Henri Estienne. These songs of love and wine fitted well the Renaissance mood. They are chaste enough in phrasing ; they invest even grossness with a dainty whimsical fancy. Love in Teos had no cruelty, fears, or sorrows. It would seem that the island lovers of Greece, like those of the Pacific today, were happily sterile. Not Aphrodite, the terrible goddess of Erycina, reigned there, but winsome Cupid. The precocious child has ruled ever since, in the art of the delicately sensual.

Ronsard wrote a book full of poems, many of them in the anacreontic manner. Wine and flowers and loves fill his pages. Silenus tramples the grapes, the rose-breasted nymphs dance amid roses, the nightingale sings his midnight sorrow. Cupid flutters through his songs, now begging asylum from the rain, now weeping with a bee sting, ever letting fly his surreptitious arrows. Once even the naughty babe appears with a pistol.

But under all the gayety persists the terror of hurrying time and the inevitable morrow, when youth will be done.

Against these celebrations of wine, these summons to magnificent drinking-bouts, we must set a dozen sober statements of Ronsard that he disliked excess, at table or in the tavern. He praises milk more feelingly than wine, and strangely honors water as a beverage. In the midst of an anacreontic to Remy Belleau, the blameless translator of Anacreon, he says : 'But no, drink not, my Belleau, if you wish to join the troop of Muses on their mountain. It is better to study to excess, as is your wont, than to ally yourself with Bacchus and his mate.' Ronsard turned fastidiously even from meat, and counsels a friend not to resemble the vulture tearing at flesh.

What delighted him, in his praise of wine, was not drunkenness in fact, but the vision of ecstasy. His intoxication was essentially literary. It was the divine attribute of Bacchus, thigh-born, protogonous, joy-shouting, twin-horned, bull-eyed, martial, ivy-crowned, raw-meat-lover, trieteric, germ of the gods. Ronsard brought Bacchus to his Vendômois, and alleged that the god had camped beside the Loir, giving his name of Dionysus to the incomparable vineyard of La Denisière. Thus the poet realized the old myths, making them a part of his own life and experience. Thus also he made drunkenness a part of his dream, separating it immeasurably from the sottish reality of staggering peasants. Indeed, most of our celebrations of wine depend on the literary connotations of the lovely word ; substitute 'gin' for 'wine' and your poems vanish.

Ronsard's praise of fleshly love was similarly literary. The pleasures of sense could not possess him long. They were transformed into poetry, and much exaggerated in the process. With uneasy consciousness of the inferences men would draw from his *Folastries,* he put at the head of the collection the distich of Catullus :

> *Nam castum esse decet pium poetam*
> *Ipsum ; versiculos nihil necesse est.*

'The good poet should himself be chaste ; his verses need not be.' He wrote to his friend and neighbor, Julien Pacate, rector of Thoré : 'You are always lecturing me, Julien, because I talk only of drinking. You say that's not the way to gain wealth and glory. But tell me, my proud friend, isn't it better to write of it than to do it ?' Julien replied : 'Ah, you are trying to play the sophist. My dear Pierre, you should neither write of it nor do it.' For the word 'drinking,' Pierre and Julien might well have substituted another.

We have other significant testimony about his habits. His friend, Doctor Pierre des Mireurs, wrote to Jean de Morel, after the appearance of the *Folastries* : 'It is high

time that Ronsard should put his writings in accordance
with the integrity of his life.'

His life was certainly not free from a moralist's reproach. Nevertheless, most of his pornography existed
in the imagination, as probably it does in the case of
other celebrated pornographs. He was passing through
a stage of eroticism, in reaction from his vain devotion
to Cassandre. The erotic stage did not persist, for it was
his nature to make love a holy thing, dwelling in a distant garden of dream. Love was too dear to him to be
forever debased. 'Love, I love thee well,' he wrote, and
affectionately noted all its maleficence :

The rocks know naught of love, nor oak-trees, nor the sea,
But love is man's affair, his proper destiny.
To love, to hate, to doubt, to feel the urgent breast
Now hot with love, and now by jealousy possessed ;
To long for endless life, to cry for death ; to groan,
To think, to dream ; to talk, while wandering alone ;
One's self to give and bind, condemn, forget, oppress ;
To have the face turn pale with secret tristfulness ;
To ope the mouth to speak, and find no utterance there ;
To hope a baseless hope, and dive into despair ;
To hide an inward flame under an icy cloak ;
The mind to alembicate, and feed on cloudy smoke ;
To mask the palsied heart with a demeanor gay ;
To feel the tear in the eye, to waste with care away :
Such is the lot of him who eats love's sickly fruit
Borne on a tainted tree corrupted at the root.

> *Un rocher n'aime point, un chêne ni la mer :*
> *Mais le propre sujet des hommes, c'est aimer.*
> *Aimer, haïr, douter, avoir la fantaisie*
> *Tantôt chaude d'amour, tantôt de jalousie,*
> *Vouloir vivre tantôt, tantôt vouloir mourir,*
> *Rêver, penser, songer, à part soi discourir,*
> *Se donner, s'engager, se condamner soi-même,*
> *Se perdre, s'oublier, avoir la face blême,*

Ouvrir tantôt la bouche, et n'oser proférer,
Espérer à crédit et se désespérer,
Cacher sous un glaçon des flammes allumées,
S'alembiquer l'esprit, se paître de fumées,
Dessous un front joyeux avoir le cœur transi,
Avoir la larme à l'œil, s'amaigrir de souci :
Voilà les fruits qu'Amour de son arbre nous donne,
Dont ni feuille ni fleur ni racine n'est bonne.

Love had used him ill, yet he must love forever.
Might he only die in love, and be led amid the odor of
her flowers to the orchard-paradise of Cnidus ! Love
was the doom upon him, which he would not protest :

> I am thy servant, Love ; I wish no other king.
> Beardless I was thy serf ; I'm still thy underling.
> I shall be always thine, though sadly I grow old,
> Faithful to love alone, and by love unconsoled.

> *Je suis ton serviteur, je ne veux d'autre roi,*
> *Sans barbe je fus tien, barbu je suis à toi :*
> *Tien je serai toujours, et dussé-je en tristesse*
> *User ma pauvre vie avecques ma maîtresse.*

In this temper, but with no idol for his heart's sighs,
he returned to Paris. His friends did not recognize in
him the sickly lover. To all people of taste he was the
unrivalled master of French poetry, and the chief star
of his Pléiade. He was an admired figure throughout
the Latin Quarter. He accepted adulation gracefully
but as his due. To support his position, he took a page
into his service, a likely boy named Amadis Jamyn. The
page paid his master by service and devotion, and the
master, struck by the boy's promise, repaid him by setting him to school to the best masters, Dorat and other
Grecians. Jamyn later put off the page's livery to become Ronsard's secretary and lifelong companion, and
to become a poet with his own transitory fame.

Ronsard now felt that he had outgrown the schools ; he was ready to advance from the Left Bank to the Right. He visited the court, and swaggered in the halls of literary patrons. He was much to be seen in the salon of Jean de Morel, maître d'hôtel of King Henri II, and a gentleman of culture. Antoinette, wife of Jean de Morel, was noteworthy for her erudition and intelligence, and the three beautiful and accomplished daughters were the subject of much poetic praise. The daughter Camille, 'the tenth Muse,' wrote poems, highly admired, in French, Latin, and Greek. This was the first literary salon in French history.

Ronsard, who was commonly addressed as 'the Petrarch of Vendôme,' let fall in this salon a literary bomb. He announced that he was done with Petrarch, and done with hopeless sighing. 'Those lovers so cold in summer,' he said, 'those admirers of chastity who clammily petrarchize are always fools ! They despise love, which is by its nature ardent and prompt.' When the ladies made a pretty outcry, he added scandal to shock. He blustered : 'If some sweet, worthy lady, horrified by inconstancy and change, reproves me, frowning, for abandoning Cassandre, who first wounded my heart with a shaft of love ; and if she says that the good Petrarch would never have committed such a sin, he who was thirty-one years in love with his lady, without ever permitting any other to inflame his soul ; tell her that Petrarch had no authority over me, to lay down the law to me, nor to those who would come after him, to make them live so long without a chance of freedom. He wasn't that sort himself. If you look close at his writings, you will see that he was too intelligent to play the fool for thirty years, wasting his youth and his art at the knees of one single mistress. Either he took his

fun with his Lauretta, or else he was a great nincom-
poop to love and get nothing. I can't believe it, and it
isn't credible. No, he had his fun with her, and then he
made her admirable afterwards, "chaste, divine, and
holy," as he says. Just so every lover should praise the
one with whom he has his pleasure ; for the man who
blames her after their bliss is no man, but is born of
tiger's race.'

With one accord the young men of the Pléiade abandoned Petrarch, and set to work on Gaietés, Baisers,
and Mignardises. It was as if orders had been issued
from headquarters on Parnassus.

But the man who dictates laws does not take them
so seriously as the subjects who are bound by them.
Ronsard, having given the order to be gay, labored long
on his noble volume of *Hymnes,* sober celebrations of
justice and philosophy, eloquent counsels to King
Henry and others of the great. Ronsard's mood is suggested by the tone of the *Hymne de la mort.* He will
look no more to the ancients for his themes, he says, but
will row with his own oars upon his own sea. He will
sing the praise of death, which none has sung. He re-
counts the kindnesses of death. Happy insensibility !
And happy redemption in Christ ! And glad release
from the pains of life ! How great and admirable is thy
power, O Death !

> I hail thee, happy, profitable Death,
> Sovereign physic for the pain of breath !
> When my time comes, Goddess, I ask of thee,
> Let me not languish long in malady,
> Tormented on a bed. Since thou art sure,
> Let me find suddenly my sepulture,
> Guarding God's honor, fighting for my king,
> My blood upon my own earth issuing !

Je te salue, heureuse et profitable Mort,
Des extrêmes douleurs médecin et confort !
Quand mon heure viendra, Déesse, je te prie,
Ne me laisse longtemps languir en maladie,
Tourmenté dans un lit ; mais, puisqu'il faut mourir,
Donne-moi que soudain je te puisse encourir,
Ou pour l'honneur de Dieu, ou pour servir mon prince,
Navré d'une grand'plaie au bord de ma province !

It is such a prayer as we have all made in ardent youth. Death does not grant our prayer, nor did she answer Ronsard, for all his cajolement of her, *heureuse et profitable Mort.*

VIII

Marie

THE spring of 1555 came to Paris, with the spring's troubling messages. The poet Ronsard looked at himself in the mirror, and took no great pleasure in the sight. A thin, pale, scowling face, a meagre, dishevelled beard, sprent with gray. His thinning hair was snowy. He parted his lips, and saw blackened teeth grinning from the mirror.

Yesterday his darling had mocked him, called him an ugly old man. And this at thirty ! 'You're more than a hundred years old,' she had said, 'and you still want to play the boy ! Where is that vigor you boast of ? You just whinny ! You look like a corpse being dumped into the grave. Only look at yourself in the glass ; look at that gray beard, that eye thick with rheum, and that face that seems a shrine-saint black with taper-smoke !' He had found no better answer than : 'I've never learned to stare at myself in the glass.' But as he was the frankest of men, he turned her small-talk into rhyme, and made songs of it :

> So my youth has reached its end !
> I've no store of strength to spend,
> My head is white, my teeth are black ;
> Thin red water in my veins
> Warms me little, nor sustains
> Sinews dissolute and slack.

Adieu, my lyre ; adieu, my dears,
Darling girls of careless years,
Adieu ; my frolic days have fled,
And after all youth's jubilee,
There's nothing now will comfort me
But a good fire, and wine, and bed.

Ma douce jouvence est passée,
Ma première force est cassée ;
J'ai la dent noire et le chef blanc ;
Mes nerfs sont dissous, et mes veines,
Tant j'ai le corps froid, ne sont pleines
Que d'une eau rousse en lieu de sang.

Adieu ma lyre ! adieu fillettes,
Jadis mes douces amourettes !
Adieu, je sens venir ma fin ;
Nul passetemps de ma jeunesse
Ne m'accompagne en la vieillesse
Que le feu, le lit et le vin.

In the self-torturing mood, he looked past the face to the spirit, and judged it sternly. That spirit he recognized to be idle, discourteous, sombre, rude, obstinate, indiscreet, fantastic, volatile, untidy, shy, suspicious. Other poets were the same, that was something. Their character was the consequence of drinking from the stream of Permessus, which flows down from Helicon. No wonder I never have any luck in love. The girls are always mocking me under their breath, thinking me too deaf to hear their whispers. And when I really love with all my heart, I get only disdain. Look at Cassandre, walking her proud way ! What has she given me ? Only a few cold kisses, to make me stop annoying her ! Less than she gives her yapping dog !

He whipped himself with his thoughts, a flagellation not without its perverse pleasure. After, he took thoughts of balm to rub upon his wounds. There had

been good times, after all. Plenty of fine girls had not
been shy or scornful. How they had laughed, and sighed,
and lovingly caressed him ! There was something about
him, after all. His girls ? Why, they were innumerable !
In Paris, Anjou, Vendôme. . . . There was a fine little
ode in Anacreon, Εἰ φύλλα πάντα δένδρων . . .

The poet, humming, took down his Anacreon. The
thing would go well in French. He crossed to his table,
and made from Anacreon an odelette to his friend
Olivier de Magny. 'Count me the flowers of spring, the
sands of the sea, the stars of heaven, the leaves of the
oaks, and you can count my loves. Two hundred in
Touraine, four hundred in Maine, and in Angers, Amboise, and Vendôme enough to make a hundred thousand. In Paris, six hundred at once, and in Blois a hundred million, all in Cassandre's eyes. There aren't
enough counters in France to record my total !'

Ronsard was restored to his normal mood. Love, he
knew, was the destiny of his nature. Like the salamander, he could not live unless consumed with love's fire.
He would serve love ever. Better a thousand deaths than
ever to be weary of her.

To be sure, at the moment he was not suffering particularly. There was his mocking darling, whose lack of
respect was happily matched by her lack of scruple.
Under the head of honest love, he could count two
charming Paris girls, Marie and Jeanne. In truth, he
had got no farther with them than talking, laughing,
kissing their hands and tapping jocosely their small
breasts. And if all the truth must be told, that was all
he asked of them.

Cupid winked his little cunning eyes and chose a
shaft.

In dangerous freedom of fancy Ronsard left Paris for

the country. It was the ominous month of April. He
went beyond the Vendômois to Anjou, to the village of
Bourgueil, between Tours and Saumur. He was bound
to visit his old friend and kinsman, Charles de Pisseleu,
abbé of Bourgueil, a precocious bishop, and a great
hunter of wild boars. Bourgueil is today a busy white
village ; the fame of its notable wine has succeeded to
that of its abbey, now in ruins.

Here Ronsard met the second of his great loves.

Two miles from Bourgueil the hamlet of Port-Guyet
stood on the bank of the Loire (the great Loire with
an *e*), which has since deserted its bed for another, three
miles to the south. Here dwelt a family of substantial
farmers, bearing the name, perhaps, of Dupin. (The
scholars argue bitterly about the name, and there is
hardly a chance that they will ever be sure of it.) The
Dupins, if they were Dupins, were of an intermediate
social state. They had relationships with the small gentry ; they taught their young to read and write. But
they were frankly farmers, and their girls were accus-
tomed to all the lowly duties of a country household.

One day at Port-Guyet, Ronsard saw the three pretty
Dupin girls, Antoinette, Anne, and Marie, paddling on
the river, and heard over the water their loud rustic
laughter. He fell in love with the three of them, with
their artless country grace. But as he came to know
them, he singled out the youngest, Marie, in the win-
someness of her fifteen years. Here, he thought, is the
natural beauty of the rose ; I will love her forever.

Marie was to him all the youth he had been so bitterly regretting. Capturing her, he could outwit time.
'I love a crimson bud half opening in the morning, not
the evening rose, drooping under the sun ; I love youth's
body in its flowering spring.' Her ignorances and inno-

cences delighted him ; it seemed to him an admirable
thing to forget the sour wisdom of books and the lessons
his own manhood had taught him.

He courted Marie by entering into her childish mind,
and solemnly playing her schoolgirl games. He helped
her twine a wreath of roses for her chestnut hair. She
took an ivy leaf and pricked it with a pin. He seized the
leaf, held it to the light, and read : *'Je t'aime.'* He had
a brief kiss before she escaped, nimble and laughing.

He talked, of course, of love. 'Marie,' he pointed out,
is made up of the same letters as *'aimer'* ; her name is
itself an invitation to love. He offered, unconvincingly,
to abandon the courts and join Marie in her simple
life. He proposed that at dawn the two should lead their
flocks to pasture near Port-Guyet, in the noon heat they
should lie together under an oak, and with the declin-
ing sun conduct the cattle to drink from the grassy
streams, bringing them to the byre with the bagpipe's
whimper. Marie, who knew the stern routine of the
farm, must have laughed at his Arcadian picture.

He wrote a jolly dawn-song to gladden her, a song
which Robert Herrick imitated in the next century,
one which students of every land find in their Antholo-
gies of French Poetry :

> Up, up, my sweeting ! Up, my slug-abed !
> The skylark, high in heaven, sings in the morn ;
> Long has the nightingale upon the thorn
> Sweetly complained of love, how love has fled.
> Up, then, and see the grass bediamonded,
> And the new rosebuds to your rose-tree born,
> And your dear pinks, that yester-eve forlorn,
> Till you baptized them, hung the sorrowful head.
> Only last night you promised me anew
> You'd be awake to greet me with the light.
> But sleep has sealed those little eyes so tight !

So for the sin of sloth I'll punish you ;
I'll kiss a hundred times your eyes and breast —
That's how I'll teach you to be up and dressed !

Marie, levez-vous, ma jeune paresseuse,
Jà la gaie alouette au ciel a fredonné,
Et jà le rossignol doucement jargonné,
Dessus l'épine assis, sa complainte amoureuse.
Sus debout ! allons voir l'herbelette perleuse,
Et votre beau rosier de boutons couronné,
Et vos œillets mignons auxquels aviez donné,
Hier au soir, de l'eau d'une main si soigneuse.
Harsoir, en vous couchant vous jurâtes vos yeux
D'être plus tôt que moi ce matin éveillée ;
Mais le dormir de l'Aube aux filles gracieux
Vous tient d'un doux sommeil la paupière sillée.
Je vais baiser vos yeux et votre beau tétin
Cent fois pour vous apprendre à vous lever matin.

Together they heard the nightingale singing in the willows, and Ronsard made the old comparison of the poet's laments and the bird's. Only, he said, the nightingale can move his beloved by his song, but when the poet sweetly murmurs of love, Marie claps her hands to her ears. He gave her a nightingale in a cage, a prisoner's gift of a prisoner.

He became ever more urgent in his dalliance. 'I love you so much, I am crazy for you !' he cried ; *'Ha, je vous aime tant que je suis fol pour vous.'* Marie replied with the instinctive coquetry of her age and country. 'You are too inconstant, too light in love,' she told him, and he found it hard to deny the testimony of his published works. When he tried to take a kiss by surprise, she turned her face away. 'Go get a kiss from your Cassandre,' she pouted. 'Why don't you take your pleasure from all those fine ladies you boast of, instead of telling stories to a mere village girl ?' Laboriously he

explained that they were no whit better than herself,
that he was sick of fine ladies, that rather than love in
high place he preferred to love in low. His explanation
ended the love-talk for that day.

There were days when he would frankly bore her,
with his boast that all his words were immortal, that
with his art he would liberate her from time, and make
her a goddess. Immortality is a meaningless word to
those who live simply in the present. She murmured a
mocking reply, too low for him to hear. He asked her
to repeat it, and she said, all too loud, that it is no pleasure to shout in love-making. True, he answered, but
this you overlook : that the lover, to hear you better,
comes close to your scarlet lips, and scatters with his
kisses the pretty words they make.

He was always asking. There are five points in love,
poets before his time had said : sight, speech, touch, and
the kiss, and the last point, most longed for, to which
all the others tend, which is called for decency's sake the
Gift of Mercy. Country frankness had left Marie in no
ignorance of the poets' meaning. But she had no gift of
mercy for her suffering suitor. Marie would only laugh,
and turn aside her face, or even flee in anger. Why was
she so cruel ?

> '*Vous le voulez et ne le voulez pas,*
> *Vous le voulez et si ne l'osez dire*'

cried Ronsard, furious with exasperation. It was not the
Church's code that restrained her, nor the menace of her
glowering mother. Her heart was her simple guide. Surrender would come with love, and if she did not quite
want to surrender, she was not quite in love. 'I am very
fond of you, but . . . I don't love you in that way.'
Calamitous words, to all lovers, of all the centuries !

In tortured mood Pierre left Marie, at the summer's
end of 1555. On his departure, he protested that the
separation would certainly cause his death. Nevertheless, he departed. Very important business. His poems
to Cassandre were proving very popular, and he had to
get out a new edition, with a number of added poems.
He had to see his publisher. Love conquers all, and
Venus rules the world, but even Venus strikes her standard to the publisher.

The agonizing courtship was resumed in the summer
of 1556. A winter of absence had not cooled the poet's
ardor, nor had it inclined Marie to love. The contrary,
indeed. The gallants of Bourgueil had discovered the
charms which enraptured Ronsard. If they did not
promise immortal fame, they proposed the more immediate satisfactions of mortality. There was one in particular, a young gentleman, a ranging beau, and 'a fool
of a young man,' says Ronsard. It was probably Charles
de Pisseleu, Ronsard's relative, the recipient of the local
abbey's revenues, the precocious bishop.

Ronsard was suspicious and jealous. He was jealous,
even, of Marie's doctor, who came night and morning
to examine Marie in an illness, but in fact, vowed the
poet, only to examine her bosom unprofessionally. He
was the more jealous of the hearty hunting bishop.
There were no patent proofs, only the look and manner
of the two. Marie scoffed at his suspicions, but they
would not be gone. 'This is my fate,' he said, in an
agony of self-pity. 'If there is any girl anywhere who is
inexorable, inhuman, and cruel, I must needs choose
her for my love. And if some maid is sweet, amiable,
and lovely, I cannot capture her, courtly and faithful
though I be ; she will always fall in love with a fool.
I was born under a malign star. But that is love ; those

who deserve reward live in grief, while the fool is well
treated.

> *O traître et lâche Amour, que tu es malheureux ;*
> *Malheureux est celui qui devient amoureux.'*

Marie had, indeed, a little pity for his forlornness.
She cajoled away momentarily his ugly surmises, and
allowed him some unimportant caresses. When summer
was over, and it came time to part, he was more deeply
in love than ever. He bade farewell to her, his dear life
and soul, in whom he lived and breathed :

Adieu, my lovely, frank, and simple maid, adieu.
   Adieu the servitude where I was fain to dwell,
   The travail and the joy that constantly I knew.
   The time has come to part, and I can only tell
My old love over. Here, my gentle damosel,
   Here is my heart to keep, a trifling gift to you.
   Take it ; and kiss me, dearest maid. And then farewell.

Adieu, belle, humble, honnête, et gentille maîtresse,
   Adieu les doux liens où vous m'avez tenu
   Maintenant en travail, maintenant en liesse :
   Il est temps de partir, le jour en est venu.
Mais avant que partir je vous supplie, en lieu
   De moi, prendre mon cœur, tenez, je le vous laisse,
   Voy le là, baisez-moi, maîtresse, et puis adieu.

It was with renewed confidence and hope that he returned to Bourgueil, evidently in the spring of the next
year, 1557. He brought a gift for Marie from Montoire,
the Vendômois market town nearest to La Possonnière.
It was an appropriate and useful present : a distaff, one
of the smooth sticks, artfully shaped, with which one
pulls raw wool into threads. Still in the French countryside one may watch the peasant women flicking their
distaffs as they guard their cows or geese. Ronsard's gift

was prettily tied with a ribbon, and accompanied with a poem which celebrated the antiquity of the distaff (which was invented by Pallas Athena) and the domestic accomplishments of Marie. His present seemed to him exquisitely apt, a symbol of rustic simplicity and a defiance of courtly snobbishness. We may suppose that Marie would have preferred something a little more showy, and, perhaps, a little more expensive. We may suppose further that the philandering bishop bought more ostentatious gifts, with the money he was accused of extorting from his abbey's almoner, cellarer, and provost.

Marie had yielded to Ronsard's rival what she had never given to him. Village gossip corroborated the testimony of his own jealous heart. There was an angry parting. The poet returned to the Vendômois to lick his wounds of love and pride. He took a literary revenge on Charles de Pisseleu ; in the next edition of his works he erased several laudatory dedications to his supplanter. That wenching priest ! May he languish through his life, and add the hate of himself to the common hate of men ! May he gnaw his own heart, and see his purposes escape from his hands like wind ! May he die without fire and water ! May the light of heaven never be agreeable to his eyes ! May poverty make perpetual war upon him, may he go helpless from land to land, seeking his bread, and at the end die naked, hungry, by the roadside, and be the food of wolves ! And may his unshriven spirit wander among the tombs, and lament in raven's plumes upon the housetops !

The supplanter thus disposed of, Ronsard consoled himself with the Muse, faithful even to faithless bards.

Two instalments of the *Amours de Marie* had already been published. Probably most of the sonnets and songs

were written far from Anjou. Ronsard wrote easily of
love, as he admits. He confesses also, disastrously, that
he loved better in absence than by his beloved's side.
He was a true poet. In solitude, remembered joy or
bitterness would fill his heart with bliss or pain, unen-
durable until he should convert them into beautiful
words. An experience, an impression of the past, would
obsess him. A summer meadow near Bourgueil, the torturing laughter of Marie, would return with a clarity
that he must capture and reproduce. But the actual
Marie in her actual meadow might distract intolerably
the creative mood.

The story of the *Amours de Marie* is that of the
Amours de Cassandre. It is the old tale of the poet's
ardor rebuffed and unappreciated. The difference of the
two series is in the manner of the telling.

Ronsard alleges that for Marie he adopted a new low
and simple style, in order to be understood by his peasant dear, ignorant of the recondite beauties of Greek
mythology. He was fitting his form to his subject, as he
had done in the praises of Cassandre. But it is true also
that his new style was a logical stage in his poetic development, and Marie appeared conveniently to illustrate it, as the perfect model knocks at the artist's studio
when his theories are ready for paint.

He was tired of the Greeks and Petrarch, and a little
tired of his whole method of imitation. 'I know that I
should cease to borrow foreign subjects from the lying
Greeks,' he wrote. The learned obscurity of his Pindaric
odes had been no less blamed by persons of taste than
exalted by the erudite. On the whole, he wanted the
wider audience, popular acclaim rather than the appro-
bation of the scholars. He felt also confidence in his
own power, and the need to assert his independence.

Rather than the French Pindar or the French Petrarch, he wished to be Ronsard.

He could not attempt complete originality, freedom from all literary influence, as indeed no writer can. He re-read the old poets of simple love, Ovid and Tibullus ; and Theocritus, the Sicilian shepherd with his rustic pipe ; and the neo-Latins, especially Marullus. From them he took many a theme and many a toothsome phrase. But on the whole the share of imitation is much smaller in the *Marie* series than in his previous work.

The new low style is boldly colloquial, as I have tried to suggest in my translations. Ronsard describes the rustic scene realistically, its fields, birds, cattle, and the life of its inhabitants. He makes lowly comparisons ; thus he tells of the lark mounting by great leaps into the sky, then falling, like a spindleful of thread that a drowsy girl by the fireside drops, her head swaying forward. He chooses the direct, familiar word, not kine but cows, not bosom but breast. To make poetry out of these everyday words, black with handling, one must so order them that they shine suddenly and amazingly. One must make great music on the oaten pipe ; one must, in short, be a poet.

'If anyone should blame me,' he said, 'because I am no longer so grave in my verse as I was at my beginning, when the Pindaric humor filled with great wind my magniloquent mouth, tell him that one does not sigh of love in a high solemn mode, but with a beautiful low style, popular and pleasant, as did Tibullus, the ingenious Ovid, and the learned Catullus. The son of Venus hates ostentations ; he asks only that one sing one's passions truly, without bombast or color, in a sweet and dainty style, flowing with a little murmur like dropping water. Those who do otherwise cheat Venus and her son, Love.'

He found a style which murmurs like dropping water. It is a style which still murmurs of tenderness, and grace, and evanescence. In it he has caught the attitude of the wilful maid, listening distraught to the shepherd piping on his reed. The sweet low words preserve for us this moment of beauty.

The *Amours de Marie* delighted that singing age. Their vogue spread far and fast, and ere long they were sung throughout Europe. One of the lovely songs, set to music by Roland de Lassus, is to be found in the Virginal Book of Queen Elizabeth of England :

> *Bon jour mon cœur, bon jour ma douce vie,*
> *Bon jour mon œil, bon jour ma chère amie,*
> *Hé bon jour, ma toute belle,*
> *Ma mignardise, bon jour,*
> *Mes délices, mon amour,*
> *Mon doux printemps, ma douce fleur nouvelle,*
> *Mon doux plaisir, ma douce colombelle,*
> *Mon passereau, ma gente tourterelle,*
> *Bon jour, ma douce rebelle.*

Mary Queen of Scots consoled herself, in the dour north, with such cajoling words as these, too delicate for translation :

> *Ma maîtresse est toute angelette,*
> *Ma toute rose nouvelette,*
> *Toute mon gracieux orgueil,*
> *Toute ma petite brunette,*
> *Toute ma douce mignonnette,*
> *Toute mon cœur, toute mon œil.*
> *Toute ma Muse, ma Charite,*
> *Ma toute où mon penser habite,*
> *Toute mon tout, toute mon rien,*
> *Toute ma maîtresse Marie,*

Toute ma douce tromperie,
Toute mon mal, toute mon bien.
Toute fiel, toute ma sucrée,
Toute ma jeune Cythérée,
Toute ma joie et ma langueur,
Toute ma petite Angevine,
Ma toute simple et toute fine,
Toute mon âme et tout mon cœur.
Encore un envieux me nie
Que je ne dois aimer Marie.
Mais quoi ? si ce sot envieux
Disait que mes yeux je n'aimasse,
Voudriez-vous bien que je laissasse
Pour un sot à n'aimer mes yeux ?

It was such songs as these that moved a Cambridge don, sitting under a plum tree in his garden, to write : 'Behind rises the gaunt skeleton of the new University Library, gaping for the coming deluge of books in their lorry-loads, of massed periodicals briefer in their life, and far less lovely, than a rose. How many of the writers that scribble in the one and squabble in the other, know Ronsard ? Yet, irresistibly, we are drawn to read these things in their fussy novelty, knowing quite well that in the states of feeling they will give us they cannot compare with him. Doubtless one must live in one's own age too ; he would have been the first to echo that. But how fantastically we allocate our days ! When I think that till a couple of years ago Ronsard was not much more than a name to me, and recall the shelves of learned trash I read instead, and that such is the common way of our world, I wonder if secretly we are half dead and shun living things, lest they should shame our shallowness. Until by some chance we suddenly hear again one of the immortals ; and ask ourselves wonderingly in what frivolous and somnolent owl-light, among what fugitive cobwebs of futility we have wandered so long, deaf to Dionysus dancing by our blindly shuttered walls.' 1

Time did its healing work. Ronsard found some consolations in Paris for his heart and mind. But he did not forget Marie.

In the spring of 1560 Ronsard learned that Marie was bidden to the wedding of a cousin, at Saint-Cosme, a little island in the Loire on the outskirts of Tours. Of the ancient abbey of Saint-Cosme Ronsard's brother Charles was prior.

By a happy chance a certain Françoise, or Francine, de Gennes was to be present at the wedding. Francine belonged to the upper bourgeoisie of Tours ; she had once been the idol of Ronsard's fast friend Antoine de Baïf. The two rejected suitors determined to see again their old loves, and to try the effect upon their hearts.

At La Possonnière Ronsard met Baïf, whose country home was at La Flèche, about forty miles distant. In the voluptuous stir of April the two set out afoot. All the morning they walked under the new green of Gastine forest. By noon they reached the château of Beaumont-la-Ronce, whose high tower still looks down on the clustering village. Its lord, Philippe de Ronsard, something of a cousin, received them royally. Justifying his nickname of 'jolly Phelippot,' he kept his visitors at table for hours. They were barely able to do the six miles to Langennerie before sunset. There, where the road fords the little Choisilles, they camped under some willows bordering a field. Next morning they were up at dawn, and soon pushing south to Tours. (Had they halted in a great field to the left of the road, and urged time to

1 F. L. Lucas, *Studies French and English* (Cassell and Co., Ltd., London, 1934), p. 113.

go astray, they would have heard in premonition a strange roaring in the air, and seen the aviation camp where the Americans were trained in 1918, amid the pine barracks and the mud, and the frequent wrecks of rickety training planes.)

Ronsard and Baïf topped the rise to the north of the Loire, and saw the towers of Saint-Gatien of Tours, and, off to the right, the little belfry of Saint-Cosme, half obscured by the willows of its tiny island.

On the island the travellers found the wedding party in full frolic. Francine and Marie welcomed their swains, Antoine and Pierre, by their nicknames of Thoinet and Perrot. There was dancing in a field, and the two newcomers joined in, forgetting their thirty-mile walk. There was plenty of wine, and Touraine dainties, and hearty joking, and humorous public love-making. It was such a *noce* as the French have always loved.

Baïf took Francine aside, and, as Ronsard reports, recalled the story of his love. It was six years since they had first met, in April, when every tree is in bloom, when the earth passes from old age to youth, when the swallow, that foreigner, builds his home against a beam, when the snail, carrying his house upon his back, leaves a shining track on the flowers, when the caterpillar puts on a yellow fleece, and when the butterflies with dia-pered wings flutter over the fields. How he had loved her ! The two had gone, in fun, to a country witch, who had spat three times on her own breast, and vented three ritual sneezes. Then she had modelled an image of Francine in dough, turned about and muttered three times, and had taken Francine's garter and hung it about the lover's neck, as a sign that he would be for-ever in hopeless bondage to her. Again, on Saint John's

Eve, June 23, that white night when Europe still feels
a rouse of old paganism, the two had cut reeds and set
them out to grow. Baïf's had become of great length, a
symbol of lasting love, and Francine's had not grown at
all.

Could they not reawaken the old romance ? Baïf tried
the fates once more. He put hazel-leaves in the palm
of his hand, and tapped upon them. They made no
crackle ; hence her heart did not answer his.

> *O belle au doux regard, Francine au beau sourci,*
> *Baise-moi je te prie, et m'embrasses ainsi*
> *Qu'un arbre est embrassé d'une vigne bien forte.*

She would not listen, nor take his hand in the dance,
nor accept the flowers he had picked for her. He threatened to fling himself into the Loire, 'there, where you
see that boy fishing.' But Francine laughed, and refused
even by a glance to appease his ill. Baïf did not throw
himself into the Loire ; he contented himself with
swooning.

Ronsard was about to take up the song, to tell how
his Marie had surpassed even Francine in cruelty, when
Marie's mother, always his enemy, insisted (the old
maternal trick) that it was time to go. Their boat was
untied from the willow tree, the menfolk took their
places at the oars, the sail was hoisted. Amid boisterous
farewells and thigh-slapping jests Marie took her seat
for the journey home to Port-Guyet. Ronsard sat on the
sandy shore and imagined a song of good speed for the
craft. 'May the blue-black swift fly before you, with the
gull, and may the loon forget his sad fate and his Hes-
peria, and plunge not in the water, and may the screaming heron, which flees the storm, hang high and silent
in the air, and may all sweet birds that seek their prey

in the fishy waters convoy you to your port.' Why could
he not be magically transformed into the water that
bore the boat? Then he might lap it round, and amor-
ously kiss the trailing hand of Marie, and leap in spray
to her lips, and carry her safe to her haven of the
Chapelle blanche. But he could make no such meta-
morphosis ; the old herbs had lost their power to trans-
form men. He had no recourse but to carve the name
of Marie on the tree trunks. He vowed that he would
make a fine bed of leafy periwinkle, and sweet thyme,
and spiky lavender, and creeping pennyroyal, and green,
cool waterlilies, and riverside weeds. He would crown
his hair with roses and lilies, and broach a pipe of Anjou
wine, and drink it to the lees, in memory of Marie, all
divine, all his sweet care.

His despair is not convincing. He had had a happy
journey, and a golden day on the island of Saint-Cosme.
No premonitions crossed that April sun. And that is
fortunate, for on this little island of Saint-Cosme he was
destined, a quarter of a century later, to die.

Marie returned often to his thoughts. Very likely he
saw her again in Bourgueil, where for a time he kept a
brace of hunting dogs. He wrote for her an elegy, to
conclude the edition of his *Amours* which appeared in
1560. 'My second soul,' he said, 'that the age to come
may remember our young loves, that your beauty which
I loved so long may not waste with the years and perish
in the tomb without leaving some spark of itself behind,
I here consecrate to you the most galliard of myself, the
spirit of my spirit, to make you live again.' He took up
again a conceit he had used for Cassandre. If only he
were a great king, he would build a temple on the
Loire's banks : the temple of Ronsard and his Marie.

To their marble images would come all the young lovers
of that country, to compete in a contest of Cytherean
kisses. The victors in these idyllic games would be
crowned with an odorous weight of flowers, in memory
of Ronsard and of Marie.

Ah, why, my pretty miss, did Love not deign
To join and bind us with a single chain ?
Then, after death had hid us with his wing,
We'd be the song that lips of lovers sing.
The men of Vendômois would say in wonder,
Viewing the tomb that we'd be lying under :
'Ronsard, who left his Loir and his Gastine,
Loved in Bourgueil a lovely Angevine !'
And all the Angevins would say in awe :
'Here is Marie, who loved a Vendômois !
Their hearts were one heart, where love lived alway
Perdurable, until their latest day !'

O ma belle maîtresse ! hé ! que je voudrais bien
Qu'Amour nous eût conjoints d'un semblable lien,
Et qu'après nos trépas dans nos fosses ombreuses
Nous fussions la chanson des bouches amoureuses !
Que ceux du Vendômois dissent tous d'un accord,
Visitant le tombeau sous qui je serais mort :
'Notre Ronsard, quittant son Loir et sa Gastine,
A Bourgueil fut épris d'une belle Angevine !'
Et que les Angevins dissent tous d'une voix :
'Notre belle Marie aimait un Vendômois ;
Les deux n'avaient qu'un cœur, et l'amour mutuelle
Qu'on ne voit plus ici leur fut perpétuelle.'

Some dozen years later, a visitor informed Ronsard
casually that Marie of Bourgueil was dead. The word
rang like a knell in the heart of the poet, now sobered,
middle-aged, and half a churchman. Marie was dead
then, and so was youth, and so was love ! Her companion soul was calling him from heaven :

Prends courage, mon âme, il faut suivre sa fin ;
Je l'entends dans le ciel comme elle nous appelle ;
Mes pieds avec les siens ont fait même chemin.

The poet suffered, as he had suffered in the days of his love. He reviewed dolorously the past, and wept the flow and disappearance of all things. The look of Marie haunted him ; her half-forgotten words, her pretty graceful ways returned.

O beaux yeux, qui m'étiez si cruels et si doux !
Je ne puis lasser de repenser en vous,
Qui fûtes le flambeau de ma lumière unique.

But in his pain was a new understanding. He no longer hated her for her obduracy, which now seemed unimportant, even lovely, charged with sweet wistful memory. He had loved her vainly and bitterly ; at least he had loved. Marie had gone forever, with the roses, and the old gayeties, and the youth of his own heart. Something remained : the knowledge she had given him of his own capacity for love and despair. 'In your service,' he said, 'I learned what it is to love.' That is to learn some truth, indeed.

He wove for her a beautiful garland of elegiac verse, some of the tenderest melodies of French poetry. They are so harmoniously moving, in their union of simple phrase with delicately falling sound !

Hélas ! où est ce doux parler,
Ce voir, cet ouïr, cet aller,
Ce ris qui me faisait apprendre
Que c'est d'aimer ! ah, doux refus !
Ah, doux dédains ! vous n'êtes plus,
Vous n'êtes plus qu'un peu de cendre.
Hélas ! où est cette beauté,
Ce printemps, cette nouveauté
Qui n'aura jamais de seconde ?

Du ciel tous les dons elle avait ;
Aussi parfaite ne devait
Longtemps demeurer en ce monde . . .
Si je n'eusse eu l'esprit chargé
De vaine erreur, prenant congé
De sa belle et vive figure,
Oyant sa voix, qui sonnait mieux
Que de coutume, et ses beaux yeux
Qui reluisaient outre mesure,
Et son soupir qui m'embrasait,
J'eusse bien vu qu'ell' me disait :
'Or' saoule-toi de mon visage,
Si jamais tu en eus souci ;
Tu ne me verras plus ici,
Je m'en vais faire un long voyage.'

In his heart he buried Marie with the roses, still
framing the memory of her young face.

As on the branch one sees the rose, in May,
   In its first glorious youthful arrogance,
   While jealous heaven looks down with sullen glance,
   Shedding in dew its tears, at point of day ;
And grace and love are nodding on its spray,
   Its balm the gardens and the groves enchants ;
   But then the rain, or the heat's puissance,
   Petal by petal, plucks it all away ;
So, when your delicate beauty's early bloom
   Was earth and heaven's rapture, a hard doom
   Brought beauty low, where dust in dust reposes.
Take, for your obsequies, these tears I shed,
   This jar of milk, these flowers flaming red,
   That, living or dead, your body be but roses.

Comme on voit sur la branche, au mois de mai, la rose
   En sa belle jeunesse, en sa première fleur,
   Rendre le ciel jaloux le sa vive couleur,
   Quand l'aube de ses pleurs au point du jour l'arrose ;
La grâce dans sa feuille et l'amour se repose,
   Embaumant les jardins et les arbres d'odeur ;
   Mais, battue ou de pluie ou d'excessive ardeur,

Languissante elle meurt feuille à feuille déclose.
Ainsi en ta première et jeune nouveauté,
   Quand la terre et le ciel honoraient ta beauté,
   La Parque t'a tuée, et cendre tu reposes.
Pour obsèques reçois mes larmes et mes pleurs,
   Ce vase plein de lait, ce panier plein de fleurs,
   Afin que vif et mort ton corps ne soit que roses.

IX

The Trade of Poetry

RONSARD'S father was right ; the trade of the Muses is a barren one, and even mighty Homer had to beg his bread. The man of letters' cares were more grievous in the mid-sixteenth century than they are today. He could look adoringly at no publisher ; the blessed word 'royalty,' which makes the bard feel momentarily a king, was unknown. One gave one's manuscript to a printer, at most receiving some trifle in return. It was thought base to accept money for one's heart's chants. Even a century later the great Boileau boasted that he had never taken a penny for his work.

But since presumably one had to live, one sought the patronage of the great, whose gifts do not demean. One hunted an honorable secretaryship in the house of a noble, or a more honorable post as *valet de chambre* of the king. If one had qualified, as had Ronsard, for the right to draw ecclesiastical revenues, one harried the king and those great lords who held the livings in their hands. In converse with the high nobility, one turned forever the talk toward the quiet little abbey in the country, the fat priory ringed with thriving fields.

To gain such a reward was an exacting business, demanding every quality of the applicant. He must show some fitness, and in addition he must capture the favor of those with gifts to bestow. He must stand well at court. It was the effort to stand well at court that occupied many of Ronsard's days in Paris, and that produced the unreadable half of his work.

At dawn or earlier the poet was astir, in his quarters on the hill of Sainte-Geneviève. He made his toilet, wiping his face with cotton dipped in weak aromatic alcohol. (Water was thought to render the face over-sensitive to cold and heat.) Through the tangle of narrow streets, walled with schools, convents, and jut-ting half-timbered houses, he made his way to the Seine. He picked his way carefully through the stinking mud, which smelled of sulphur and seemed to burn what it touched. He skirted playing children, bargaining women, perhaps a man slaughtering a pig in the com-mon quarters of the roadway. For his protection, he carried a flower to smell, or, when the pest was raging, a sponge of vinegar in his hand and a curl of angelica in his mouth. He kept a wary eye on the upper win-dows, fearful of a housewife too lazy, or too malignant, to cry *gare l'eau* ! as she emptied a chamberpot into the street.

He crossed the Petit Pont or the Pont-Saint-Michel to the Ile de la Cité, and cast a glance at Notre-Dame, black with age. He had his choice of three bridges, all bordered by precarious shops, to reach the right bank. He then turned to the left, descending the stream to the Louvre.

The Louvre bore little resemblance to the palace of today. It was still in part the towered and crenelated fortress of the thirteenth century. And it was still very tiny, the mere kernel from which the great Louvre has grown, almost year by year.

The present visitor, wandering amid endless antiqui-ties in endless halls, is apt to lose all sense of the palace's design. He may remember, however, the great enclosed square court at the east, from which extend the two interminable wings, with the gardens between. The enclosed court, the *Cour du Louvre,* has exactly four times the area of the Louvre of Philippe Auguste, of Henri II, and of Ronsard. Their Louvre occupied the southwest quarter of the present court. There remains of it only an L-shaped section, half the present western wing between the court and the gardens, half the southern wing between the court and the river. In this oldest part of the Louvre the Venus de Milo stands, with her embarrassed smile.

Ronsard entered the palace through a low, dark, vaulted passage. He came out into the square court, filled with gentlemen of the household, important visitors, hurrying servants, and larking pages. Couriers' horses stamped on the cobblestones. Magnificent prelates swished by with a silken rustle, and bearded monks trotted in coarse gowns of gray or black. Women passed, great bells of brocade. From the windows peered pretty faces, under black velvet hoods.

Through a door in the western wall Ronsard entered the guard-room, where the Swiss guards, in their feathered velvet caps, and doublets and hose with vertical red and yellow stripes, inspected the visitors. Four lovely caryatids by Jean Goujon supported a balcony, used by the musicians when the hall was turned into a ballroom. The caryatids still stand there, serenely bearing their burden, in the company of Demosthenes, and Mercury attaching his sandal, and the child with a goose.

Ronsard turned to the right, and mounted the new staircase now known as the Escalier Henri II. He entered the large room above the guard-room, the *grande salle,* which served as the general waiting-room. Today it is the Salle Lacaze, occupied by Chardin, Watteau, Fragonard, and others, save when it is in use for special exhibitions.

Here Ronsard stood and chatted with other circumspect courtiers with petitions concealed in their breasts. (Pockets were not invented till 1560.) The gentlemen wore, at a becoming angle, coquettish velvet caps, cockfeathered. Their heads were held to a stiff dignity by the wide starched ruffs which the king had introduced to hide the scar of an abscess on his neck. They wore flaring cloaks, and doublets, puffed and slashed, of velvet or silk ; only prelates and great nobles were permitted to wear silk on silk. Below the doublet, tight smallclothes of tender fabric, with a built-up codpiece. Skintight stockings, gartered at the mid-thigh, displayed a handsome leg to advantage. Fashion required a great weight of clothing above the waist, and almost nothing below. The ladies, by contrast, were tight-bodiced, but from the waist down they were enormous tents.

The courtiers waited the appearance of King Henri II. The waiting was a dreary task, trying to impatient tempers. Reminiscent followers of the court confess that their trade was particularly hard on the feet ; one must learn to stand motionless, hour after hour, day after day.

At last the king appeared, surrounded by those fortunate ones who had had the felicity of helping him dress. He passed among his faithful, with a nod, a smile, a welcome, and here and there a hard stare which dismissed a man from his own favor and the friendship of all the court. He accepted a few petitions from eager hands, and was soon on his way to his council meeting. It was about seven in the morning.

To most historians, Henri seems a dull king, heavywitted, a great fighter with curious timidities. As a boy of seven he had been sent to prison in Madrid, with Ronsard's father for companion. Four years of jail perhaps put the print of fear on his mind and darkened his spirit forever. Slow and melancholy, but conscientious in his royal duties, he countersigned his ministers' blunders, and led his country through profitless wars. He had at least the physique of a king. He was tall, strong, and handsome, and was one of the best athletes of a sport-loving age. None could equal him in the broad jump. Mounted, he seemed a centaur. He loved horses, and loved to display his skill on fine beasts trained to whirl and dance and curtsey. In autumn he hunted the stag; in winter he slid on the ice, built snow forts, and led snowball battles. At other seasons he fenced, played football and pall mall and especially tennis. Ambidextrous, he defeated all opponents, fairly, not by privilege of rank. The tennis court in his new addition to the Louvre was the model for all Europe. It was so arranged that the ladies could look down upon the players. Henri was happiest when he could hear their applause for his victories. His unathletic companions lived in perpetual terror; thus when he leaped lightly over a broad ditch Colonel de Bonnivet leaped after him and was nearly drowned.

Ronsard could not look upon his king with the eyes of a modern historian. He joined in the chorus of adulation, and tried to be heard above it. He found his superlatives in the realm of the fantastic. 'The King of the French is almost a god; thou art so well obeyed, wherever thou art, that from the Breton sea to the sea of Provence and from the Pyrenees to the gates of Italy, if thou shouldst only cough thou wouldst be heard.'

The queen, Catherine de Médicis, was likely to be absent, for the best of reasons, from the public ceremonials. After a ten-year delay in producing a dauphin, she was now almost constantly pregnant, achieving ten children in twelve years. She was frankly ugly, with large, heavy features, an olive skin, bulging eyes, and a short figure which was becoming a mound, a hummock, a great fertile hive. She was extremely intelligent, a patron of art and letters, fond of luxury, festivities, and food. She had a room with 119 mirrors, and another with 81 Limoges enamels set in the wainscoting. She loved cock's kidneys and artichoke hearts, and once nearly died of over-eating.

Ronsard praised her, with a wealth of classical allusion and a total lack of humor. He compared the three nights required for the conception of Hercules with the ten years necessary to make the dauphin, François. He described her youthful hunts on her daring side-saddle. He alleged that Jupiter tiptoed away from Juno to force Catherine in her sleep, and would have succeeded had not the river Arno risen in fury to save her. The queen was certainly not offended, but she may have been amused.

The royal pair was in fact a trio. Catherine shared the royal bed and throne with her astonishing rival, Diane de Poitiers. Henri had fallen in love with Diane when he was seventeen and she thirty-six. He remained infatuated with her until his death at the age of forty, when Diane was almost sixty. King, queen, and royal mistress appeared in public together. On the royal progresses the three were greeted by triple welcomes, and by arches of triumph in which Diane's crescent figured equally with the arms of the king and queen. (The vulgar took the crescent's points to betoken the cuckoldom of the queen.) In Fontainebleau and elsewhere one still sees endlessly repeated the symbol that united the initials of the three. Catherine appeared to be on the best of terms with her slim rival, whose naked beauty, sculptured by Jean Goujon, we still admire. But the queen cherished a secret hate, which exploded only when her adored husband was dead. Diane was banished from the court and degraded ; Catherine was tempted even by the offer of a courtier to cut off her rival's nose.

To Diane Ronsard paid his meed of praise, with strong hints that Diana, sister of Phoebus, should give presents to Phoebus's band of poets. He asserted that she surpassed in beauty Helen of Greece, and Lucrece, curiously enough, in chastity.

The court and the country lived in an atmosphere of perpetual unrest. The war with Charles V, Holy Roman Emperor, was incessant, bloodying the fields of France, Lorraine, and the Low Countries. Over all Europe hung the fear of the Turk, who had besieged Vienna in 1529, who seemed ever ready to pounce upon a Christendom that had opened its own veins. War drained the treasury of France, took all the country's wealth in taxes, paralyzed its economy, and brought hordes of honest workers to beggary and famine. The steadily rising costs of all goods bewildered and angered the people, who were not economists enough to recognize the effects of the gold and silver pouring into Europe from America.

The nobles of the court suffered, in their noble way, as much as their serfs. The feudal system obliged them to equip and pay their own levied troops in the country's wars. Competition in courtly display had become acute, with the introduction of the new Renaissance luxuries from Italy. Debt harassed and ruined the great families of France. Even the household of the king was reduced to mean economies and ignoble shifts. In such a pass the lot of the scholar-beggar was hard indeed. To capture a patron or the payment of a royal gift was a task requiring rare ingenuity, diplomacy, and perseverance.

Ronsard played the game according to the rules. He sang the praises of the great, such as his school-friend, the mean-spirited Cardinal de Lorraine, and doffed his cap, hopefully. He attached himself to the skirts of the cultured and sceptical prelate, Odet de Coligny, Cardinal de Chastillon. He snarled at the Italian painters, receiving money that should go to good French poets. He demanded as a right alms for poets, descendants of those old father philosophers whose whole wealth was a stick, a ragged mantle, and the cupped hand. He heaped scorn on the nobles who were annoyed by the poets' praise, who dodged giving the proper largesse. They would rather build palaces than gain the grace of the Muses, ha ! Their castles will tumble down, and their names, unknown, will be confounded with the common dust, unless they have their immortality from the bards ! Even the kings, he dared to tell Catherine de Médicis, lie like logs in Saint-Denis, forgotten, except those few wise enough to be liberal to good writers.

He played the game. He wrote volumes of adulation, dull even to those who read therein their own virtues. He bored his patron, the Cardinal de Chastillon, with his importunities, like those of a fly that has tasted honey. But he had his reward. He attained the favor of King Henri, who called him his *nourriture,* his meat. He was admitted occasionally to the very *chambre de parade* of the king, with its gilt wainscoting, its sculptured ceiling, its carved vipers, centaurs, Neptunes, its sweet smell of thyme and juniper, battling the foul

odors from the old moat beneath the windows. (The
room is today the *Salle des Sept Cheminées*, with its
overwhelming Gros and Davids.) There the king recalled the bad days of his imprisonment in Madrid, with
Ronsard's father, and the good days when he and Ronsard, young men together, had played football in the
Pré aux Clercs.

To Ronsard's clamor there was some response. In
1552 he received the cure of Marolles, near Meaux, in
1554 the cure of Challes, in the diocese of Le Mans, in
1555 or 1556 the cure of Évaillé, near Le Mans and
not far from the Vendômois. By 1559 he had lost or
sold the cure of Challes, but in that year he was bene-
ficiary of Champfleur, in the Maine, and in the following year he received the archdiaconate of Château-du-
Loir and the canonical prebend of Saint-Julien-du-
Mans. In 1561 he resigned the benefice of Champfleur.
If the list seems imposing, one must recall that all the
benefices were small, and that Ronsard, who had not
taken the final orders, and who resided in none of his
cures (except briefly at Évaillé and Saint-Julien-du-
Mans), was obliged to pay working priests to do the
parish duties.

The poet received finally the official post of 'councilor
and almoner' of the king. His only duties were to attend
the court from April to June ; his reward was an annual
pension of 100 crowns.

He was, on the whole, successful, and in full cry after
more success. He had no illusions about poverty. To the
familiar paradox of the rich, that wealth brings only
care, and poverty joy and heart's-ease, he replied with
the common-sense observation that rich men seem gen-
erally cheerful and secure, while the poor have only
their choice of miseries. The poor man can sleep under

the trees without fear of robbers, true, but with the cer-
tainty of fever, catarrh, and deadly coughs. No, Poverty
is the mother of error and all despair ; damned and
louse-bitten be he who will praise her.

Though he had his success, he found that it did not
bring him happiness. Old friends turned jealous, and
old companions in poetic arms shook their heads, saying
that their leader was selling his genius for a handful of
silver. The accusation he knew to be just. He no longer
had time for laboring at his arduous trade. Worse, he
no longer had repose of mind. In his hours of solitude,
he must fill his thoughts with devices to gain advantage.
The dream of beauty will not come to a heart full of
plots.

He hated the cost of his success, and hated his own
sycophancy. He reproached himself bitterly :

> I sought no more to study in solitude, alone.
> I burned with one desire : to get, to have, to own.
> I hid the natural look resolving on my face,
> I learned to spy and listen, to run from place to place,
> Dogging the death of others. Oh, wretched way to pelf,
> If death of other men is profit to one's self !

> *Si qu'en lieu d'être seul, d'apprendre et de savoir,*
> *Je brûlai du désir d'amasser et d'avoir.*
> *J'appris à déguiser le naïf de ma face,*
> *Épier, écouter, aller de place en place,*
> *Cherchant la mort d'autrui : misérable moyen,*
> *Quand par la mort d'autrui on augmente son bien !*

'Wealth ! Poetry will not bring you thereto, nor praying to Phoebus, who has gone deaf. You must pray to
the great Gods of the Court, follow them, serve them,
be at their table, tell them funny stories, court them,
see them, solicit them often, else your labor will be only
wind, and all your learning pass in smoke. Poetry is a

headache, and frenzy is its name !' Thus he tortured
himself, thinking of the great works he had written,
and of the small profit he had drawn from courtiership.

Yet surely he had many pleasant hours at court. He
enjoyed the condescension of the king, and the respect
of cultivated nobles, and especially of great and kindly
ladies. All treated him as the unquestioned master of
French poetry. The title : 'Prince of Poets,' followed his
name like an honorary degree. This eminence he had
won as a young man, after only a brief struggle.

Before Ronsard came, the court's pet singer was
Mellin de Saint-Gelais. Part poet and part court jester,
he had a witty verse commentary in pocket for every
public triumph and private scandal. It was light verse
in every sense, *vers de société,* still capable of provoking
a wan smile. But the earnest young men of the Pléiade
were shocked that the holy Muse should be brought so
low. Mellin de Saint-Gelais himself, the ever welcome
wit, seemed to take everything as a joke, while in secret
he defended his position with grim tenacity.

When Ronsard's first volume of *Odes* appeared, in
1550, the court was first oblivious and then contemptu-
ous. Poetry, said the courtiers, is something light and
graceful, a game ; it is not a set of interminable strophes
and antistrophes, half in Greek, requiring a set of
learned footnotes ! Above all things, poetry should not
be a bore.

Mellin de Saint-Gelais waited his opportunity. One
day, in the presence of King Henri and his sister, the
wise Marguerite, he brought the conversation round to
the new poetry. He then drew from his pocket the little
volume of *Odes,* and read a selection, falling afoul of
the learned metre, stumbling over the Greek words,
wagging his long beard as he simulated the poet in

frenzy. He was irresistible ; he was marvellous. But
Marguerite was not amused, and uttered her anger and
her praise of the new poet.

The Pléiade rallied to the defense of their master.
Nicolas Denisot and others wrote scathing mockeries.
Olivier de Magny called on the Furies to apply a lizard
to Mellin's breast and a thousand fanged serpents to his
hair, to whip the record of his crime on his back, and
to torment his bowels with red-hot pincers. The chancellor of Marguerite, Michel de l'Hospital, joined with
them. And Ronsard sounded a dreadful blast, comparing Mellin de Saint-Gelais to a dog grinding his enven-
omed tooth and baying at the moon of Ronsard's glory.
He vowed that he would trumpet the insult to the ears
of all posterity.

Peacemakers then stepped in, to point out to the
rivals that they stood to gain nothing by a public dispute. Within two years the quarrel was composed, the
poetic honorable amend made, and the offensive verses
on both sides suppressed. The two remained outwardly
in the court's favor. But by this time it was patent to
all that Mellin de Saint-Gelais was a witty verse-maker,
and that Ronsard was the Prince of Poets.

To justify his royal standing, he dreamed of a royal
poem, a Louvre in verse. This was to be his *Franciade,*
conceived in his chill study at Coqueret. In an ode of
1550, he revealed to King Henri the device of his epic.
Cassandra (the Greek Cassandra) would foretell in a
poetic frenzy the journey of Francus, the foundation
of a new monarchy on the banks of the Seine and its
glorious destiny.

Ronsard suggested a subsidy to permit the writing
of the great work. But King Henri listened distraught.
He had other needs more urgent than an epic poem.

So the *Franciade* remained for years an outline. Ronsard hesitated to set seriously to work, to choose the perfect first line, to follow it with a second and a third. He needed always more preparation, more skill. No doubt the tentative drafts seemed to him sadly insufficient, in comparison with the shining vision in his mind. He could almost hear the plaudits of the happy people welcoming the *Franciade* ; he could almost see the book, a noble folio, with the lines of large type marching in platoons down the middle of the wide page. Unfortunately he could not quite read the words.

In the meantime, he had almost fame enough for his touchy vanity. An adulator proposed that a temple should be built by the Seine to the Greek and Roman Muses, and that Ronsard, the high priest, should sit there in the smoke of the altar, his brow bound with sacred fillets. The Academy of the *Jeux Floraux* of Toulouse awarded him in 1554 its honorary wild rose, and in the following year named him *Poète François par excellence,* and sent him a Minerva of massy silver. Ronsard, not to be outdone in magnificence, presented the Minerva to King Henri, to show that poets' gifts were not vain words alone.

His eminence was recorded even in enduring stone. Pierre Lescot, architect and artist, was embellishing the new Louvre. He sculptured in relief a goddess with negligent blown draperies ; her puffed cheeks were set to a trumpet, which sounded in the ear of another goddess, holding a crown of laurel and a palm. The king, at table, asked the significance of the figures. Lescot replied that by the first goddess he meant Ronsard, and by the trumpet, the virtue of his poems, especially the *Franciade,* which would waft the king's name and that of France to all quarters of the universe.

In the southwest corner of the *Cour du Louvre,* one may still see that goddess, still puffing her silent trumpet, in memory of Ronsard.

The poet's life was one that most poets would envy. He was the intimate of the great, and the recipient of their occasional favors. He was known as one of the Guises' men, and celebrated the triumphs of that family, next in power to royalty. He visited often the château of the Cardinal de Lorraine, the great Guise, at Meudon, on the site of the present observatory. There he was the lion of the literary parties that met in the grotto which the Cardinal had had dug in the hillside, to be the sojourn of the Muses. There he listened to the musician Ferabosco, singing to his three-lyre accompaniment. And he dined in the great hall, at a flower-strewn table, where chiselled silver dishes filled with precious sugar-plums rested on white linen table-cloths perfumed with medlar-water and melilot. The fare was mostly rich meats, strongly spiced with ginger, coriander, fennel, aniseed, caraway, saffron, and nutmeg. Elaborate pastries were displayed, rather to impress the eye than to tickle the taste. Vegetables and salads, the fare of the poor, were banished.

At the tables of the great the convives are likely to forget the deference due to poets, even to the prince of poets. Ronsard perhaps felt more at ease in the literary salon of Jean de Morel, on the left bank, just off the Seine, in the present rue Séguier. Or, as the French have always found the café table the fittest altar for a literary chapel, he would join his friends at one of the popular taverns, Le More's, Sanson's, Innocent's, Havart's.

There were literary functions demanding his presence. There was, notably, the memorable production of Jodelle's *Argonautes.*

Good Étienne Jodelle had shown in 1552 the first French tragedy, in the modern definition, his *Cléopâtre captive*. It had been appropriately celebrated, one may remember, by the humorous sacrifice of a goat, with correct classical rites. Jodelle continued to write plays and to gather fame, and, with fame, an unreasonable self-confidence.

When, in January 1558, the king captured Calais and returned to Paris, the city organized a banquet of welcome in the Hôtel de Ville. To Jodelle the committee appealed, to arrange for the production of an after-dinner playlet and a pantomime. By the way, would he write some Latin inscriptions, and see to the decoration of the hall, with perhaps a couple of arches of triumph ? It would be a good idea to have some appropriate music. And he would take care of the costumes ? They could give him just four days.

Jodelle, in what must have been a poetic frenzy indeed, consented. Four sleepless days passed, in a kind of hallucination.

The festival began badly. A pelting rain beat down. When Their Majesties arrived in their carriage, they were greeted by an artillery salute. The royal horses took fright, and the Majesties narrowly missed being upset. As the hall was jammed to suffocation with the bourgeois of Paris, the noble escort had trouble finding place to stand. Jodelle's decorations and inscriptions were half finished. The classical Latinity, beyond most comprehensions, lent itself to burlesque translations. In the crowd, the service of dinner collapsed ; some of the great had no wine to their meat, and a parched throat is the enemy of goodwill.

After the dry dinner, the Cardinal de Lorraine said grace. The order was given to remove the tables. But

the crush was so great that the servitors could not suc-
ceed in lifting them and carrying them away. The frantic master of ceremonies, recognizing that the removal
of the tables was impossible, ordered another impossi-
bility. He signalled that Jodelle and his troupe should
enter and give their play.

Jodelle had dashed off a pleasing half-hour masque
in verse, presenting Orpheus and his singing rocks,
Minerva, Jason, and the Argonauts. He had chosen,
patly, the episode in which the Argonauts carried their
craft through Libya on their shoulders, and his crafts-
men had constructed a painted boat which should sym-
bolize the heraldic skiff of Paris. He had foreseen even
to equip his craft with a demountable mast, so that it
could pass through the entrance door. But there had
been great trouble about costumes. And Jodelle had
been unable to rehearse his troupe of fourteen till half
an hour before the banquet, and then he had found, to
his horror, that his actors only knew half their lines.

At the entrance cue Orpheus appeared, struck his
lyre, and proclaimed that if ever the rocks had answered
him, they should now follow, and sing the triumph of
the great king. Orpheus paused, and two painted belfries entered. The hall roared with laughter, and Jodelle
nearly fainted. He had written his order to construct
two rocks, *rochers*. No doubt his handwriting was feverish ; the scene-painter had prepared two *clochers,* belfries.

There was nothing to do but go forward. The actors
plunged amid the spectators, trying to clear a path
toward the king and queen. The singers hidden in the
painted belfries stumbled blindly ; the uncertainty of
their song was drowned in laughter and the furious
cries of trampled guests. The entry of the mastless ship

Argo was greeted with uproarious shouts, which increased with the efforts of the unhandy sailors to mount their mast. Jodelle, who played the part of Jason, was stricken speechless. No matter ; if he had remembered his lines no one would have heard them.

The masque was hustled off the floor, and the second part of the entertainment began. Jodelle had imagined a pantomime in which Virtue, Victory, and Mnemosyne (the goddess of memory, of all things) would enter with a group of naked cupids, and would present crowns, with poetic compliments, to the noblest guests. But the cupids' parents had evidently insisted that, in the cold February rain, their children should be warmly dressed. They appeared well bundled up ; their golden wings would not fit them, clothed, and hung at ridiculous angles. And only one of the crowns, that of the king, was ready.

Jodelle, who would endure, he said, rather an elephant in his eye than a spot on his honor, fell into a tertian fever. In fact, he never recovered from the shame of the *Argonauts,* and wrote long brooding justifications. 'The tail of joy is grief,' he said. He could not let his discomfiture be forgotten, and neither, I hope, will we.

Whether Ronsard laughed or wept at Jodelle's disaster is not recorded. He was soon to have other concerns, shared with the rest of France.

In July 1559 Paris was in fête, to celebrate the peace of Cateau-Cambrésis and two royal marriages. And King Henri, jousting on horseback with Montgomery, captain of the Scottish Guard, received a lance-thrust which penetrated his eye and brain. The king was dead ; long live King François II and his spouse, Mary Stuart !

The new king gave, indeed, no promise of long life. A puny, pimply boy of fifteen, subject to giddy fits, suffering from a chronic discharge of the ears, he was weak in mind and body. Husband of the most loved queen in modern memory, he could give her no fleshly evidence of his love. His usual apathy was broken only by occasional fits of violence. Suddenly furious at the buzzing swarm of place-seekers, he threatened to have them all hanged, and erected to that end a gallows higher than a parish church-tower.

Ronsard must have shown remarkable discretion in his suit, for his post of *conseiller et aumônier ordinaire du Roi* was renewed. The honor brought him no great profit. At the accession of the new king the finances of the kingdom were in a most parlous state, the payment of pensions from two to five years in arrears.

The poet had, at any rate, the privilege of attendance upon His Majesty, and upon his adorable queen. Ronsard had loved her since, a child of six, she had come from Scotland to live with her uncle, Ronsard's patron, the Cardinal de Lorraine. It was the tragic fate of this Mary, Queen of France and Queen of Scots, to draw love fatally to her, as she draws it still.

To Ronsard, the pale, slender, studious girl brought the memory of his old master, her father, James V. She recalled his boyhood in bleak Scotland, especially when, whimsically, she dressed in kilts, tartan, and bonnet, and sang a barbarous ballad to the lute. He loved her because she loved poetry, and mostly his own, and most of all the poems he wrote for her.

She was Queen of France for only a year. Her pitiable spouse died of his accumulated ills, toward the end of 1560. For the second time the court put on its deep mourning. All the royal rooms of the Louvre were hung

with black drapes horrid with skulls and crossed thigh-
bones, and even the chairs grinned of death. Mary removed to Fontainebleau, and there, clad in a long robe
of mourning white, she walked pensive in the long
alleys, while the white swans glided placid on the lake
beyond. So Ronsard remembered her always, when the
news came of all her griefs and errors in her sullen
northern kingdom.

Mary quitted France forever, ousted by her mother-
in-law, Catherine de Médicis, who would have no rival
in the regency. Ronsard wished he might be a bird, to
fly beside her dwindling coach.

He felt very old and abandoned. He had seen three
kings of France die. On January 1, 1560, he saw the
death, at thirty-seven, of dear Joachim du Bellay, his
only peer in French poetry. He wrote : 'The other day,
as I was wandering, solitary and pensive, as is my constant mood, I went so far that I got lost on the Seine-
side, below the Louvre, where the Bonshommes convent is shut straitly between the shore and the hill.
There, as if beside myself, I accused Fortune, mother
of flatterers. . . . I hated my life, and confessed that
antique virtue dwelt no more here. I wept Du Bellay
who was of my age, my craft, my temper, my kin, who
died, poor and wretched, after singing so often and so
learnedly the praise of princes and of kings.'

He looked back sombrely on his own life. He had
pursued gain and office, and had indeed received some
trifling posts, such as might be tossed to a favored keeper
of the king's hounds. For this reward he had turned his
Muse to the trade of flattery, and had harnessed her to
the car of royal triumphs. He had composed elegies at
the command of the great, and though he held that an
elegy should not exceed thirty or forty lines, he was

obliged to prolong them interminably, for the great judged a poem by its length, even though they would not listen to the end. In this business he had written poems of which he was not proud. (Did he esteem as little as do we his lament for the death of Albert, the king's lute-player, from gall-stones ?

> *Quelle mort le tua ? Une pierre qui vint*
> *Lui boucher la vessie, et le conduit lui print*
> *En cette part où l'eau par son canal chemine,*
> *Et tout d'un coup boucha sa vie et son urine.*

The conclusion is, indeed, pretty : that Albert's lute-playing was of a sweetness well capable of dissolving the gall-stones.)

For five years he had barely attempted the lyric form. Official verse and the routine of courtiership had taken all his strength. More essentially, the concern for place and advancement was paralyzing the nobler feelings. He felt the pains of frustrated ambition, no longer those of love. His imagination had ceased to soar birdlike, singing on its flight.

Well, there was another king, the boy Charles IX. And perhaps under the new reign the poet would be better rewarded. With security and a little ease, he might at last produce his *Franciade,* the national epic of France for all future times. And he might once more set free his spirit, and let his genius do its proper work.

X

Bleeding France

THE traveller, striking south from Paris's center, might cross the Seine by the bridge of Notre-Dame, and turn left through the Place Maubert, where he would cross himself before the hanging bodies slowly turning on their ropes, as if for a last look at the world. He held his nostrils as he crossed the open sewer, which Erasmus remembered when he said that a soldier returning from the wars brings his wife only the itch and a soul as pure as the sewer of the rue Maubert, or a public latrine. The traveller climbed the Mont-Sainte-Geneviève, keeping the church of Saint-Étienne-du-Mont to his right. He passed beneath the Porte Bordelle, under the inspection of slouching archers, and emerged amid a cluster of houses, to cross a disused moat and continue through thinning suburbs along the Grand' Rue Saint-Marceau.

Just beyond the Porte Bordelle, in the space between wall and moat, stood the house of the poet Ronsard. A painted angel above its door gave it the fitting name of *la maison de l'ange*. A poet might look on such a lodging with complacence. It was comfortably large, with a pleasant garden where the master might toil to ease his spleen and to refresh himself with the touch and smell of clean earth. A mulberry tree stood there, as in the garden of Shakespeare. Under the tree was a large stone table. The garden was separated from the court by a

155

balustrade and grill, with stone pillars surmounted by lions of stone. The house belonged to Antoine de Baïf, who lived just within the walls. The king permitted, by a special and most unmilitary dispensation, a passage-way to be pierced in the city wall, that the two poets might meet, on urgent business of the Muses.

A century later the house was the property of the poet Colletet, whose literary *cénacle* met about Ronsard's table, under Ronsard's mulberry tree. The site may be sought today on the rue Rollin, in whose little length Descartes and Bernardin de Saint-Pierre lived, and Pascal died.

In the *maison de l'ange* Ronsard took his pride and his pleasure. For diversion, he made his rendezvous by preference at the *Trois Poissons* tavern, whose sign-board showed, by an agreeable chance, the three fish of his own heraldic shield. He had lost his taste for the noisy meetings at the *Pomme de pin,* round the corner, where the book was soon drowned in the bowl. Even the parties at Dorat's seemed to him tiresome, and be-wildering to his deaf ears. For Dorat, at fifty-three, kept his youth in the fashion of schoolmasters, a youth of the mind that seems naïve even to the young. In drink and song, as well as erudition, he must excel, at whatever cost in the haggard dawn.

Ronsard found his happiness rather in quiet evenings before his fire. Baïf would slip over from his house, through the private passage. Or perhaps Jodelle would come, with his ravaged face and his bombastic actor's gestures. Or young blond-bearded Jacques Grévin, the author of tragedies on classic models. To them Ronsard confided the troubles of his heart.

'By labor,' he said, 'one becomes a lawyer, a philos-opher, an orator ; but not a poet. The gift of poetry is

like that fire which comes as a presage on winter nights,
over the river or the meadow or a sacred forest, leaping
and flashing and darting rays through the night's obscure. People watch the holy flame in terror, their souls
beating their bodies. But finally its brightness dwindles,
it turns pale and livid, and ceases altogether. It never
dwells long in any land, nor returns to a place it has
once visited. Thus neither the Hebrews, nor the Greeks,
nor the Romans, have held Poetry entire in their hands.
It has seen Germany, and has thriven on the shores of
England, Scotland, and France. Its delight is to choose
diverse men in strange countries, illumining a whole
land by its beams. But soon its light is consumed away
in the wide air. As for me, my dear Grévin, if celebrity
has been mine, it has been sold me too dear. I don't
know if another would be content with it, but I know
that my art torments me cruelly, though now, in my
lifetime, I enjoy that acclaim which is given after death
to the unfeeling dead. Because I have tasted of the
waters of Permessus, I am now smitten by sleep and
sloth. I am unskillful, useless. And what is worse, I cannot overcome that sluggard humor which possesses me.
If to reward me Calliope had made me the best of her
troop, if I were perfect in the art she teaches, I would
stomach my woes and my shortcomings. But since I see
myself, when all's said, to be only half a poet, I could
wish for a trade less divine than ours.

'Look you, there are two sorts of poets : the versifiers,
who invent verses and verses alone, cold and frozen
fellows, whose work serves, in the end, only to package
cinnamon, sugar, ginger, and rice ; apprentices, ink-
wasters, whose hide Apollo has never pricked. And the
others, whose minds are consumed by poetic fire, who
are full of fear and divinity. Of these there have been

how many ? Only four or five, who coupled mystery to
eloquence, and who by fables hid under a motley veil
the true sense of their song, that the common clown,
the friend of ignorance, might not understand the craft
of their sweet wisdom. Such poets God keeps in torment, and never leaves them free, but urges and presses
them with a burning goad. Their feet are on the earth,
their spirits in heaven. They wander through the woods,
the mountains, and the fields, and all alone enjoy the
nymphs and the fairies. But the people call them raging
mad.

'And what is their reward in this world ? They labor,
and another enjoys the fruits of their toil. They bear
every shame and indignity, only to fill their bellies, and
the great forget them, as if they were court beggars,
court fools.

'Look at my own case. I have sung the fame of two
kings, untimely dead, and all my work is to be begun
again. Incessantly I have served the Guises, since the
days when the Cardinal and I were boys together, on
the benches of the Collège de Navarre. I have celebrated
their achievements in war and statecraft, and defended
the Cardinal against the poisonous slanders of the
Huguenots, exposing myself to their venom. And who
receives the vacant benefices in his gift ? A fat protono-
tary, an envious dandy, a buffoonish courtier, a patcher-
up of history, a self-styled Cicero of our times ! Hungry
crows, swag-bellied harpies ! Thus the great oxen plow
the plain, the fat sheep bear wool upon their backs, the
industrious bee in his dark refuge labors, and all for
others' profit ! Ah, how mad were our poor fathers, to
teach their sons the literary trade ! It would have been
better to teach us the business of the vine-dresser, the
plowman, the mason, or the carpenter, rather than that

of Apollo, whereby we are considered insensate, mad !'

Policy counselled Ronsard to stifle his resentment against the Guises. They were growing daily greater, leading their own party, the Ligue, which defended Catholicism and the family interests. Meanwhile the Protestants, under the lead of the Condés and the King of Navarre, waxed in power, ominously confronting the Guises and the Ligue. Between the two great parties the royalty of France, represented by the foreign Queen-Regent, Catherine de Médicis, and the ten-year-old king, Charles IX, stood weak and wary, taking buffets from both sides. It was commonly whispered that the Guises, all pride and ambition, would find a way to seize the throne of France, ousting the boy king and his mother. But it was the king's party that Ronsard chose, less from fidelity, it would seem, than from spite toward the Guises, whose appreciation of poetry was so exclusively aesthetic.

The King of France was a thin reed to lean on. A solemn child of ten, a little bent, slack-jawed, forever sick, feverish, or frozen, he seemed cursed in his inheritance and doomed to a poor, brief life. But such thoughts were not to be spoken. Ronsard wrote for him poetic counsels, excellent advice : flee liars and flatterers, do not give offices for money, do not oppress your people with taxes, do not make war. The people must look to you favorably, and love you without fear ; thus have great kings kept their supremacy, not by harnessing their folk.

The King of France accepted the advice politely, and returned to his solemn games. Statecraft was left to his mother and her invaluable chancellor, Michel de l'Hospital, humanist, poet, and friend of Ronsard's. Their policy was, at first, one of conciliation of the two opposing parties and of the rival fanaticisms. Catherine de Médicis wished the Guises and the Condés to neutralize each other ; she wished Catholics and Protestants to live at peace in a quiet land. It was a hard end to attain, when hatred hung over France like a mist.

Many of Ronsard's friends, radical-minded intellectuals, went over to the new teaching of the Huguenots. They lamented that their master in poetry would not join them. He was hiding his talent in the ground, they said, with his songs of love and myth. If he would devote his genius to the praise of Christ, they said, he would be perfect ; but Satan, father of lies, has seduced him, making him sing only his fables and falsehoods.

The converts' words could not touch Ronsard with Protestant grace. In his youth, as he admitted, he had been for a moment tempted by the poisoned honey of the reformers' sweet brew. Now, however, he was firm in the faith, and was repelled by the insolence of his old friends, who thought they knew more than all Christ's church :

> *Tenez-vous en vos peaux, et ne jugez personne,*
> *Je suis ce que je suis, ma conscience est bonne.*

Not for him the radicals' easy sense of superiority, by a mere declaration of enmity to the established order. To be sure, he recognized the abuses of the Church : the sale of benefices to boys of fifteen, to ignorant louts, to fops and popinjays. 'What would Saint Paul say of our young prelates, who have no care for their poor flocks, whose fleece they steal, and sometimes their very hide ? Who live without trouble, without preaching, without praying, perfumed and elegant, courtiers, philanderers, hunters and hawkers, spending God's substance with lewd harridans ?' (Ronsard, absentee cleric, who spent the tithes of his priories on his ease and pleasure, might have been accusing himself. But moralists do not accuse themselves.) 'What would Saint Paul say to see the Church's wealth, its puffed-up ministers, its Popes clad pompously in silk and cloth of gold ? He would repent that he had suffered for her so many beatings, pains, and exiles, and would pray that a fiery shaft might strike her very head. Indeed, there are cruel abuses to be redressed. Nevertheless, the reform should take place within the Church. In this hard moment for France, it is dreadful to take arms against her, to weaken her against watchful enemies beyond the frontier. Inward division, in the face of external danger, is the calamitous character of the French nation !'

(*Plus ça change,* say the French, *plus c'est la même chose.*)

The troubles of France grew rapidly worse in the year 1561. The Guises assembled a private army, with the evident intention of seizing the young king and ruling as his regents, eventually, perhaps, as his successors. The Condés and the Protestants drilled for war. And the Queen-Regent fought desperately for peace, and for time, till her son should be grown and strong.

Catherine de Médicis believed, or hoped, that controversies could be settled and hatreds appeased by the meeting of enemies in an atmosphere pulsing with goodwill. Since her own religious faith was no more than a state policy, a vestment that rulers wear before their people, she could not understand the passions of believers, aspiring to the martyrs' crown. Her temper was rather that of the Elector of Saxony and the Duke of Bavaria, who threw dice to decide if their realms should be Catholic or Protestant. Her pathetic trust was in mediation, arbitration, reason and reasonableness.

Catherine summoned, therefore, an assembly of Catholic and Protestant spokesmen, to find a common ground on which peace might be built.

The spokesmen obeyed, but with no peace in their hearts. They gathered at Poissy on the Seine, the native town of Saint Louis, where today Sunday trippers from Paris sit day-long on the shore, fishing through the river's oily iridescence for legendary fish. It was the *Colloque de Poissy* that met here, in September 1561. Its sessions were held in the high gothic refectory of the Dominican convent. Ronsard was among the spectators.

The prelates, with their brilliant robes, lace rochets, glittering pectoral crosses, confronted the black-gowned, white-banded ministers. For the queen, the Chancellor Michel de l'Hospital addressed the assembly, asking Christ's spirit of forgiveness and love. Then spoke, for the Protestants, Théodore de Bèze. He had been a humanist in his time, a friend of the young Pléiade, and had written pagan love poems with the best of them. But while teaching Greek at Lausanne he had deserted Apollo for the god of Israel. At Poissy, De Bèze, arrogant, would abate nothing of his faith. He proclaimed that in the Eucharist the body of Christ is as far distant from the bread as is the top of heaven from this earth. The Catholic prelates replied in fury, and the *Colloque* served only to widen the cleavage between the two parties.

Ronsard was much interested to see again his old friend, now inspired by the devil's grace. De Bèze had a noble presence, with great forked beard and gray hair above broad brows. His eloquence captured many. Ronsard heard him preach, a few days after, in a temple of the Faubourg Saint-Marceau ; he watched his compelling gestures and observed the ardor of his hearers. 'He offered Paradise to the mob, thinking that God would owe him Paradise in return.' But Ronsard thanked God for his deafness, obscuring the resonant voice. He escaped from the assembly, feeling like a sailor safe on shore, who watches his companions perish in the storm. He called on De Bèze to preach no more in France a gospel in arms, a bepistolled Christ, black with powder-smoke, bearing in his hand, like Mahomet, a great cutlass red with human blood. Better, he said, for the preacher to retire to Lausanne, there to read again of the prowess and wrath of Achilles, and in verse to make Ajax fight, and Nestor speak, and to wound Venus once more with lovely wounds.

Ronsard loathed war, and sedition, and cruelty, and these earnest hate-mongers, tense with righteousness. His own religious convictions were mild enough, just sufficient for his Church and prince. Men of great faith bewildered and bored him. What fools, to prate at such dreary length of dogma and doctrine ! What tiresome ardor ! How could reasonable men busy themselves with such concerns, rather than with love, and the world's beauty, and the sacred secret bliss that sometimes mysteriously fills the soul ?

Ronsard had the sense that he had outgrown the world, or that the world had hurried past him, to leave him standing nonplussed, with the fading rose in his hand.

During the winter of 1561-2, men's folly turned ever more tragic. While Queen Catherine issued an Edict of Tolerance, Catholics and Protestants vied in intolerance. Protestants sacked and gutted churches ; Catholics hunted notorious Protestants to lonely roadside deaths. Everywhere, in secluded valleys and forest clearings, men were marching and counter-marching to the shout of sergeants.

On the first of March was provided the incident to unsheathe the ready swords. The duc de Guise and his men assaulted a barn filled with Protestants at worship, killed thirty, and wounded a hundred and thirty. It was the Massacre of Vassy, setting an official opening date for the First Civil War. The Protestants seized many cities, including Vendôme, where they hacked merrily at the heads of gothic saints, and desecrated Christ's Holy Tear.

Ronsard heard the news probably in Le Mans, where he was fulfilling his very occasional duties to the church of Saint-Julien. On April 3, he or his agent in Le Mans rented for his use the house of La Poterne, on the little cathedral-crowned hill above the Sarthe. His occupation of it must have been brief. In May he was in Paris, and was present at a test of cannon at the Arsenal. Soon after, he retreated from the tumults of the capital to his church of Évaillé, a dozen miles north of La Possonnière. There he found no country peace.

Évaillé is a dismal village today, a score of dark houses haphazard round a dark café-bakery. The surrounding landscape looks gray even in midsummer. The church, Ronsard's church, is queasy with age. Tremendous pillars, which could bear a cathedral roof, uphold a dirty wooden barrel-vault. The interior is chill and clammy ; the hand-blackened plaster has fallen here and there. The tawdry brightness of cheap modern ornament only adds to the slattern look. The church is now too poor to support a curate ; a priest comes on high days from Écorpain, two miles distant. But in Ronsard's time it bore the title of barony, and the poet, whether from need or some ecclesiastical requirement, or because of some vanished charm, chose to spend there the summer of 1562.

The countryside was filled with alarms. Nearby Saint-Calais was captured by a Huguenot expedition from Vendôme, and recaptured in a rising for which the monks gave the signal, with a mad ringing of bells. Hatred and vengeance led to atrocities, which were answered by vengeance, atrocities, and hate. A country gentleman was strangled, his wife stoned and thrown down a well.

Ronsard remembered that before he was a cleric he had been a warrior. He formed a troop of squires and gentry, a vigilante committee to preserve order and oppose Huguenot aggression. His leadership attracted, perhaps, the truculent Protestants. They attacked the church in force. But Ronsard and his men were ready; they drove off the assailants with well-placed musket-fire. Ronsard, the captain-priest, was the chief target of the attackers. Five arquebus-shots, fired at close range, missed him, through God's evident favor toward the Muse.

When he was reproached for such deeds unbecoming to the cloth, he mildly answered: 'Being unable to defend the Church with the keys of Peter, I had to use the sword of Paul.'

The pen was still his handiest weapon. In May of 1561 he wrote his *Discours des Misères de ce Temps,* a noble poetic appeal to Catherine to appease France's troubles. He describes in tragic words the distresses of his country. Fell Opinion, child of Pride, has set all men at odds, arming son against father, brother against brother, wife against husband. Weak women interpret the sense of Scripture; unreasoning children dispute about faith; the artisan leaves his shop, the pastor his flock, the lawyer his trade, the sailor his ship, the merchant his stall at the fair. The student is distraught from study. From his scythe the farmer fashions a pointed dagger, a pike from his rake-handle, while his steel plowshare becomes a broad knife. The churches are turned into stables, brigandage reigns, and all authority is dead. France is destroying herself. Let the queen assert herself and impose stern order on both factions.

To this stirring *Discours* anonymous Huguenots replied, with that vigor of abuse which is the special talent of the righteous. They neglected Ronsard's argument, to concentrate their attack on his person. They accused him of atheism, of plagiarism, of avarice in the accumulation of church livings, of eating meat in Lent, of lewd life, of pederasty, of suffering from syphilis. They revived the old tale of Jodelle's goat sacrificed to Bacchus. To make Ronsard's sins the more heinous, they insisted that he was an ordained priest.

The poet was goaded to reply, with answering abuse which would have been more salty if he had known who his opponents were. Contenting himself with mockery of the more ridiculous accusations, he insisted on the genuineness of his faith, and soberly contested the charges that had some appearance of reason. A priest ? Would to God he were ! He would enjoy the weight of a good bishopric on his back ! He would be glad to wear a mitre on his head, which the razor would shave for holy days, with a great wide crescent tonsure !

As the little dispute continued, with charge and countercharge, the great war filled France with its terrors. The nobles of the land took sides, following religious conviction or political advantage. Many were inspired only by a purpose to attack the central government, weakening it to the profit of their own dwindling feudal

powers. Armies scoured the country, the Ligueurs in
red, the Huguenots in long white woolen coats over
their armor, which gave them the nickname of 'the mill-
ers.' The base, the violent, the greedy, enlisted. Swiss
and German mercenaries joined the Huguenots, for the
business-like looting of monasteries, while many of the
Catholics were no better than freebooting bands, oper-
ating against rich Protestant merchants. The hatreds of
civil war were set free ; the smell of blood maddened
men to more bloodshed. It was every one's pious duty
to torture, shoot, or drown his neighbor. The gentle
Michel de Montaigne observed with horror that man
can kill for pleasure, inventing new deaths and tortures,
delighting in anguish. With men were burned their
books, their thoughts. No great loss, most of them ; such
pamphlets as *Spiritual Sugar to Sweeten the Sour Misfortunes of these Times.* Beauty was the Huguenots'
hated victim ; it was their joy to pull down sculptured
saints, to hack at carved tombs, to deface ancient paintings, to bring great red and purple singing windows
crashing to the ground. Man's desire was all fixed on
destruction, on death.

Ronsard put the blame squarely on the Protestants.
France's troubles were their doing. The aristocrat in
him despised the presumptuous plebs, usurping the
rights of nobles, diploma'd scholars, and divinely consecrated churchmen. The Huguenots' face of piety was
to him insufferable hypocrisy. 'They are simple in dress,
ambitious of honor, gentle in speech, arrogant of heart ;
their look is shamefaced, their souls shameless ; some
are apostates, some atheists, some demand the first place
above all men, some are jealous of God's Paradise,
promising it to those who follow their dreams ; and
some are sophistical liars, who write on Holy Scripture,

and torment the Gospel in a thousand ways, and turn
it into songs !' They would break down God's appointed
order of mankind ! 'The street-porter calls himself the
citizen's equal, and everything is turned to wind and
mockery, when the old law of our fathers is despised,
when the Gospel is the common property of pastors,
women, children, workmen, servants, even of brigands,
who call themselves the sons of God, and sing some
psalm between their murders !'

The wars dragged their bloody track across France.
The duc de Guise was assassinated by a Huguenot
zealot. Catherine abandoned her policy of mediation
between the extremes, and strove to head the Catholic
party. An ill-boding peace, or rather truce, was signed
at Amboise in March 1563.

During that year the trace of Ronsard disappears.
Presumably he was in Paris, observing the troubles, paying his duties at court, talking with secure friends. He
thought seriously of leaving ungrateful France, and
seeking his fortune in some land where the Muse was
still honored.

He was out of tune with his time. His Christianity, a
strange mingling of orthodoxy with Renaissance paganism, no longer fitted men's murderous conviction. Ten
years before, he had written a long parallel of Christ
and Hercules, comparing, for instance, the three nights
which Jupiter fused in one for the conception of the
hero with the mystery of the Saviour's birth. Now the
Protestants called his poem scandalous ; he could not
see why. He soberly proposed that modern men should
revive, in honor of Christian saints, the festivals of the
dear Greek gods. He would see the rose-crowned vil-
lagers singing before the holy altars, and dancing drunk-

enly under the elms to the hoarse hautboy, just as David
had leaped before the ark. He longed for the return of
that old innocent age of gold, before the use of steel and
fire was guessed. Then the gods showed themselves vis-
ibly to men, and the cattle spoke presages in human
voices, and envy and rancor did not reign. The fields
had no boundaries of ownership, and the grateful earth
yielded its fruits without men's labor, and the old gently
left this life as in a dream.

To Ronsard, the imaginations of the Greek bards
were more real than any visions of Christian prophets,
more real even than his own recollections of fact. He
could not picture the Christian heaven as he could the
timeless gayeties of the Elysian Fields :

> Poet, to you came Death, the gladness-giver ;
> You crossed the black irremeable river,
> And blessèd, to the blessèd fields you come
> To greet your Homer in Elysium.
> There the old Fathers sit in grassy bowers,
> And heart-free, talk of love among the flowers,
> Each in his lady's lap ; and one lies long
> Under a myrtle ; and one sings a song.
> Some wrestle on the sand ; and others fall
> To leaping combat with the bounding ball.
> And there is Orpheus, amply gowned in white,
> Leaning against a laurel-tree, to smite
> His hornèd lyre, a song of dawn to sing
> To the brigade, that dances in a ring.
> There, in that innocent earth, untended grows
> The Panacea ; and the crimson rose
> Blows amid lilies. By the river-side
> Daisies and pinks are looking, candid-eyed,
> And there the birds incessantly outpour
> Their lovely jargon over grove and shore.
> And Zephyr there and Flora harmonize
> Their gracious, sweet, and everlasting sighs.
> There Fate and Fortune keep not men forlorn,

There does not evening hasten toward the morn,
Nor morn toward evening ; nor does there the rage
For rank and goods keep men in vassalage.
There does the sad-eyed, shouldering ox not wend
With upturned plowshare home, at the day's end.
Nor does the sailor, off forbidding shores,
Tickle the back of Neptune with his oars ;
But on abundant honey are they fed,
And drink the nectar that the heavens shed.

Ainsi toi bienheureux, si poëte heureux se treuve,
Plus dispos, et plus gai, tu traversas le fleuve,
Qui n'est point repassable, et t'en allas joyeux
Rencontrer ton Homère aux champs délicieux,
Où, sur des bancs herbus ces vieux Pères s'assisent,
Et sans soin, de l'amour parmi les fleurs devisent
Au giron de leur dame : un se couche à l'envers
Sous un myrte égaré, l'autre chante des vers,
L'un lutte sur le sable, et l'autre à l'écart saute
Et fait bondir la balle, où l'herbe est la moins haute.
Là, Orphée habillé d'un long sourpelis blanc
Contre quelque laurier se reposant le flanc
Tient sa lyre cornue, et d'une douce aubade
En rond parmi les prés fait danser la brigade.
Là, les terres sans art portent de leur bon gré
L'heureuse Panacée, et le rosier pourpré,
Fleurit entre les lis, et sur les rives franches
Naissent les beaux œillets, et les paq'rettes blanches.
Là, sans jamais cesser, jargonnent les oiseaux
Ore dans un bocage, et ore près des eaux,
Et en toute saison avec Flore y soupire
D'un soupir éternel le gracieux Zéphire.
Là, comme ici, n'a lieu fortune ni destin,
Et le soir comme ici ne court vers le matin,
Le matin vers le soir, et comme ici la rage
D'acquérir des honneurs ne ronge leur courage.
Là le bœuf laboureur, d'un col morne et lassé,
Ne reporte au logis le coutre renversé,
Et là le marinier d'avirons n'importune,
Chargé de lingots d'or, l'échine de Neptune ;

Mais oisifs dans les prés toujours boivent du ciel
Le nectar qui distille, et se paissent de miel.

In sum, both sides bored him, the fanatic Catholics
and the fanatic Protestants. For his own faith, he found
it easy to subscribe to whatever his fathers had believed.
Such a faith did not forbid a pagan rule of life and a
pagan trust in Nature's goodness. 'Do not break your
tranquil ease for Papishers or Huguenots,' he wrote to
a friend. 'Be neither friend nor foe of either, but believe
that God, our gentle Father, who is not partisan like us,
knows what is needful for us. Lie in a wood's shadow,
or by a stream-bank or a gurgling spring, and while
your years are green cheat age with play. For we die incontinent, and will go in the obscure skiff to the far
unremembering exile, whence none returns. For thus
has Nature willed.'

Death is sure, though it be but the change of form,
as the silk-worm becomes the butterfly with diapered
wings, as the egg becomes the peacock. *Omnia mors
poscit. Lex est, non poena, perire.* In the face of the
universal doom, how frantic are our ideologies ! 'Everyone prates of his windy imaginations, and vows that he
alone is in the right way ; everyone is dogged for his
own truth ; but after one season comes another season,
and man is only an old fabled tale !'

In the hurry toward death, Nature counsels us to
delay, to enjoy the shining world, to follow our hearts'
dictates. Most clearly the heart bids us love. Not all the
hate of the civil war could turn Ronsard from love.

There was the mysterious Sinope, a sixteen-year-old
maid of high rank. Ronsard loved her through a springtime with an 'almost furious affection,' said his friend
Belleau. He dreamed wildly of marriage, of renouncing

for her his clerical station, his tonsure, and the round
bonnet that indicated the clerk. But if he should annul
the vow that forbade marriage, he must abandon at the
same time the revenues that would make marriage possible. He settled his problem as poets do, by writing
poems on his anguish, and by doing nothing, till the
problem somehow settled itself.

There was Genèvre, whom he met romantically on a
hot July day of 1561. The poet was bathing in the
Seine ; he observed on the opposite shore a picnic party,
singing and dancing. Loveliest of the ladies was one
with long yellow hair, hanging in two tresses. Ronsard
was allured. He swam to the party, and emerged from
the river, like a Triton, naked, to join the dance. He
capered to the ladies' laughing shrieks, then plunged
into the stream and swam away.

The memory of the unknown beauty tormented him,
till one day he encountered her standing in her doorway. Without ado he declared his love, and demanded
its return. Genèvre replied merely that he was wasting
his trouble, writing in water, sowing sand.

He suffered an appropriate time, living in a kind of
trance. His servants had to plead with him to go to bed :

> *Monsieur, il est bien tard, un chacun se retire ;*
> *Jà minuit est sonné, qu'avez-vous à gémir ?*
> *La chandelle est faillie ; il est temps de dormir.*

He set siege to Genèvre, and after a proper courtship
won his point. The amorous rage was succeeded by love.
Genèvre had quaint seductive ways, pinching, tickling,
curling his hair about the ear. She had a trick of folding
his shirt in pleats, and kissing him with each pleat. She
was kind. But her heart was elsewhere, with a lover
whom she had adored totally, and who had died of a

dropsy after six years of mutual bliss. And Ronsard found, with interest, that the thought of Genèvre excited him more than Genèvre herself. He told his beloved of this curious discovery : 'Certainly I have tested by many an experience that love augments and is strengthened in absence ; whether that in meditation, the pleasant memory cajoles the mind, or whether the portraits of past joys are freshly printed on the soul, or whether the soul regrets what it has lost, or whether delight is too soon perishable, while the memory of it lasts longer. In short, I know not what it is ; but assuredly I know well that I love better in absence than by my darling's side.'

This tactless description of the literary mind in love had its inevitable effect on the beloved. Genèvre, annoyed with the poet's frank egotism, returned to her interrupted fidelity to the dead. Ronsard marked his poems to Genèvre for publication.

For several years, it seems, he kept his heart free from any searching passion. He had his amourettes, his follies of a month or a night :

> Maintenant je poursuis toute amour vagabonde ;
> Ores j'aime la noire, ores j'aime la blonde ;
> Je cherche ma fortune où je la puis trouver.

But he avoided the afflictions of love, and so love passed him by. He was very busy, anyway ; first with the civil troubles, then with a renewal of courtiership. He was trying to secure his fortunes, at the court of the young king, Charles IX.

XI

The Court of the Boy King

THE majority of King Charles IX was celebrated in 1563, on his thirteenth birthday. By decree, manhood comes quick to kings ; they command even Nature. But to the look, Charles was still a tall, thin, sickly boy. He hung his head constantly, staring at the floor. He seemed to bow under the crown's weight, to wear his golden robes like a burden. He had always been perfectly subject to his masterful mother ; 'ma mère !' was his incessant cry. As a child he was carried screaming to his Royal Council, and all his life the duties of government were as hateful to him as they were incomprehensible.

In adolescence the docility of boyhood turned into a queer violence. He had unfortunate masters ; he learned to swear and dissemble from his favorite Gondi, Maréchal de Retz, the greatest denier of God of his times. The king came to believe, says Brantôme, that swearing and blaspheming were a form of conversation, rather indicating gentility than sin.

To defy the constant menace of consumption and to show his new manhood, he became a passionate hunter. All his joy was in running the stag through the royal forests. The meetings of the Royal Council were postponed till evening, when the king, back from the chase, drowsed through the discussions of national policy.

Like his father, he loved to show his muscles and his prowess at games. When a great tourney was held at

174

Fontainebleau, the thirteen-year-old king was inconsolable because his mother, remembering her husband's fatal joust, would not permit him to take part. At last relenting, she allowed the king to fight with sword and dagger against his fencing-master. To no courtier's surprise, the king brought down the fencing-master, and delivered to him, as he lay upon the ground, a simulated death-blow.

With the bold women of his court his violence gave place to a shamefaced timidity. He had his mistresses, as a testimony to his manhood, 'whether for honor's sake or pleasure's,' says Brantôme quaintly, adding that the king dallied *plus par réputation que lasciveté*. He fell in with convention so far as to have a bastard son, by a well-born lady, a Huguenot. But he was no lover. He tried an amorous bout as a solace for the toothache, and had hard words from his companion when he told her that his pains had not been a moment forgotten.

He was more at ease with his stud-grooms and whippers-in, whose language he spoke by preference. Next in his favor were the rowdy young nobles with stud-groom minds. He had curious whims. Once, in a coachman's costume, with a wide green hat, he drove his sister and mother through Paris. Catching sight of a friend on foot, he lashed at him with his whip. The furious noble drew his sword for murder ; recognizing the monarch, he changed his fury to labored laughter. Charles would rouse his young companions from their beds with his ready whip. He was a skillful artisan, and on his own forge made horse-shoes and arquebus-barrels. He made coins, the crown, the double ducat, the teston, both of honest metal and of counterfeit, and defied the Cardinal de Lorraine to tell which was which. For a solemn ball he had his police assemble a dozen pickpockets and

cut-purses, and delightedly watched their deft work.
Their loot, worth three thousand crowns, was afterwards returned to the victims. It was rumored that he
employed an apostate monk to celebrate the black mass,
and that he summoned a condemned sorcerer and offered to pardon him in return for an account of the
orgies at a witches' sabbath.

Among his whimsicalities was a taste for poetry. Naturally he took for his tutors the first poets of his realm,
and of them his favorites were Ronsard, Dorat, and
Baïf. He turned some tolerable quatrains, which were
received with rapture by his masters. Their sycophancy
confirmed him in his scornful way with them ; he gave
them niggardly rewards and hints of more, saying to his
familiars that poets were like horses, who need to be fed
sparingly, for too much grain makes them fat and wind-
broken. Poetry with him was a rainy-day diversion.
Baïf, in an eloquent moment, was interrupted by the
quarrelling of dogs under the royal table, and the king
abandoned his poet for his dearer pets.

Ronsard was beside himself with the honor granted
him of poetic intimacy with his monarch. His heart
a-flutter, he would enter the sacred bed-chamber, for-
mally saluting the bed if the king happened to be absent. He read the boy's quatrains with transport, and
replied with long poems, comparing his master to Hercules and to the sun. He wrote an epitaph on the king's
bitch, Courte, noting that Courte had a kind of life
after death, for her hide was made into gloves for the
queen.

Friendship with petulant royalty is not all bliss. The
poet suffered from the king's adolescent humor, which
expressed itself in mean mockeries of his age. Charles

had his shrewdness ; he knew what would cause his companions to wince.

Now that Ronsard had the highest of all patrons, he revived an old, dear project. He took from his cabinet the fragments of the *Franciade,* the great epic poem with which he proposed to endow the French language and the French nation. King Charles gave him encouragement, and even advice. He suggested that Ronsard abandon the twelve-syllable alexandrine line, and rewrite the whole in ten-syllable lines. A king's suggestion, even in poetic technique, is law. Ronsard set to work, writing and re-writing. All modern critics agree in condemning the change. Yet surely the *Franciade* in alexandrines would have been just as dull as in the ten-syllable form, and longer by a fifth.

By 1564 the civil wars had fallen into a lull, and the court was eager to forget cruelties and hatred. As spring came on, the royal family felt restless within the walls of the Louvre. Their restlessness was augmented by the horrible springtime task of cleaning the Louvre's moats. The court removed to the country palace of Fontainebleau.

The great palace was lovely in its freshness, its Rossos and Primaticcios bright and new, its walls ungrimed by time and tourists' hands. In the niches, on the ceilings, the naked gods and goddesses posed with antique grace, delightful to the Renaissance mind. Here the Apollo Belvedere stood serene, and the Laocoön writhed, and the Gioconda smiled. From the new balustrades the ladies tossed bread-crumbs to the carp. They say at Fontainebleau that some of these deathless carp still fight for bread. They may be recognized by their gold nose-rings, stamped with the arms of François I. The woodlands heard the packs in cry, the winding horn, the pound of galloping hooves. The palace and the parks were filled with courtly diversions. There were elaborate jousts, acting out stories of maidens imprisoned in ogres' castles ; a combat of twelve Greek knights and twelve Trojans, fighting for love ; serenades at dawn, and plays in which the greatest nobles of France were the actors. At night there were concerts, and nautical spectacles on the dainty lake, under a shower of fireworks. And balls in the great golden hall of Henri II, the fine ladies in billowing satin, wearing pearl necklaces twined in their hair. Masquerades flitted from room to room of the palace, and occupied the lanterned glades.

It is true that many courtiers were quietly ruined by the obligatory pleasures. A carnival was reckoned to cost 7,500 livres to a participant. In distant provinces peasants groaned under new exactions invented to pay for noble wardrobes at Fontainebleau.

In the endless festivities Ronsard had his share. It was his task to organize poetic masques and plays, and to provide incidental verse for gold-armored heralds and for adulators of His Majesty. He wrote a pastorale for the young brothers and sisters of the king, and a masque for sirens rising from the canal in Fontainebleau gardens, and poetic challenges for the king in his tourneys, and the text for a ballet on horseback. It was all well enough in its way, amusing and profitable to the writer. But Ronsard, in his dark moods, must sometimes have felt that the poet, the consecrated one, god-communing, lawgiver, freedom-giver, revealer, had become a sort of upper servant of a stupid boy, who happened to wear a crown. He had sold his birthright for a little money, given grudgingly and with ill grace.

He had still, to be sure, the consolations and the torments of love. In the ambience of court gallantry, Ronsard loved, and, as usual, furiously and futilely. For three months at Fontainebleau he gave his angry devotion to his Astrée, the lovely young wife of Antoine d'Estrées, marquis de Cœuvres. At their first meeting Astrée had prettily given him candies to eat, but later, he complains, she fed him only gall and venom. He watched her, in a pageant, arming a knight-errant, kissing him before he donned his glittering helmet and rode away on her hest. 'Happy knight,' he cried, 'and unhappy poet in his clerkly disguise !' Once Astrée wore a laurel wreath in his honor, and once, after an absence, she gave him a kiss. It was an icy kiss, tasteless, a corpse-like kiss, such as Diana gave her brother, such as a girl gives her grandmother. 'Are my lips so bitter ? Ha, you should imitate the pigeons, who beak to beak make love on a tree-top, with kisses sweet and long.' His reproaches brought him nothing, not even another corpse-like kiss. 'You love only in ideas !' he said.

The poet misread her ; she had other kisses for others. She loved a friend of Ronsard's, Le Guast, Captain of the Guards. Later, she saw her lover killed by the ruffian baron de Vitteaux. And when Vitteaux was slain in his turn by the young marquis de Tourzel d'Alègre, who was avenging his father's death at Vitteaux's bloody hands, Astrée gave her person as a reward to the slayer. A violent heart beat beneath her demure brocades. When certain butchers and tradesmen insolently demanded money due for supplies furnished to herself and the marquis de Tourzel d'Alègre, she had them soundly beaten. The tradesmen, merchants of spirit, invaded her house, found the couple in bed, stabbed the two of them, and threw the bodies out the window.

Perhaps Isabeau de la Tour d'Auvergne, demoiselle

de Limeuil, was briefly kinder to the poet than was his obdurate Astrée. Isabeau was one of Queen Catherine's troop of maids of honor, a glorious bevy who lived and slept together, under the watchful eye of a princess-governess. They passed their days in gentlewomen's occupations, music, dance, and embroidery. They were on show at every festival and function, surrounding the ugly queen-mother with beauty, exchanging decorous badinage with the gentlemen of the court. It was 'a true paradise of this world, a school of behavior and virtue, the ornament of France,' says Brantôme. The maids of honor were goddesses, creatures rather divine than human, he says; in a ball-room they shone like stars in the serene night. Their duty, beyond that of being lovely, was to entertain distinguished guests, and to train the rough young nobles to some sort of civility. The young nobles complained loudly of their training, which put them to unaccustomed tortures. 'These maids of honor,' says Brantôme again, 'were all of them enough to set fire to the whole world; and so they burned a good share of us gentlemen of the court.'

Some of the maids of honor were irked by the imposed decorum, and found hours for secret pleasures. Of such was Isabeau de Limeuil, a ripe, high-colored, blue-eyed blonde, with a voice that led all the others in the choral songs. A daughter of one of the great families of France, she had the hauteur and insolence of her caste, and a frank and careless sensuality that might more fittingly have lodged in one of her brothers.

She gave Ronsard her kisses; perhaps, in a stir of sense, more than kisses. But he could not take and return them in her own light-hearted temper. For all his boasts of amorous skill, when the holy moment came he was likely to fall into a musing fit, examining his

own mind, forgetting his eager partner. Isabeau drew
away indignant at the fantastical-melancholy mood interrupting her pleasures. Ronsard justified himself at
length in verse. 'When I am beside you, seeing you so
beautiful, watching your hair, a dainty golden mesh that
could capture and bind the Scythian swordsman, seeing
your smile, your lips that Love alone kisses, seeing your
grace and beauty, your wild sweetness, your humble
cruelty, and seeing that I cannot attain to your perfection, I have cause to be melancholy.

> I doubt and fear, lest hurrying Time efface
> Your love, and lest another win your grace,
> And lest some god may bear you to the skies.
> I'm jealous of myself, my heart, my eyes,
> My steps, my shadow ; and I fear and rue
> Each moment that another talks with you.
> Alas, I'm like the horrid serpent-wardens
> Of the Hesperian golden-apple gardens,
> Whose task is all to frighten and annoy,
> Though the sweet fruit they never can enjoy.

> *J'ai peur que votre amour par le temps ne s'efface,*
> *Je doute qu'un plus grand ne gagne votre grâce,*
> *J'ai peur que quelque dieu ne vous emporte aux cieux ;*
> *Je suis jaloux de moi, de mon cœur, de mes yeux,*
> *De mes pas, de mon ombre ; et mon âme est éprise*
> *De frayeur, si quelqu'un avecque vous devise.*
> *Je ressemble aux serpents, qui gardent les vergers*
> *Où sont les pommes d'or ; si quelques passagers*
> *Approchent du jardin, ces serpents les bannissent,*
> *Bien que d'un si beau fruit eux-mêmes ne jouissent.*

'Incessantly and everywhere your lovely presentment
floats before my eyes, tormenting my blood and heart
and soul with the desire to see again your absent self.
My thought is forever conversing with you. I am like
the miser who buries his treasure deep. Though he

travel to far lands, by new seas and countries and cities, his avarice still hangs heavy round his neck, for his heart is always where his treasure is hidden. Forever, my treasure, I think of you, and I cannot live unless I am with you in thought. As spring brings the flowers, summer the heat, autumn the grapes, and winter the cold, so cruel love by its nature brings to the lover's heart care and grief, sadness, weariness, tears and misfortune, fear, suspicion, and pain. And then you ask me the cause of my sadness and my languor ! If on your part you had felt any spark of the flame with which you burn me, you would know my own distress by your own experience. Your brow would be sad, and you would know all the sorrows that love gives for a boon which is nothing !'

A boon which is nothing, *un bien qui n'est rien* ! The women Ronsard loved seem very chary of the boon which is nothing. He could not understand their ultimate reluctance, and vowed that some fate, some curse of fortune, was to blame. To Isabeau he protested that he had every accomplishment of the lover. 'Adventurously I have loved in various quarters, and am esteemed by the ladies to be understanding and discreet. I know with what honor a great lady is respected, I know well what service a widow requires, and a maiden, and a wife ; and I know well how in such cases one should govern oneself sagely. I never made an error therein, nor could I do so. I am, you might say, predestined to please the ladies, *comme prédestiné pour aux Dames complaire.*'

Isabeau evidently found these recommendations from satisfied customers a little too fatuous. In such tones he could demand 'a boon which is nothing !' Nothing, indeed ! He would learn, *parbleu,* that the boon was something to the giver ! And there were others who would prize it higher, and no starveling poets, either !

There was, indeed, another, and no less a person than the Great Condé himself, leader of the Protestant party. When Catherine de Médicis made a truce with Condé, on an island in the Loire, below Orléans, she took with her in her skiff the lovely Isabeau de Limeuil. The ambassadress was well chosen. Isabeau's charms served to detach Condé from his austere associates. The two loved in the stormy fashion of the Valois court. Their amour, and the peace of France, was declared in 1563 ; in the following year Isabeau bore a son to the *joli petit homme*. But in 1565 Condé married Françoise d'Orléans. He sent to Isabeau for the portrait of himself he had given her. She returned it decorated with a pretty pair of horns. She married Scipio Sardini, an Italian banker who had made his fortune in France. ('This sardine has become a great whale,' said France.)

In 1569 Mme Sardini was journeying across France. Her coach was shouldered off the road by a troop of ragged, bloody soldiers. They were returning from the great Catholic victory of Jarnac. Their leader, the duc d'Anjou, recognized the beautiful Isabeau, and prepared a malicious jest. He haled forward some men carrying a stretcher. 'Could you identify this corpse for me ?' he inquired. He whipped off the blanket, to reveal the mangled form of Louis, prince de Condé, killed at Jarnac. Mme Sardini looked at the pretty little man, the father of her child. She said one word : *'Enfin* !' At last !

When Ronsard heard this news, he may have felt that he was in some measure avenged upon Isabeau for her disdain. Or he may have felt simply that love is all a burden and a weariness, a punishment of men. It was about this time that he told his secretary, Jamyn, to beware of love, not to anchor at its shores, or he would grow old there, without hope of escape. 'Love? It is only an ardent frenzy, which fills the mind with smoke, error, wind, and an importunate dream. Dreaming and loving, my friend, they are all one.'

In bitterness with love, he hunted more substantial gains. By the kindness of young King Charles, he obtained a canonry in the church of Saint Martin of Tours. And as well, a home, a place to live and die in, the priory of Saint-Cosme, on the outskirts of Tours.

This was in the spring of 1565. Just five years before, Ronsard had come to Saint-Cosme, to frolic with Marie, to say a last farewell to her, and to write for her one of the loveliest of his happy-melancholy poems. The little island was dear to him, with its weeping willows, its level meadow where he had danced with the wedding party, its sandy shore where he had bidden Marie goodbye, and had watched her boat dwindling down the Loire. Was it chance that brought him the gift of this island? Or Apollo, who still had in heaven a little influence with the Christian gods in office? More likely his brother Charles, the incumbent of the priory, saw a chance for an ecclesiastical transaction, and Pierre prayed to the king that he might rule where he had sweetly suffered.

In the year 1182 certain canons of Saint Martin of Tours abandoned the ease of their comfortable city to live austerely at Saint-Cosme. They built there a little Romanesque church, a casket for the Host. Today the apse remains, the round-arched windows, an altar of rain-resisting marble, the tiny side-chapel that could scarcely contain a priest and his acolyte. Beside the church stands the old half-timbered priory, now a farm dwelling. Only a few years ago the society of the *Sauve-*

garde de l'Art Français rescued the site from the rats, the destroying ivy, the stone-quarrying neighbors, and banished the horses stabled in the sanctuary. The pious visitor today is shown the open gallery whence Ronsard surveyed his island and the soft-flowing Loire, and the large bright room with a great fireplace and carved roof-beams. It is the room where the poet lived and worked, the room in which he died.

Saint-Cosme is no longer an island, for part of the river bed has been reclaimed, and has become the demesne of swarming after-hours gardeners from the city. The pine-tree has gone, the glory of Ronsard's little realm. To the pine the poet intoned a psalm ; in the tree he could still perceive the form of Atys, the self-mutilator, metamorphosed into a pine by merciful Cybele. Our strange prior made his prayer to Cybele, the Berecynthian, the Great Mother of the Gods. This is the saint whom he begged to save him from error and mischief. For, in his theology, Cybele is philosophy, and her pine is nature, which has mutilated itself of human grossness.

Here Ronsard spent the summer of 1565, reading, writing, working in his garden, listening to the drowsy enchantment of the offices in his church. He had for constant companion his secretary, Amadis Jamyn, who had been his page and had grown to be a scholar and a poet.

In November he received the most exalted of visitors.

King Charles and his mother were making a tour of the kingdom. Their billeting officers arrived in Tours, choosing quarters. They marked with white chalk the château of Plessis-les-Tours, setting it aside for royalty. Yellow chalk indicated the temporary homes of nobles. The occupants were told to be gone, and not to re-enter

their houses till the royal progress had passed on. Profit-
eering, and even profit, were checked by the publication
of official prices for foodstuffs, well below the market
value. The court descended on the town like an invad-
ing army. But the people cheered their king, it seems ;
a city's honor and a fine show in the streets are worth
paying for.

King Charles turned from his official ceremonies to
greet the poet in his new priory. Ronsard, with a perhaps affected simplicity, presented his king with a white
melon from his garden. They exchanged rhymes ; the
king, in some clumsy lines, invited Ronsard to return
his visit in the royal palace of Amboise. Ronsard, overcome, lauded his pupil's poor verses as words of revela-
tion, vowing that he was vanquished in his own art.
'Thus great Augustus wrote to Vergil !'

Ronsard was on a tide of fortune. In the following
year he received two more homes. The first was the
priory of Saint-Gilles, in the comfortable market-town
of Montoire, ten miles from La Possonnière. Ronsards
of La Denisière had been its priors from 1454 to 1480.
The coquettish Romanesque chapel, hardly higher than
a cottage, still stands beside the little Loir, still flowing
unconcerned by time. It is very ancient. It was built in
the eleventh century by the Cluniac Benedictines, as a
halt for pilgrims on their way to the shrine of Saint
Martin of Tours, and thence to Saint James's tomb in
Compostela, in the northwest corner of Spain. Saint-
Gilles is now a shrine for archaeologists, who there admire the red and green frescoes, done in the Byzantine
style brought from the East by way of Monte Cassino
and Cluny. The archaeologists look delightedly at the
beardless Christ of the frescoes, and explain that this
was the Christ of the Greeks, a lovely adolescent, all

beauty, charm, and sweetness. Ronsard, no doubt, admired less than present scholars the awkward angularities of the Byzantine convention, and found the Saviour a queer pop-eyed pot-bellied creature, a great insect, crooking uncomfortably his enormous knees to fit in an insufficient space. No wonder an indignant Renaissance, conscious of its new, free art of painting, plastered over these fantasia of a ruder age.

Ronsard dwelt little at Saint-Gilles. Even the town of Montoire was too crowded for him, in his country mood. He preferred the nearby priory of Croixval, which chanced to be in the hands of his secretary. It lay only four miles from La Possonnière, where Ronsard's nephew Louis dwelt with his newly-married second wife. The poet, coveting the benefice, found a way to make it his own. He was appointed its prior, in exchange for an annual payment of 120 livres to Jamyn. Croixval became, a few years later, his favorite dwelling.

The priory stood where the plateau between the little Loir and the great Loire breaks down into the broad valley of the smaller stream. It had been built in the twelfth century, as an outpost against the wide hostile forest of Gastine. In Ronsard's time the deep woods still covered the plateau, which is today an endless field of wheat. Down from the forest flowed two streams, the Cendrine and another too small to have a name. At their junction was Croixval, the Crossing of the Valleys.

The priory church and the quarters for the few monks have now disappeared. The little that remains has been rebuilt to make a peasant cottage. The visitor picks his way among the chickens, the simple machines, the refuse of an untidy farm. His call brings forth a slattern, who points silently to the house, built of the pale stone of the cliff and of plastered wood. She makes

no attempt to describe the dwelling; there is hardly
anything to describe. It is just a peasant house, like any
other house. But the informed visitor will notice that
the pitch of the roof is steeper than those the peasants
build today, and he will perceive, on the jogs at the
gable-ends, two ancient carved beasts, lions or dogs.
Within, a staircase with a carved balustrade leads to the
room where Ronsard lived and wrote. The cellar is the
slattern's pride. Her candle lights massive arches and
groined vaults, built with the Church's confidence in
eternity. Near by is the well, heavily curbed and capped,
probably the same well from which Ronsard drew the
water for his garden. And all about are farm lands, vines
and grain, and peace, comfortable to tired men growing
old.

Whether because his quarters were not yet made liv-
able or for another reason, Ronsard seems to have spent
little time at Croixval in 1566. He preferred his river
island of Saint-Cosme. The following year he resumed
his attendance on King Charles. He put off his country
character to become once more the courtier.

During 1567 he followed in the king's train. The
civil wars broke out again with new fury. Condé and
Coligny, for the Protestants, tried to kidnap the king.
The court galloped in terror to Meaux, and took shelter
behind solid walls of Swiss mercenaries. Ronsard was
there. He offered his stout hand and heart to serve the
king. The Church's laws bound him less than men's
honor.

Inwardly he was sick of the foolish bloodshed, these
wars of hatred that men took so seriously. He was sick
of the courts, their empty shows, the jealous struggle
for place and power, and sick of his own position as a
minister of the king's minor pleasures, the *menus plai-*

sirs. He hated the indignities to which he was some-times put, Poetry herself being shamed in his person. There was a fop, a curled and painted court minion, who dared, in the midst of dinner, to mock Ronsard's poetry, reciting it with false emphasis and comic asides. Ronsard's rage proves that the fop got his laughs, that the great deigned to be amused. He wrote a violent in-vective, praying that the offender might be well cuck-olded, that he would have a malodorous wife (two in-congruous wishes, one would say), that cats and dogs would befoul him in the streets, and that he would end on the gibbet of Montfaucon, with the carrion crows picking at his eyes and mastiffs pulling at his feet. Such a fate seemed to Ronsard reasonable, for one who had slandered divinity and blasphemed against the Poet.

As the wars waxed in violence, and angry men had no ears for the gentle Muses, Ronsard retreated to his priories. Most of 1568 and 1569 he spent at Saint-Cosme, where, for a long year, he struggled with a quartan ague. In the intervals of fever he led a pious, sober life, be-fitting the cloth. Neither the gay companions of Co-queret nor the ruffed lordlings of the court would have recognized their Ronsard in this tranquil half-priest.

'When I wake in the morning,' he wrote, 'my first task is to invoke the Eternal Father of all good, praying humbly that he may give me his grace, and that I may pass the newborn day without offending him, and that he may chase from me all error and sectarian opinion, and that he may be pleased to keep me in my first faith, humbly subject to the laws and to my prince. Then I rise from my bed ; when I am dressed I give myself to study, learning virtue, and reading and writing, in ac-cordance with my destiny, which from my childhood has bound me to the Muses. For four or five hours I remain alone in my room. Then, feeling wearied with too much reading, I drop my book and visit the church. Returning, I talk an idle hour with my friends, and then dine frugally, and render my thanks to God.

'The rest of the day I take my pleasure. If the afternoon is pleasant and serene, I go to walk, in the fields, or in a village, or in a wood, or I seek out silent, solitary places. I love gardens that have a wild look ; I love the flowing water that twitters by the shore.

'Often, talking with a friend on some grassy bank, I have fallen asleep among the flowers, in a willow's shade. Or reading there, I have hunted the means to live again in men's minds.

'But when the skies turn sad and dark and the unwelcoming fields are grim, I seek out company ; or I play at cards ; I do the *voltige* on my wooden horse ; I broad-jump, wrestle, or fence. I joke and tell stories ; in truth, too much severity does not lodge with me. I like to make love, to talk to ladies, to record in verse my amorous flame. I like the dance, the masque, music and the lute, the foes of care.

'But in those places where one must show the office and duty of a devout heart, then I am a firm pillar of the Church. I arm my shoulders with a rippling surplice, my arm with an amice, my back with a cope. I lose no moment of the divine prayers. At daybreak I am at matins ; I have my breviary in my fist, I sing sometimes (though rarely, for my voice is not good). In nothing do I scant my duty of service. I am at prime, at sexts, at tierce, at nones. I hear the High Mass sung, and with the incense perfuming the church, I honor my prelate. And when my duty is done I return to rest. So from morning till the return of evening we sing praises and canticles to the Lord.

'Then, when russet night has ranged the stars, cur-
taining sky and earth with veils, care-free I bed, and
raising my eyes, my lips, my heart toward heaven's
vault, I make my prayer, beseeching that high Goodness to pardon sweetly all my fault.

'That is how I live ; and if your life is better, I am
not envious of it.'

It was a good life. Ronsard, growing older, felt that
sympathy with the earth which forecasts the ultimate
return of the body to its home. He was happy in his
gardens, planting, grafting, dressing his vines. With
Jamyn by his side and an Ovid in pocket, he would set
forth in search of a salad of herbs, salutary for his fever.
In the ditches and fields' edges he would gather the
tufted lamb's-lettuce, the tiny-leafed daisy, the pimper-
nel excellent for the blood and spleen, the sweet root of
the rampion, and the buds of currant-bushes. Returning to the priory, he would prepare the simple feast,
with rosy vinegar and olive-oil from Provence, for he
scorned the northern walnut-oil, fatiguing to the stomach. And after a little conversation, a little game with
his pet hunting-dogs (he hated cats, the very sight of
them made him shudder and quake), he would tranquilly seek his bed. He slept by preference on his left
side.

He proclaimed his happiness, and his scorn of the
base courtier :

> Let him who will laboriously cling
> To the uncertain favor of a king ;
> For me, I'd rather feed on naught but bread,
> Drink with a cupping hand from a brook's bed,
> Play on the country lawns, or lie and dream,
> Or make my verses by a murmuring stream,
> Watch in a cave the Muses dance by night,

Or hear the pell-mell noise in the last light
Of sheep and oxen from the haughs returning.
How happier I, in these dear fields sojourning,
To plant and sow, heart-whole and fancy-free,
Than sell myself to a king's slavery !

Or aille qui voudra mendier à grand'peine
D'un prince ou d'un grand roi la faveur incertaine :
Quant à moi, j'aime mieux ne manger que du pain,
Et boire d'un ruisseau puisé dedans la main,
Sauter ou m'endormir sur la belle verdure,
Ou composer des vers près d'une eau qui murmure,
Voir les Muses baller dans un antre de nuit,
Ouïr au soir bien tard pêle-mêle le bruit
Des bœufs et des agneaux qui reviennent de paître :
Et bref, j'aime trop mieux cette vie champêtre,
Semer, enter, planter, franc d'usure et d'émoi,
Que me vendre moi-même au service du Roi.

It was a good life, indeed. But we have learned to be
suspicious of those who are loud in the praise of obscurity, and of those who noisily renounce the world.
We shall see them again in our city. One does not ab-
jure the love of fame, nor the love of women. He who
has loved yesterday will love tomorrow ; *cras amet qui*
nunquam amavit quique amavit cras amet. And he who
has been tortured in love may expect only further tortures. We learn nothing from experience, and we always
fall in love with the same person.

XII

Hélène

RONSARD, in his jocund priory of Saint-Cosme, heard troubling tales from literary visitors, late from the royal court. There was a new poet in Paris, the darling of the great. This Philippe Desportes, a mere boy of twenty-four, wrote court poetry with a quality of its own ; *mignardise*, it was called, a dainty, precious, Italian quality that accorded with the current vogue in art, dress, speech, and manners. Ronsard was still the Prince of Poets, no doubt ; but he was a prince in exile, out of sight and out of mind. 'Ronsard ? What has happened to old Ronsard ? I thought he was dead !' the witlings would say.

'I write for myself alone,' Ronsard proudly proclaimed in 1569. The boast, written for others to read, was patently absurd. He gave the proof of its absurdity by leaving his dear countryside in the country's opulent August of 1570. He returned to the courts he had so loudly scorned, to defend his poetic primacy, to show to the world that Ronsard was still master, and the only master.

He re-entered immediately the literary life of the capital. He found pleasurable hours at the *Académie de Poésie et de Musique*, founded by good Antoine de Baïf in this year 1570. The Academy's ambition was 'to represent words in a song confected of sound, harmony, and melody,' or, briefly, to blend music and poetry into

193

a single thing. In a way, the opera is the realization of
Baïf's dream. His theories were elaborate. He wished to
renew in French the classic prosody based on the length
of syllables, to establish a new art of poetry, and to train
musicians and poets in their united craft. The first task
he proposed to his Academy was to classify all the syllables of the French language into longs and shorts. But
of this curious effort, and of Baïf's own exemplary volumes in *vers mesurés* we need not speak. His Academy
was far more than a school of instruction in his own
theories. It was a gathering of the most celebrated poets
of the time, Dorat, Ronsard, Jamyn, Jodelle, Belleau,
Pontus de Tyard, and others, joining with the country's
eminent musicians to sing and hear sung their produc-
tions, to work for the betterment of the French language, and to talk to exhaustion about art and literature.

The Academicians met in Baïf's house in the faubourg Saint-Marceau, and occasionally in the Collège de
Boncourt near by. Some of the Academy's rules are in-
teresting. The poets were forbidden to touch the musicians' instruments or music ; sick musicians were
granted a kind of health insurance ; no members of the
Academy were allowed to quarrel within one hundred
feet of the house.

The meetings were for some time successful. King
Charles lent his favor, and often his presence. He loved
music ; in fact, at mass he was known to rise and take
his place with the choristers. But after the Saint Bartholomew Massacre in 1572, the brooding king retired
from the world and allowed the Academy to languish.
It has its fame, however, as the first forerunner of the
Académie Française.

Ronsard was welcome in certain fine houses, where
the arts were honored. He had the friendship of Nicolas

de Neufville, sieur de Villeroy, Secretary of State. A
patron of the Muses, Villeroy opened to poets and
scholars his house at Conflans, where the Marne joins
the Seine, at the edge of present Paris. The mansion
stood in the midst of elaborate landscaping, with lawns,
and sanded walks, and orange-trees in boxes. There was
a circular pool, and a sunken garden, with a fountain
and a summer-house, adorned with statues of Tiberius
and Germanicus, and all about were trellises, cypresses,
laurel hedges, espaliered fruits and sweet-odored plants.
It was the delight of Villeroy and his friends to row on
the two rivers, like any Sunday bourgeois of our day.
Of some such happy moments Ronsard has left a poetic
record.

He was faithful also in the parlors of the maréchale
de Retz. Here was a seminary of poets, a forcing-house
of the spirit. The hostess was a lady of condition, the
governess of the royal children. She was learned in
poetry, in the oratorical art, in philosophy, mathematics,
history. She knew Greek, Italian, Spanish, and some He-
brew, and made speeches in Latin. She was the tenth
Muse, the fourth Grace. The poets who fed at her table
crowned her with every superlative in their verbal stores.
She was Artemis, Pasithée ; her flowered boudoir was
the *cabinet de Dictynne.* The painters, led by Jean de
Court, successor at court of François de Clouet, did portraits of her, which belie a little the poets' insistence on
her beauty. The musicians came with their instruments,
and dedicated to her the compositions which they had
first rendered in her parlor. There still exists a pretty
manuscript volume of the habitués' ecstatic tributes to
the hostess, done in a fine hand, with the titles richly
gilt and interlaced. Here was such a précieux salon as

later throve in France. Preciosity was no discovery of
the seventeenth century.

The maréchale's particular pet was Philippe Desportes, whose airy, fine-drawn conceits were in key with
the ladies' imported delicacy. Platonism and Petrarchism
reigned, the fleshless adoration of womanhood, pure
and purified speech (though indeed the lady's coarse
husband, Albert de Gondi, was King Charles's master
in blasphemy).

Ronsard, who had served his time to Petrarch and
had then outgrown and forsworn his master, had the
strange sense of watching, ghost-like, his own youth.
These young men were repeating his own development,
his own errors of twenty years back! Even Amadis
Jamyn was tempted from Ronsard by Petrarch, and was
rewarded by a popularity in constant proportion to his
infidelity. Must Ronsard, then, turn back time, adopt
the vogue he had long abandoned, in order to prove
his mastery? Or might he, perhaps, return to the Petrarchan manner, but mark it with his own stamp, blend
Petrarch and Ronsard to something greater than either?

Such thoughts possessed him as he spoke his share
of flowered compliments, sweeping his bonnet to the
floor before the lovely ladies, with that dignity which
seems always a relic of more formal days, but is perhaps a quality of aging muscles. The ladies were, in fact,
a charming bevy, bearing names as richly fantastic as
their costumes. There was Callipante, known to the
world as Marguerite de Valois, the king's sister. Callipante was soon to be famous, to be remembered still,
by the milkmaid name of Margot, Queen Margot. There
was Pistère, the title in gallantry of Henriette de
Clèves, duchesse de Nevers. And Imérée, Statyre, Sca-
ride, Fysée, Sigifile, and Calitée. Of these it was Statyre

who moved strangely the heart of Ronsard. Her name, without the portals of the hôtel de Retz, was Hélène de Surgères.

Hélène was one of the famous band of Catherine de Médicis' maids of honor. Her membership in that lovely chorus is proof of her high birth and her beauty. She was celebrated, besides, for her precocious learning ; 'Minerva' was already her nickname. Three other maids of honor, two of them her cousins, formed with her an erudite quartet that intimidated the young gallants and ravished the poets. The four girls would walk together, carrying books, reading one to the other in several tongues, especially in the Italian Hélène had known from childhood. Any one of them could turn a pretty sonnet in her own right. Even the honored poets protested against this bookish passion, swearing that the maidens were defrauding their precious youth with the consolations of age.

Hélène had a Spanish darkness, inherited from the Fonsecas, her father's race. Her voice was charming, her hair dark and abundant. She was beautiful, else Ronsard would hardly have loved her ; 'an ill-shaped body hides an ugly soul,' he said. But her beauty had a sombre air of dream. Though she was still in her teens, she had been marked by indelible grief. Her affianced suitor, Jacques de la Rivière, had been killed fighting the Protestants, in 1569, apparently. Ever after, until her death, Hélène wore by preference mourning gray. The color chimed with the ghostly pallor of her face, beneath its superficial olive tint. She was often ill, and always cold, even in August. She was a spirit, in whom the blood ran thin. Her greatest favor was to give her cool hand. In the gusty, lusty, full-fed court of the Valois her ethereal grace bewitched the gentlemen like a vision from another purer world. It bewitched, among many, Ronsard.

The poet met her, evidently, in the salon of Mme de Retz, in 1570. Her charm, her youth, her learning, and her respect for the Prince of Poets attracted him. Perhaps immediately he conceived the thought of making her the pretext for a poetic venture which would put young upstart Desportes in his place. For a time, however, he was stubborn against love, as he admits. The old heart did not leap so readily as in times past.

He was also very much occupied. He was obliged to work hard at the courtier's trade, to re-establish his position among the short-memoried great. From November 1570 till the following March, the court was in a tumult, with the festivities connected with the king's marriage to Elisabeth of Bavaria. Ronsard was the chief superintendent of the triumphal entry into Paris. He supervised the arches of triumph, the allegorical sculptures, paintings, and decorations. He wrote the devices and inscriptions, great sonnets to be enormously lettered and hung across the streets. For his work he received the useful sum of 270 livres.

He was also grimly at work on the calamitous *Franciade*. Four books out of the projected twenty-four, nearly six thousand laborious lines, were put together. All the epic requirements were fulfilled ; there were heroic wanderings, interventions of gods in human form, the obligatory storm at sea. Everything was there but life, the mysterious radio-activity of true poetry. And at the end he had not got his Francus beyond Crete, on his way to France.

At last the *Franciade* went to the printer. It was the summer of 1572. There was a sense of excitement in the Paris streets, a sense of menace. The politic wedding of

Marguerite de Valois, sister of King Charles, to Protestant Henry, King of Navarre, was in preparation. Their union was intended to bring union to France. But the Huguenots, swarming to Paris for the ceremony, showed an arrogance that infuriated the Catholic city. The taverns fumed with hatred, with dark talk of bloodshed.

On Sunday, August 17, a great ball was given in the Louvre, in honor of bride and groom. Ronsard took advantage of the old tradition of epithalamia, in which the poet shared strangely in the nuptials, to describe Marguerite in luxurious detail, from her dark hair powdered with gold dust, and the ruby hanging in her ear, to the veined marble of her legs. On Monday the marriage was solemnized in Notre-Dame. The bride, it seems, cherished a spark of rebellion. When the priest asked her for the words, 'I do,' she was mute. The groom put out his rough hand, and bobbed her head to the priest. The ceremony proceeded. In fact, she detested her husband, with his heresy, his insolent swagger, his bad breath.

On Wednesday there was a fine celebration in the Palais-Bourbon. A revolving stage, with twelve reclining nymphs, represented Paradise. Adjoining Paradise bloomed the Elysian Fields, lit by candles burning within crystal stars. Near by was hell, with its capering demons. Henry of Navarre led a band of knights-errant, who strove to carry off the nymphs, defended by King Charles and his two brothers. Cupid then appeared and made peace, and all the knights and nymphs joined in a dance.

There are some quarrels that Cupid cannot appease. In the midst of this festival the revellers were surprised by fireworks. At the sudden boom the knights put their hands to their swords, and faced about, looking for an enemy. The king sent secretly for a company of arque-busiers. And then calm returned, and the swords slipped back in place, and the dance went forward.

On Friday Coligny, the great Protestant leader, was shot and wounded by a Guises' man, as he walked toward the Louvre.

Saturday was a day of fear, plot, and preparation.

Sunday the twenty-fourth was Saint Bartholomew's Day. Queen Catherine and her council determined to settle matters. By their order, and with the forced consent of the king, the wounded Coligny was assassinated. The populace of Paris picked up their cue, and for three days killed Protestants, some four thousand in all. King Charles himself caught the frenzy, and shot at fugitives from his Louvre window, crying : 'Kill ! Kill !'

For a time Catholic France was proud of its work. A month later there was a celebration of the massacre in the palace of the Bishop of Paris. The guests, in high spirits, threw bread and apple-cores at one another. 'The king,' says a witness, 'dipped his napkin into the wine and flung it into the face of an aged knight, without the slightest respect for his gray hairs, and completely ruined his costly dress. The knights regarded the king's merry and intimate jesting with them as a mark of favor.'

But Ronsard never mentions the evil days of Saint Bartholomew. There was nothing he could say. He would not, like old Dorat, celebrate the carnage for pay. Nor could he, a churchman and the king's man, reprove the authors and perpetrators of the crime. But his silence is significant, as is a curious poem, found among his papers, in which he attacks Catherine de Médicis, saying that her best palace is not her Tuileries, but Saint-Denis, where she will lie in the tomb beside her dead husband.

Saint Bartholomew was disaster enough to Ronsard. His *Franciade* appeared only a few weeks later, when no minds were calm enough to settle down to an epic. The poet received a perfunctory royal gift of 600 livres, but none of that public acclaim which he had been predicting, and which others had predicted for him, since the days in Coqueret, more than twenty years past. The *Franciade* was born dead, in a moment marked by calamity.

By this time he was obtaining some consolation from Hélène de Surgères. Though he seems to date his servitude from 1570, he apparently made no great effort to urge his suit until a certain day of May, probably the May of 1572. He had often watched her walking, dreaming and pensive, and had feared to accost her. He did not wish to interrupt her meditation, and he feared a little for himself. He was almost fifty, old in look as men of fifty were in those days, when doctors, dentists, and oculists had not yet learned to fend off Time's ruin. He had been blessedly free of love for several years past. He might coolly use Hélène as the subject of a sonnet-sequence, to shame young Desportes ; could he be sure that he would not be wounded by his own words ? Was he sure that he did not wish to suffer once more ? Is not suffering better than insensibility ?

He ceased to argue with himself, and chose that May day to break in upon Hélène's meditation. They walked together in Queen Catherine's royal garden of the Tuileries, that well-ordered geometrical pleasance, with its labyrinths, bosquets, clipped rosemary in fantastic human forms, its palisades of box, privet, and jasmine, its alleys of sycamores, elms, and pines, its horse-shoe structure to make an echo, its trim-edged water-courses, its grotto representing the seasons of the year and the

signs of the zodiac in fine majolicas, with snails, tor-
toises, lizards, and frogs perpetually spouting water.
Catherine's château of the Tuileries, in course of con-
struction, showed above the trees, with the medieval
towers of the old Louvre.

The poet talked of flowers, for Hélène loved them
and studied in her earnest way their names, qualities,
species, and medicinal use. They talked of poetry, of
Ronsard's past works and of his dreams for the future.
Hélène confessed that she liked best sad songs, and
Ronsard's own melancholy mood better than his galliard manner. Ronsard reminded her, a little later, when
he had grown bolder :

> You told me, darling, as we walked alone,
>   You did not like a song that was too sweet ;
>   You loved the plaints of lovers who entreat
>   With lamentable melancholy moan.
> 'Often,' you said, 'in secret I intone
>   Those songs of yours where mood and subject meet
>   In sorrow's homage ; for my own conceit
>   Is one that grief has taken for its own.'
> Your words are cheats. If you had any care
>   For hearts fordone with anguish and despair,
>   Some little pity you would have for me.
> You sing my verses, and you weep the while,
>   Like that Egyptian subtle crocodile,
>   Better to filch my life by treachery.

> *Nous promenant tout seuls, vous me dîtes, Maîtresse,*
>   *Qu'un chant vous déplaisait, s'il était doucereux ;*
>   *Que vous aimiez les plaintes des tristes amoureux,*
>   *Toute voix lamentable et pleine de tristesse.*
> *'Et pour ce (disiez-vous) quand je suis loin de presse,*
>   *Je choisis vos sonnets qui sont plus douloureux :*
>   *Puis d'un chant qui est propre au sujet langoureux,*
>   *Ma nature et Amour veulent que je me paisse.'*
> *Vos propos sont trompeurs. Si vous aviez souci*

De ceux qui ont un cœur larmoyant et transi,
Je vous ferais pitié par une sympathie ;
Mais votre œil cauteleux, trop finement subtil,
Pleure en chantant mes vers, comme le Crocodil,
Pour mieux me dérober par feintise la vie.

By way of her melancholy he sought to touch her heart. He dwelt with her on the memory of her dead lover, Jacques de la Rivière. He accompanied her to the grave of Mlle de Baqueville, one of the inseparable four poetic maids of honor, separated finally by death. Hélène laid upon the grave her sheaf of flowers, and sighed and wept, showing that death had taken part of her own life. And Ronsard swore that he would die, since she despised the living and loved death more than anything.

Beside a fountain in the Tuileries garden he made an outright declaration to her. She smiled and did not check him. He would have thought himself a very god, had it not been for her duenna, who kept interrupting. Later, at the thought of that hour, he would feel a sweetness running in his veins, and nearly faint with pleasure.

She permitted him little favors. She drank, and passed him the cup, bidding him finish the drink, in which a little of her heart was swimming. They went to church together, and Ronsard looked in her eyes, heedless of the priest at his altar. Together they visited a sorcerer. Ronsard cries : 'Oh, happy was that magic, and the hair burnt, the murmur, the incense, the wine poured upon the waxen image ; O happy servitude !' He sent her gifts : a pot of ivy, which coils and climbs and brings down trees and towers. If only he might twine like the ivy about her lovely limbs !

We'll find our blessèd time, I pray, beholding
  The dawn above the boughs of a wide tree ;
  We'll waken to the sound of the birds' scolding,
And you will turn your half-closed lips to me,
  And I will murmur all my pain, enfolding
  Your rose-and-ivory body, sleepily.

Ne viendra point le temps que dessous les rameaux,
  Au matin où l'Aurore éveille toutes choses,
  En un ciel bien tranquille, au caquet des oiseaux,
Je vous puisse baiser aux lèvres demi-closes,
  Et vous conter mon mal, et de mes bras jumeaux
  Embrasser à souhait votre ivoire et vos roses ?

He addressed her in the dainty finicking style with
which the courtiers disguised their eventual fleshly purpose. He called to his aid legions of cupids, and half the
gods of Greece. He found subtle allegories, the more admirable as they were farther-fetched. He spoke to the
gnat, elephant-trunked, and bade him not suck his darling's blood, but feast on that of Ronsard. Then he
changed his conceit, and told the gnat to bite Hélène
and bring him the precious blood to taste, and then to
carry his own to her. (A transfer of malarias, the sar-
donic reader will say.) He gave her an agate, marked
with a crab, the sun's symbol, and regretted only that he
could not give her the sun itself. He sent her an immortelle, and developed the obvious meaning. Imitating
the ancients, he hung flowers, bedewed with his tears,
above her doorway, so that the opening door would
bring them down about her head, uttering their message.

He grew more urgent, and the manner of his pleading
pleased her less. When he kissed her hand she withdrew
it ; it was no good for him to cry that the kiss filled
him with a sweetness beyond telling, that the mere look

of her made him faint. Such words alarmed her. Once when he merely touched her hand she turned pale with anger. It was her beauty, he insisted, that was to blame ; she must pardon herself, not him.

He was proud, too proud, of his capacity for ardor. Too complacently he described how every artery, vein, nerve, tendon, and pulse was filled with love's fever. Too indelicately he pointed to the doves of the Tuileries, wooing beak to beak.

Love had taught him nothing. Pleased with his own fury, he could not see himself with her eyes, nor understand the cool fastidiousness of her spirit. He followed her everywhere, and she was often annoyed by the fidelity of this doting lover. Poet or no poet, he was ridiculous to the court, with his white hairs, his deafness, his noisy exhalings of woe. Hélène felt a little ridiculous too. She liked him, but better in private than in public. She enjoyed her own anodine coquetries with him ; she was annoyed when he took them too seriously. One day as they conversed by a window, a ray of sunshine fell between them, and then vanished. 'The sun came to look at you, and, dazzled, retreated !' exclaimed Ronsard. 'I have faced down that god and vanquished him !' 'The sun is tiresome,' said Hélène playfully ; 'I like you much better !' An incredible joy at the words filled Ronsard's heart ; but as he gloried, a younger man came to address her. She turned to him with a welcome, and left, standing alone, the poet who had conquered a god.

The two were mentally, as well as physically, incompatible. Ronsard's temper was formed by the lusty poets of Greece and Rome, who honored the play of sense ; Hélène found her spiritual food in the Platonism imported from Italy. She believed that beauty on earth is an emanation of divine harmony. The purest, the truest

love, is satisfied by the union of two spirits, quitting
and annihilating two gross bodies. She loves best who
can dominate and purify man's passion. And human
love is but an example and a stage ; it develops those
spiritual qualities which will serve for the ultimate
love, the contemplation of God.

As Hélène, ardent-eyed, set forth her Platonic doctrine, Ronsard argued or coarsely sneered. The spirit
feels nothing save by the aid of the body, he said.
'Though the human mind puff itself up with Plato's
doctrine, which boasts that the mind is an influxion of
heaven, it would be helpless without the body, and
would find it hard to praise its own celestial origin. By
the senses the soul sees, hears, imagines ; it has its actions through body's cordial aid. The mind must be in-
corporate to have any power ; matter renders it more
perfect and more worthy. You love the mind, and ex-
travagantly say that love is polluted by the body. Such
a word is only wild imagination, which embraces the
false for the true ; it is a renewal of the fable of Ixion,
who fed on wind, and loved nothing but the clouds. No,
I will be no pupil of Plato, who preached virtue and
notoriously did not practise it.'

His misjudgment of Plato was not, to Hélène, a mere
literary vagary ; it was an attack on the faith which she
held as much by instinct as by reason. She was cold by
nature. Even her body was anaemic, disposing her to
that purity which charmed and exasperated Ronsard. 'I
am sulphur and saltpetre, and you are only ice !' he
shouted. He found her in mid-August huddling by her
fire. She looked very pale in her gray gown. 'Why do
you sit there in your chair, complaining ?' said the poet,
ruddy from a brisk walk. 'I shiver,' she replied, 'and
the summer day could not warm me. All my body pains

me ; I have not been really well for six years, such has been my grief of mind.' Ronsard nodded his head. 'If summer, and youth, and the world's warmth cannot heat your blood, how shall I rouse an answering glow from your frozen soul ?'

She took to her bed, frankly ill. Ronsard visited her, and found her lovely in her pallor. Her head was framed in an embroidered silk wimple ; her white hand lay idly on the coverlet sewn with red roses. She was so beautiful, framing words with her thin voice, that Ronsard felt his reason shaken on its base.

Even when summer and winter had passed and the spring had returned, she felt no effervescence in her veins. '*O perte de jeunesse !*' he cried ; 'Venus is displeasing to you, and her son hateful !' Ronsard encountered her with her girl cousin. The cousin greeted him with a gay welcome, but Hélène continued with her private thoughts, pensive, head bent, loving only herself, disdaining the interrupter with a frowning eye. 'I took fright at your silence, and turned pale and went away, fearing that my salute had offended you.'

She loved only herself. And Ronsard, embittered, fell back on his old refrain. She will be old some day, and have her regrets. 'Let her glory now in her green youth, her crisp curls, her flashing eyes. They will pass. Beauty is only blowing wind, which will blow, and pass, and be forgotten.'

In his imagination he had his will of her. 'In these long winter nights, when the idle moon so slowly moves her chariot through the sky, when the late-lying cock announces day, when the night seems a year to the care-worn soul, I'd have been dead of grief without your spectral shape, which comes to ease my love, reposing naked in my arms, cheating me sweetly with a lying joy.

Truly you are cruel, and proud in your cruelty; but with your feigned person I may take my private pleasure, and slip into the place of your dead darling. Nothing is refused me. Thus does good sleep trick my amorous care with falsity. To trick oneself in love, why, that is no bad thing.'

No doubt this was one of the sonnets that Hélène did not see until they appeared in print.

Love was to Ronsard the whole business of earth; to fastidious Hélène it was an ugly thing, a threat to the soul. She had a nun's temperament. One day as the two stood at a high window of the Louvre, they looked across the jagged roofs of Paris to the hill of Montmartre, and the queenly convent with its skirt of steep hillside fields.

When at the Louvre's window, dear, we stood,
    You said, fixing Montmartre with your gaze:
    'I'd leave the court, and choose the quiet ways,
    The solitary desert, if I could.
The senses would be bound to lowlihood,
    In prayer and fasting I would pass my days,
    And love I would defy, that burns and preys.
    It could not cruelly feed upon my blood.'
'Oh, you are wrong to think,' I answered you,
    'That fire's less fire when ashes hide its glare.
    Love in the empty desert's born anew,
Above the cloister love makes bright the air.
    Against the god that can the gods subdue,
    Vain is your fasting, idle is your prayer!'

Vous me dîtes, Maîtresse, étant à la fenêtre,
    Regardant vers Montmartre et les champs d'alentour:
    'La solitaire vie et le désert séjour
    Valent mieux que la cour; je voudrais bien y être.
A l'heure mon esprit de mes sens serait maître,
    En jeûne et oraison je passerais le jour,
    Je défierais les traits et les flammes d'Amour;
    Ce cruel de mon sang ne pourrait se repaître.'

Quand je vous répondis : 'Vous trompez de penser
Qu'un feu ne soit pas feu pour se couvrir de cendre :
Sur les cloîtres sacrés la flamme on voit passer ;
Amour dans les déserts comme aux villes s'engendre ;
Contre un Dieu si puissant, qui les Dieux peut forcer,
Jeûnes et oraisons ne se peuvent défendre.'

In fact, Hélène never seriously planned a conventual retirement from the world. She loved the court's magnificence and its festivities. Especially she loved the dance, not for its amorous drama and its opportunities but for its own sake. An excellent dancer, she took an important part in the elaborate ballets in the gardens and palace halls.

There was one such, noteworthy in its time and memorable still, in August 1573. The diplomats had arranged that Henri, duc d'Anjou, younger brother of King Charles, should become the king of Poland. The Polish ambassadors came to Paris to make the formal request. The French court welcomed them fittingly. In the gardens of the Tuileries a grove of new trees was cut down, to make a great green outdoor hall. After the banquet an enormous artificial rock, silver colored, was trundled forward, while thirty musicians played. In niches of the rock sixteen lovely maids of honor posed, representing the provinces of France and various generalities. The rock made a precarious circuit of the glade. The nymph figuring France recited an ode of praise, by Ronsard, in honor of the new king. Then all the nymphs descended, and for an hour executed a ballet, doing great honor to their memories, as to their persons. The ballet concluded with the presentation of golden gifts to the most eminent spectators.

It is most likely that Ronsard arranged that Hélène should be the nymph France, to speak his ode.

Everyone was happy at this fête : Henri of Anjou because he was to be a king, Charles because he was to be rid of his younger brother, and Ronsard because Henri was taking with him, as companion and poet, the intolerable Desportes. Ronsard could have thought of no better place than Poland for his rival.

There were many other festivals in the Louvre and the new Tuileries, for the court loved the dance. The more intimate routs were held in the Salle des Cariatides, with a half dozen musicians fiddling in the marble gallery. The great balls took place in the present Salle Lacaze, on the floor above. The maids of honor, following the style set by Catherine de Médicis, wore enormous billowing skirts, high red-heeled slippers with a gush of lace emerging over the foot's arch, ruffs and high collars. The gentlemen who bowed to them in cadence glittered in brilliant silks, slashed and pinked ; their cloaks were negligently clasped to their shoulders with silver buckles. They wore their plumed hats, which in the dances were ceremoniously doffed and donned.

They danced, perhaps, the *branle de Bourgogne*, which was forever linked in Ronsard's mind with Cassandre. Countryfolk danced it to the rebec, the primitive fiddle of wandering minstrels. The courts adapted it to the small oboe, violin, and tabor. There were other *branles* : the *branle des lavandières*, wherein the performers imitate with hands and feet the sound of washerwomen's paddles slapping the wet clothes. And the *branle des mathématiques,* in which the dancers describe various geometrical figures on the floor. (Have we not read of a Ballet of Atoms, before the scientists of Baltimore ?) And the elaborate coranto, a mimed story. Three young men dance forward with three girls, who try to escape, while the young men reassure them.

The girls repulse their partners. These retire, and, dancing, readjust their laces and finery, and return, leaping, bowing, pirouetting, rhythmically beseeching and despairing. The girls at last are moved to pity, and all take hands for the final figure.

Hungrily, Ronsard watched Hélène threading her way through such dances. 'The ballet was divine,' he told her, 'assembling, breaking, reassembling, again and again intertwining, separating, swirling, imitating the course of the river Meander. Now it was round, now long, now narrow, now triangular, like the cranes' squadron flying south. No, you were not dancing, rather you were fluttering over earth ; for on that evening your body had been transformed into divine nature.'

The ballet, with its rhythmical advances and retreats, was a figure of Ronsard's own frustrated love. These old dances were the picture of woman's mastery, as our modern ones show the male's triumph. The poet footed forward, expressing his grim intention with grace ; and his lady as gracefully twirled just beyond his grasp.

So while another summer and winter passed, the distance between the two remained constant. Hélène danced in the pre-Lenten carnival, masking her face as well as her heart. 'For Ash-Wednesday,' cried Ronsard, 'you can take in my heart the ashes to mark your brow !'

In the spring of 1574, there was an interruption from the world without. King Charles yielded to his various ills ; a consumption found lodgment in his body. His mind was shaken by long brooding on the horrors of Saint Bartholomew's Day. On his sickbed he cried, sobbing : 'Ha ! My nurse, my dear, my nurse ! So much blood, so many murders ! What shall I do ? I am lost, I see it well !' His last words were : 'And my mother ?'

He died on the thirty-first of May, at the age of twenty-four. His physician, the famous Ambroise Paré, opined that his death was due to too much sounding the hunting-horn, but others alleged that his brother's partisans had poisoned him with the powdered horn of the sea-hare.

The death of his patron was a calamity for Ronsard. King Charles left no sons. The heir to the throne, Charles's brother Henri of Poland, now Henri III of France, liked the newer versifiers, and especially his personal poet, the young Desportes. When Henri received, in Cracow, the news of his brother's death, he took horse, and in a great ride of twelve hours escaped from Poland, with a furious troop of his subjects at his heels. Desportes arrived in Paris soon after his master, ready for illimitable laurels.

Ronsard's grief for his royal friend was somewhat distracted by his love for Hélène. These were months when his flame burned hottest, when his poems flowed most urgent from his heart. 'I wrote these sonnets,' he says, 'in that ill-starred month when my Prince died. Love and Death strove within me ; I felt double pain, from my lady's rigor, from my sorrow for the king I adored. The living and the dead offer me all ill hap. One loves regrets, the other tears ; for love and death are all one, in the end.' *Car l'Amour et la Mort n'est qu'une même chose.*

After this crisis of love and death, Hélène and Pierre found a calmer, happier intimacy. There were long separations, removing the exasperations of personal contact, encouraging the poetic mood of longing and sweet pain. Catherine de Médicis took her court and her maids of honor to the south of France in August 1574 and did not return until the following March. From then onward the court made many removes from Paris.

Ronsard loved excellently in absence, and Hélène too loved best with the mind. She wrote him letters, no doubt brilliant letters treating of the quintessential of love. She sent him presents from the Midi, branches of cypress, pomegranates in which he counted the seeds, equalling in number his woes, an orange and a lemon which he carried in his breast till they were cooked by his heat.

He took advantage of the court's journeys to retreat to his abbeys, especially to Croixval. There he planted in Hélène's honor a young pine, and carved upon its trunk their two names with love's symbols. He called upon the fauns to cherish the tree, and bade the summer burn it not, nor winter freeze it. He commanded the shepherd, fluting an eclogue upon his oaten pipe, to mark it annually, sprinkling it with milk and the blood of a lamb, and proclaiming : 'This pine is sacred ; it is Helen's tree !'

He consecrated to her a spring near Croixval, and wrote for it a group of limpid pastorals and sonnets.

So that your fame may flow, enrapturing
   This valley, as it's emblemed by a pine,
   I call upon the gods, I sprinkle wine,
   And in your name I consecrate this spring.
Shepherds, no more to these green purlieus bring
   Your crinkled flocks ; here let the thyme entwine,
   And sleepy flowers that wake in the dawn-shine ;
   ' 'Tis Helen's fountain !' let them, wakening, sing.
Here let the summer wanderer ease his ache,
   And on the shadowed grasses sit, and make
   Sweet songs of Helen ; and let him think of me.
Let him who drinketh here a lover be,
   Whose thirst no water's cool enough to slake.
   Water is flame to lovers' ardency.

Afin que ton honneur coule parmi la plaine
   Autant qu'il monte au ciel engravé dans un pin,
   Invoquant tous les Dieux et répandant du vin,
   Je consacre à ton nom cette belle Fontaine.
Pasteurs, que vos troupeaux frisés de blanche laine
   Ne paissent à ces bords ! y fleurisse le thym,
   Et tant de belles fleurs qui s'ouvrent au matin,
   Et soit dite à jamais la Fontaine d'Hélène.
Le passant en été s'y puisse reposer,
   Et assis dessus l'herbe à l'ombre composer
   Mille chansons d'Hélène, et de moi lui souvienne.
Quiconques en boira, qu'amoureux il devienne,
   Et puisse, en la humant, une flamme puiser
   Aussi chaude qu'au cœur je sens chaude la mienne.

Hélène was sufficiently moved by these verses to pro-
pose that she should erect a little marble monument by
her spring, in commemoration of the poet's love. Her
project was never more than a project ; there is no use
looking for her monument today. One may, however,
visit the spring, a cool stone cup under the shadow of
walnut trees. At least a few summer pilgrims have come
there to speak of love. Mme Dussane and M. Roger
Gaillard of the Comédie Française recited Ronsard's
poems by his spring, during the fêtes of the poet's fourth
centenary, in 1924. But perhaps actors do not count,
nor official celebrations of centenaries, with speeches by
the sous-préfet.

The poet returned to the court, and the torturing
intimacy was resumed. There were some happy days.
When the poet could forget his egotism and his coarse
desires he could be the most charming of companions,
and Hélène had her gay and playful mood. She sprinkled
his hair and beard with her face powder, perfumed with
the scent of Cyprus and the Indies. She wove him a
crown of myrtle and laurel, and set it on his brow, say-

ing : 'You shall be my poet, and write for me alone.'
The laurel quivered with his delight. He was sick with
a fever ; she came to see him on his sickbed, and her
glance restored him, as no mortal physician could do.

Calling on her early, he saw her rise from bed. He
caught a glimpse of her rose-and-lily breast, and was in
a transport. He duly delivered a sonnet on that milky
lawn. He was allowed to be present at her toilet, to see
her dark hair, between black and chestnut-color, un-
bound and falling to her feet.

The privileges brought him more troubled nights.
One evening he saw a candle in a neighboring window
put out. 'Would to God,' he exclaimed basely, 'that the
care and grief that Love engraves in my heart might
similarly be extinguished ! I see forever, awake or asleep,
the portrait of my beauty ! It is my hot blood that is to
blame ; my September is more hot than was my happy
June !'

After one warm and cordial evening Hélène yielded
to an unwonted impulse. As Ronsard was taking his
leave, she said, with an air of passion : 'I love you,
Ronsard, by destiny alone. Heaven forces my will to
love you. It is not your knowledge, nor your person, nor
your age, hurrying down the slope of autumn ; it is
neither your body nor your soul ; it is only the unjust
cruelty of heaven. Though I should like to forget you,
I cannot. It is Fate.'

The poet was beside himself with joy, in spite of the
galling words that Hélène contrived to put in her
sweetest declarations.

He was as absurd in love as any boy. Standing on a
stair, he saw her pass below him. The pang of her
beauty almost brought him tumbling down. She gave

him a friendly wave of the hand. Had she failed to do so, he swore, he would have fallen dead.

Again he vowed (it was the first of May) by Castor and Pollux, by the vine enlacing the elm tree, by the green-bristling meadows, by the crystal lap of the streams, and by the nightingales, that Hélène would be his last love.

It was the only vow of amorous fidelity that he ever faithfully kept.

He exacted from Hélène a mutual oath. Together they swore their faith, on a table garlanded with laurel, symbol of eternity. But the sworn words of lovers do not enter the ears of the gods. Hélène was soon false to all her plighted words. She found Ronsard's middle-aged delight importunate and compromising. Her withdrawals evoked his reproaches, and his reproaches her anger. Each found cutting words for the other. Ronsard, in the midst of his cries of passion, would make some tactless, revealing remark. 'When I'm in love,' he said, 'my spirit, utterance, and invention are better, and my Muse more strong. I must therefore love for my wit's sake, to conceive children of the word, to illumine my name at the expense of my heart's ease. What better subject could I choose than the subject which was Homer's joy, Helen, all divine, all virtuous ?'

One may imagine Hélène's response to the suggestion that his love was a form of spiritual hygiene, and Ronsard's bewilderment at her retorts. To his bewilderment succeeded resentment. 'Why can't I free myself from this ridiculous bondage ?' he raged. 'You love me only to have my songs ! My hair is not so gray that I couldn't find another girl who would gladly take your place !'

What could any maid of spirit answer to this ?

There was a three months' quarrel, when neither

spoke. Then Hélène smiled on him, and a sweet recon-
ciliation followed.

It was hopeless, Ronsard knew well. Why did he
waste his time, and the last remainder of his virile days ?
He could find no reasonable answer. It was love's doom
upon him. Clearly he observed his fever increasing, as
her affection dwindled.

His health suffered from the long martyrdom. The
barber-surgeon came to bleed him, and afterward came
Hélène. In the sickroom she caught sight of the bowl
of fresh-drawn blood. She looked at it curiously. 'How
black your blood is !' she exclaimed, smiling. And that
was all, from her who had drained the lively ichor from
his heart. 'If I am to be well and young again,' he
thought, 'I must cease to love !'

She wounded him constantly, with actions that he
took for slights, but which were only the independent
deeds of a woman who considers herself free. She drove
to Arcueil with her girl cousin, and saw a cave which he
had celebrated in rhyme. 'Why did you not ask me to go
with you ? I would have taken little room in your
coach ; I am now no more than a bodiless ghost !' She
promised him a portrait and a lock of her hair ; and
then she forgot, or was too busy. She quitted Paris with
the court on one of its abrupt departures, and left
him no memento of her.

One day he playfully bound her arm with a crimson
ribbon :

> I took a band of crimson silk, to bind
>   Your lovely arm about, in idle play ;
>   I held it captive ; 'twas my only prey.
>   I could not bind your heart, your truant mind.
> My sweet, whom I have worshipped and enshrined,
>   Now this is most unfair of you, I say !

I am a fettered slave beneath your sway,
   While love has left you free and unconfined.
Darling, I'll seek some dark magician's cell,
   Bid him subdue your spirit by a spell,
   Make us both suffer with a single pain.
No, no. Ensorcelled love but brings perdition.
   To be young, handsome, rich, soft-tongued, urbane,
   And not a poet, is to be love's magician.

Je liai d'un filet de soie cramoisie
   Votre bras l'autre jour, parlant avecques vous ;
   Mais le bras seulement fut captif de mes nouds,
   Sans vous pouvoir lier ni cœur ni fantaisie.
Beauté, que pour maîtresse unique j'ai choisie,
   Le sort est inégal : vous triomphez de nous.
   Vous me tenez esclave, esprit, bras, et genoux,
   Et Amour ne vous tient ni prise ni saisie.
Je veux parler, Maîtresse, à quelque vieux sorcier,
   Afin qu'il puisse au mien votre vouloir lier,
   Et qu'une même plaie à nos cœurs soit semblable.
Je faux ; l'amour qu'on charme est de peu de séjour.
   Être beau, jeune, riche, éloquent, agréable,
   Non les vers enchantés, sont les sorciers d'Amour.

He climbed the long spiralling stone stairs of the
Louvre to her room under its high roof. 'At every step
I lose my breath, my pulse hurries, I have sweat on my
brow, and my body quakes, and all to hear your obdurate No, in a voice that is only disdain, chill, and
pride. You are like a goddess, seated in some lofty place,
but I am no god, to mount to your heaven.'

She did not think of him, nor speak of him in his
absence. He knew it well, yet to cajole his own heart, he
pretended that she bore him in her mind, knowing all
the time that he was pretending.

The more he despaired, the more he became urgent
and demanding. 'But why, why,' he pressed, 'will you

not grant me that little boon I ask ? What is there to be afraid of ? Or ashamed of ?'

She murmured something of constancy and honor.

'They are names full of imposture, stupidity invented by our doting fathers, names by which you deny the loveliest gifts of Nature ! You are cheating your sex, insulting it. With an imagined restraint you overmaster your pleasures and desires and your very self, using the law as a vain covering. The law is a trick to catch fools ; I won't thus cheat myself of the true with the false !'

'The true ?' said Hélène. And she told him the truth, in her cool voice. 'It isn't regard for the law that holds me back,' she said, 'nor shame, nor fear, nor respect for the gods, nor any other constraint. It is merely that I have no pleasure in these pastimes. My body is cold by nature. I don't like Venus. I abhor that certain matter ; love's gifts are a poison to me. In short I do not wish to.'

'Why, that's how kings speak !' stormed Ronsard. ' "I do not wish, it is my pleasure, my will be done !" You talk of love readily enough, and draw back before love itself ! The soul without the body is a dream's falsity. In loving the intellect, you fly through empty air to disaster, like Icarus. You love a gray picture void of color. To love the mind, Madam, is to love folly. What is talking of love without doing love, if not to see the sun without loving its light ?'

Hélène, exasperated, said an unforgivable thing. 'If that is the way you feel, why not find some ready trull to ease your body ? Go visit the institution of Jeanne la grise, that you and your like point to so slyly ! I give you my permission !'

All Pierre's anger fell at the terrible words. 'No, you do not love me,' he said. 'Love's shaft has just clipped a little the top of your heart. If love had really touched its goal, the heart would be flame and sulphur. You would suspect your own shadow. Jealous, you would follow me everywhere, all alight with ardor, fury, and fear. Your love is an idle saunterer, it does not ride you at a gallop ! Your love is an amour of the courts, wherein is little fire and much smoke.'

This was the end of their love. After years of intolerable servitude, Ronsard shook himself free. 'In the midst of war, in a faithless time, when lawsuits harass me, is it not a great folly to write of love ? They put handcuffs on madmen who are not so mad as I. What an error, for one gray and sick to trust himself to love's law ! Gods, I cry my thanks to you ! Love is a fury, making its victim a blind, mad child, like love itself ! Wine, my page, wine ! Farewell, my cares, I will no longer lead such a life ! To live without pleasure is to live already buried. Nature gives us woes enough, without our hunting more. Naked I came into this world, and naked I will go out of it. What good are tears, except to fill the heart with everlasting anguish ? With wine let us chase our troubles ; I'm victor over every grief, when wine's my second !'

To cruel Hélène an everlasting farewell. 'I have sung too much of love with no reward. Serve you who will, I am going ; and I think no other squire will serve you better.'

He figured his farewell to Hélène by a ceremony of destruction. With his page he journeyed to the Mont-Valérien, which looks down on Saint-Germain, where the poet had suffered. He built a fire of juniper twigs, and sprinkled it with incense. At his word, the page opened the bag he had brought, and cast upon the sacrificial fire Hélène's gloves, her portrait, and snippets of her hair. He took her letters, tore them into scraps,

and added them to the flames. The bits of paper rose on
the column of heat and fluttered away, birds released
from their cage.

He had another farewell to make : to Love. Love, in
whose employ he had lost his wits and his life ! 'Unhappy he who trusts himself to that deceitful winged
child ! Youth gave him suck, Hot Blood fed him, Pre-
sumption bewitched him, Sloth rotted his spirit, among
joys vain as smoke. Cassandre ravished me, Marie held
me captive, and I, a graybeard at the court, again lost
myself, forgetting that love's ardor is only a bit of flaming straw !'

But the poet, fortunately, possesses an antidote to
love's despair. When love is lost, when all is lost, there
is still literature. Ronsard, making to Hélène the gift
of his heart's blood in sonnet form, had been careful to
keep copies, which were not offered up in the fire with
Hélène's letters. In an edition of his collected verse, in
1578, he published two books of love-poems, the *Sonnets
à Hélène*.

This series represents the idealized Hélène, pure and
untouchable. Some of the songs he had written did not
fit well in such a picture. Some were too intimate, some
were over-urgent summons to love, some revealed too
vividly his amorous dreams, some showed her momentary half-surrender, some reproved too crudely her
body's chill. But these poems the poet could not bear to
sacrifice. He found a device superb in its tactlessness.
After the sections devoted to the Love of Cassandre,
the Love of Marie, the Love of Hélène, he added the
rubric : *Amours diverses*. And here he grouped a set of
wanton songs to nameless and forgotten wantons : the
leering praise of certain nipples and navels, the com-
placent memory of certain ardent kisses in certain happy

bed-chambers. And into the midst of this collection he tossed the sonnets to Hélène excluded from her austere canon. Her name, to be sure, did not appear ; only initiates could identify the poet's love. But there were plenty of initiates at court.

Hélène felt that her poet had introduced her by surprise into a company of drabs and doxies. She was indignant ; she was also a little alarmed. She prized the fame of her marble purity, and she feared that Ronsard, in pique or heedlessness, might cast upon it some indelible stain. A few years later she learned that Ronsard was preparing a new edition of his works, and that he planned to transfer some of the intimate poems from *Amours diverses* to *Sonnets à Hélène*. She appealed to a common friend, Scévole de Sainte-Marthe, to intercede with Ronsard. She wished, apparently, to have the original classification kept, and to have the sonnets of her own series rearranged in chronological order.

Ronsard wrote to Scévole : 'Old friend, it is, as Aristophanes said, an unbearable burden to serve a doting master. Parodizing thereupon, it is a great misfortune to serve a mistress who has no judgment or reason in the matter of our poetry, one who does not know that poets, especially in their trifles like elegies, epigrams, and sonnets, do not keep order and time. That is the business of the historians, who write everything seriatim. I beg you, sir, not to believe therein Mademoiselle de Surgères, and not to add or subtract anything in my sonnets, if you please. If she does not like them, let her leave them, and not bother my head about them.

'They say that the King is coming to Blois and Tours, and therefore I am fleeing to Paris and will be there soon, for I hate the court like death.'

He speaks of Hélène's spring. She was still promising a marble monument for it, perhaps offering it as a fee for Ronsard's compliance with her wishes. His letter continues : 'If she wishes to make some marble design upon the fountain, she may do so. But those are women's proposals, which last only a day. By their nature women are so stingy that they wouldn't spend a crown for a noble deed. Show her this letter if you like. I kiss your hands with all affection. From our Croixval, July fifth. Your humble long-time friend, at your service. RON-SARD.'

So this is the end of all his vows, the end of love ! How often he had warned Hélène that love is wind, and smoke, and a dream !

He made her famous, as he had promised to do. His sonnets were read and re-read at the court ; Catherine de Médicis had her copies almost as soon as Hélène herself. They circulated first in manuscript, then widely in the printed versions.

Ronsard had for a time the advantage in common esteem over his rival, Desportes. He delighted in the re-newal of his popularity, while Hélène was divided be-tween satisfaction and fear that the poet would do some-thing to injure her chaste fame.

Her concern lasted even beyond the poet's death. Some years afterwards a memorial edition of his poems was in preparation. Hélène met Cardinal du Perron, an old friend of Ronsard's, at the Retz salon. She asked him to preface the *Sonnets à Hélène* with a letter, showing that Ronsard did not love her with a shameful love. The caustic Cardinal looked at Hélène's middle-aged face. For the sake of his dead friend he felt a resentment un-seemly in a cardinal. He said : 'In place of this preface, we need only put your portrait !'

So people mocked the one whom Ronsard loved. Whether, in the end, she read again Ronsard's words and regretted her cruel rebuffs, we do not know. Ronsard had prophesied she would, in the great sonnet which boys and girls memorize at school, the sonnet which English poets have loved and imitated :

When you are very old, by candle-glow
   You'll sit and spin beside the fire, and sing
   The songs I made. And you'll say, wondering :
   'Ronsard proclaimed my beauty, long ago !'
Some drowsy, shuffling servant, bending low
   To her dull labor, at my name will spring
   To wakefulness, and praise you who did bring
   A little surcease to the dead poet's woe.
I'll be a ghost, at ease beyond the tomb,
   By the Elysian myrtles' shadowy bloom ;
   You'll be an old and fireside-huddling wife,
Missing my love, rueing your own proud way.
   So wait not till tomorrow, live today,
   And gather in its hour the rose of life.

Quand vous serez bien vieille, au soir, à la chandelle,
   Assise auprès du feu, dévidant et filant,
   Direz, chantant mes vers, en vous émerveillant :
   Ronsard me célébrait du temps que j'étais belle.
Lors vous n'aurez servante oyant cette nouvelle,
   Déjà sous le labeur à demi sommeillant,
   Qui au bruit de Ronsard ne s'aille réveillant,
   Bénissant votre nom de louange immortelle.
Je serai sous la terre, et fantôme sans os ;
   Par les ombres myrteux je prendrai mon repos ;
   Vous serez au foyer une vieille accroupie,
Regrettant mon amour et votre fier dédain.
   Vivez, si m'en croyez, n'attendez à demain ;
   Cueillez dès aujourd'hui les roses de la vie.

Ronsard has kept his promise, for her who would not heed him. He brought something new into French poetry : the illumination of reality with beauty. The sonnets to Hélène are the perfection of Ronsard's poetic achievement, for in them the simplest reality is expressed with the purest art. All his skill was given to finding an exact accord between his emotion and the resources of his language. His success is measured by the emotion which his words still disengage. The sonnets to Hélène have moved innumerable hearts, more than they moved the heart of Hélène.

Hélène lived to a considerable age, cherishing her virginity, which had ceased to be of interest to anyone.

XIII

Age, That Pickpurse Envious

HENRI III, the last of the Valois kings, possessed the perverse charm which clings to last things, the bright flush which hides the secret decay. The stock was rotten. His grandfather, François I, was probably afflicted with the scourge of his century, America's first gift to Europe. The Médicis were no better off; Catherine may have presented Henri II with the red rose of Naples, as the ghoulish phrase ran. Charles IX had fought his weakness by grimly hunting from dawn to dark; Henri III hated the hunt, and accepted weakness with a kind of pride. He had, to be sure, his moments of valor, and proved his gallantry against the Huguenots, on the fields of Jarnac and Moncontour. But his panegyrists repeated endlessly 'Jarnac and Moncontour;' they were hard put to it to find a third example. The new king loved peace, ease, talk, dubious love, and his own person.

He loved his clothes, his jewels; he wore coquettish ear-pendants as well as rings, and fixed pearls in his elaborate coiffure. He introduced neck-ruffs so wide that spoons had to be made with longer handles. He was richly perfumed; his hair was besprent with a powder of violet musk. Such powder was then made with a base of fine starch; one may picture His Majesty crowned with an aureole of flies. He pomaded his face, rouged his cheeks, and dangled a fan. He carried a

bilboquet, a cup-and-ball, to beguile the tedious hours
of duty. He was fond of little dogs, and picked up the
dainty creatures in the streets, even robbed convents
of their dear pets. In the early years of his reign, he enjoyed roaring parties, that took their way from house
to house across Paris. There was a scandal on the first
Sunday of one Lent, when the royal revellers danced till
dawn in the Archbishop's Palace, while the canons were
singing their mass in Notre-Dame.

He loved regally. Among many darlings, there was a
Marie de Clèves, princesse de Condé. When she suddenly died, the king appeared in public with death's
heads decorating his jacket, his points, the ribbons he
used for boot-laces. He wore her cross at his neck, her
drops in his ears. To his courtiers he gave pendants in
the form of a skull.

As he grew older, the court resounded with the king's
scandalous affection for his mignons, the young gentlemen who formed his bodyguard. The mignons, fearing
nothing from public opinion, rivalled their master in
effeminacy. They wore their hair long and elaborately
curled, billowing above tiny feathered hats precariously
perched. Their starched and fluted ruffs were a half-
foot wide, so that, people said, their heads looked like
that of Saint John the Baptist served up on its platter.
Their effeminacy was strangely mixed with bellicosity.
At a word their swords were drawn, and they fought to
the death. It was Henri's constant grief that the duel
took his favorites almost as soon as they had gained
his favor.

His other grief was his impotency. He and his brothers had given no heir to France. Desperately, he made
his appeal to heaven. He joined the penitents, and
walked by torchlight in the processions of flagellants,

wearing a long white sack pierced with eye-holes. He
made pilgrimages to wonder-working shrines; in January he walked from Paris to Chartres, to plead with the
Black Virgin. He was accused of turning in desperation
from the worship of God to that of the Devil, of offering oblations in a demoniac mass.

He was a bad king for his country, this last fingerling
of the race that had ruled France since 1328. His life
was grotesque and not tragic, and even his death was
comical. He was stabbed by a fanatic monk, as he sat on
his *chaise percée*. That was in 1589, when Ronsard had
been dead four years.

He was a bad king, yet somehow he seems more pitiful than evil. He hunted pathetically his happiness, like
the rest of us; and the search brought him more agony
than most of us ever know.

When, in 1574, Henri arrived in Paris to assume his
sceptre, Ronsard turned wearily to the task of celebrat-
ing his new master. He could not retire to his snug
priories; he was held to the courts by his love for
Hélène. He was held also by pride, by his unwilling-
ness to yield to young Desportes. And also by money
troubles. The State, impoverished, imposed cruel bur-
dens on church livings. Ronsard was obliged to sell
some of his vineyards. The upkeep of the conventual
buildings, petty lawsuits, the inefficiency or duplicity of
bailiffs, consumed his profits.

So the poet joined the adulators of the new king, and
endeavored to out-shout the chorus. He had, at least, a
good idea. He proposed to the king that he should become a satirist, and by the power of poetry reform the
kingdom. He would be a bear, biting the false-hearted
courtiers, the prelates who do not visit their churches,

the ravens gorging on the royal treasury, and the shameless, painted dandies of the court.

The king gave no answer.

Ronsard made other efforts. He wrote outrageous
panegyrics, dubbing the king his Apollo, the court a
Delphic temple, and himself a prophet-priest who is
inspired only by the presence of his god. He could
write soberly to his abject master of his 'virtue which
reigns unequalled in the world.' At length the master
heard, and rewarded the poet with an annual pension
of 100 crowns, and an occasional commission for special
festivals. But the king's favors were grudging ; his taste
was for the Italian artifice of Desportes. Ronsard remained a poor second to the young favorite.

The elder poet was grotesquely out of place in this
equivocal court. He despised and mocked the insolent
mignons. His friend D'Aubigné pictures them for us,
waving their arms, making little dance-steps, caressing
their hair, exclaiming : 'My dear ! You're blooming
like a rose ! Are you well treated by your mistress ?
Doesn't the cruel creature surrender to that handsome
face, that curly moustache, that pretty leg ? Why, you
kill me, absolutely !'

Ronsard looked sardonically at the new elegances,
sneering at the costumes of gold and silver, woven with
jewels, at the napkins perfumed with flower sachets. But
he was too much a man of his time to notice the dis-
comfort under the elegance, the crowds that pressed
against his king at dinner, the coldness of the victuals
when they reached the royal table, the littered, unswept
state of the banquet hall.

When summoned, the old laureate did his poetic
duty. He wrote the speeches and devices for the entry
into Tours of François, the younger brother of the king.

For the wedding of the king's sister to the duc de Joyeuse, mignon and admiral of France, Ronsard and Baïf organized the fêtes, the tourneys, the masquerades, the crossing of the Seine in a boat drawn by sea-monsters. Ronsard, Baïf, and the musicians divided 2,000 crowns, their share of the total expenditure, estimated at 1,200,000 crowns.

During these years, in sum, the poet was little in evidence at court. He frequented a Paris society more to his liking. He gave up his *maison de l'ange* by the walls, and took quarters in the Collège de Boncourt, of which his friend Jean Galland was principal. Boncourt was one of that nest of semi-independent schools which made up the University of Paris. Here the students lived and pursued the ordinary course of their studies. Ronsard dined with the scholars and their masters, and with them walked daily in the college garden. He delighted them with his learned and fantastic speech, and with his extempore verse translations of Vergil and Horace. And they affectionately cared for the old poet, their Apollo come from Parnassus, during his painful attacks of gout, and they protected him from the fatiguing enthusiasm of the curious.

To Boncourt came his old friends of better days : Baïf, Dorat, Tyard, Villeroy, Passerat. Younger friends also, worshipping poets, like Claude Binet, and Davy du Perron, the king's reader, destined for political greatness and the cardinal's hat. Still unencumbered by the cassock, Du Perron delighted Ronsard by his splendid broad-jumps. 'That isn't jumping, it's flying !' cried the poet, clapping his hands in the Boncourt garden.

For a time he had a leading part in the meetings of the Academy, successor to the first French Academy of Baïf. King Henri took an interest in its reorganization,

summoned it to semi-weekly meetings in the Louvre,
filled its ranks with mignons of literary pretension.
There were several lady Academicians, Mme de Retz
among them. The present Académie Française has forgotten this precedent.

The king cared less for poetry and music than for
philosophical moralizing. His Academy subserviently
followed his taste, modelling its meetings on those of the
Florentine Platonic Academy.

Ronsard had the honor of pronouncing the official
discourse at the opening meeting in 1576. The question
for discussion, proposed by the king himself, was
whether intellectual or moral virtues are the more excellent and necessary. Ronsard chose the moral virtues,
for, he said, it is better to enjoy the sun than to know
the causes of its heat ; it is better to live than to specu-
late about life. Philippe Desportes rose to make the
rebuttal. He defended pure contemplation, wisdom better than life. This was the king's side and the side of
the sensible courtier.

The Academy continued its sessions, discussing anger,
ambition, honor, envy, fear. At the king's command,
Ronsard spoke of envy. Before long attendance dwindled, and the king found other more pressing engage-
ments, and the Academy quietly ceased to be.

Ronsard was probably bored, with the rest. He had
no great liking for abstract discussion, and still less liking for a contest in which others could outdo him. It
cut him to observe that even his good Amadis Jamyn
played the new game better than the Prince of Poets.
He laughed at the sighing Italianisms of his disciple.
To Mlle de Fontaines, dangling her fan, Jamyn exclaimed metrically : 'Is it to refresh my spirit's coals
that you make a sweet wind with your fan, or do you

wish to rouse my passion to a great roaring flame ?' In the giddy applause the elder poet could add only a perfunctory word. He had been absurd in his time, but he had devoted his artistic life to escaping the absurd, to hunting down reality. He could not, for fashion's sake, deny his lifetime's development.

The world was escaping him. He received the honor due to a relic of the past, not the ecstatic response that shows more in the eyes than on the lips. In aged spite he wrote that 'that vulgar mob, which I could never satisfy, nor ever wished to, angered me so by its yapping that our language is the less embellished as a result.' Unconvincingly, he proclaimed that he would fain be nameless and unrenowned, like a plowman with yoked oxen, upturning the fallow land to sow wheat there. He remembered an old cruel prediction of Cassandre's : 'You will become the fable of the mob ; you will build on the uncertainty of sand, and in vain will paint your colors on the sky.'

It was time for him to retire, with what grace he could. Not only was his own fame dulled by time, but the high pretensions of the Pléiade had come to nothing. Poetry had not gained the divine estate it had held among the Greeks, nor had the poet become a demigod in the world's eyes. After all the Pléiade had done to ennoble poetry, Desportes and his kind had returned to the sycophantic trifling of Mellin de Saint-Gelais. They were denying the Muse, degrading her, befouling her robes. Thus they were degrading themselves. Indeed, a chronicler wrote, a few years later : 'So many little abortions of poetry appeared that the time came when the commonalty, wishing to mock a man, called him "poet." '

Paris and the court became intolerable to the old

singer. He said : 'Here in these darkened days life is only fard, hypocrisy, brigandage, apostasy, error, and fraud. The Turk lives better than do we.' War was imminent, not the gallant wars of the past, when Venus toyed with the moustachios of Mars, but hateful civil war. The court was the home of unspeakable evil, where Ronsard toiled for no reward. He was harassed by lawsuits. And he was ill, with the slow torture of gout. His heart was no less tortured, by the cool passivity of Hélène.

The news he had was all of death. Marie was dead, in far-away Anjou. Of the old Pléiade, Du Bellay was gone, and Étienne Jodelle, and Olivier de Magny, and Jacques Grévin. Muret was exiled in Rome ; others of the jolly band of Coqueret lived in distant towns, or had turned Protestant and disavowed the Muse, or had disappeared. In March 1577 gentle Rémy Belleau died, and was carried to the tomb by Ronsard, Baïf, Jamyn, and Desportes.

He had out-stayed his time. After the accession of Henri III, after the melancholy renunciation of Hélène, Ronsard retreated more and more to his Vendômois, where he had an unfailing welcome from the land that had borne him, that would soon serenely receive him again.

Solitary Croixval was now his favorite home. Here he happily assisted at the mass, wearing his great cope, from which his head emerged like a snail from its shell. He retreated then to the treasury of his books, assembled one by one, with love, during his lifetime.

He had about him beautiful objects, in which the past was caught. Gifts of the great, and dearer gifts of friends, like the blue glass goblet presented by Jean Brinon, now long dead. He had a portrait of Mary

Queen of Scots, representing her in the long lovely folds
of her widow's weeds. And a buffet worth two thousand
crowns, which the unhappy queen had sent him from
her captivity, with a vase carved to represent Parnassus
and a flying Pegasus, and inscribed : 'To Ronsard, the
Apollo of the Muses' Spring.' Looking at these memen-
toes, he could see again Mary herself, slipping in her
white dress under the gray shadows of Fontainebleau.
He remembered the story of her boy-poet in Scotland,
Chastelard, who died for love of her, who carried Ronsard's book to the scaffold, and read the *Hymne de la
Mort* as his preparation for eternity. '*Je te salue, heureuse et profitable Mort,*' Chastelard had murmured before his head fell.

Ronsard treasured also the diamond sent him by
Mary's enemy, Queen Elizabeth of England, to whom
he had dedicated his *Élégies et Mascarades*. And a picture of a horse, which sometimes waked him by whinny-
ing in his dreams. And a ribboned, pear-shaped lute
with carven head, cracked like his own old voice.

His pleasure was in memory, and in the observation
of nature. Love was over ; he would love no more. The
thought of the past pains of love had lost all bitterness.
He recalled old joy and suffering tenderly, with a voluptuous delight, even while he rejoiced in his escape
from love's subjection.

I feel the chill of age ; my watered blood is frore,
The ardent thoughts of youth warm my old heart no more ;
No more the yoke of love shall hold imprisonèd
   My grizzled head.
I was Love's trooper once, in my young April's day ;
I bore her gonfalon gallantly to the fray.
The banner now I come to hang on Venus' altar,
   With steps that falter.

No more I'll hear the words that rapture and cajole :
'My life ; my very blood ; my eyes ; my own dear soul !'
They are for lovers' use, whose blood, hot-humored, beats
   With the heart's heats.
I'll find another fire, to keep my breast aglow.
A scholar to the earth, Nature I'll seek to know.
I'll watch the way of the stars, the troubled course they trace
   Through the void space.
My sonnets, then, adieu ! My songs of old desire,
Adieu ! Adieu, the dance, the music of the lyre !
And shafts of love, adieu ! Fly otherwhere, depart
   From Ronsard's heart !
I will be all my own, I'll serve no other one ;
No man can do him hurt who subject is to none.
I'll banish all the cares that trouble and torment,
   And find content.

    Mon âge et mon sang ne sont plus en vigueur,
    Les ardents pensers ne m'échauffent le cœur,
    Plus mon chef grison ne se veut enfermer
       Sous le joug d'aimer.
    En mon jeune avril, d'Amour je fus soudard,
    Et vaillant guerrier portai son étendard ;
    Ores à l'autel de Vénus je l'appends
       Et forcé me rends.
    Plus ne veux ouïr ces mots délicieux :
    Ma vie, mon sang, ma chère âme, mes yeux !
    C'est pour les amants à qui le sang tressaut
       Autour du cœur chaud.
    Je veux d'autre feu ma poitrine échauffer,
    Connaître Nature et bien philosopher,
    Du monde savoir et des astres le cours,
       Retours et détours.
    Donc, sonnets, adieu ! adieu, douces chansons !
    Adieu, danse ! adieu, de la lyre les sons !
    Adieu, traits d'amour ! volez en autre part
       Qu'au cœur de Ronsard.
    Je veux être à moi, non plus servir autrui ;
    Pour autrui ne veux me donner plus d'ennui ;

Il faut essayer, sans plus me tourmenter,
De me contenter.

He vowed to devote himself to the study of Nature, as, in fact, he had always done, but as now he could do with perfect tranquillity of spirit. He watched the summer come in, 'Summer, prince of the year, child of the Sun, maker of all life, kind Father, wheat-giver, wine-giver, male, perfect, entire, all-great, all-divine, cinct with rays, guide of the Sun who at daybreak holds his horses curbed ; desired by men, wheat-crowned, who dost mark men's years, who dost forge thunderbolts and lightning-shafts, mariner, voyager, courier, warrior.' With the autumn the poet watched the labors and jollities of the harvest, of the vintage. He joked with the peasants, who stood in no awe of him, and no longer in fear of his lordly ways with maids in bloom. He catalogued their rakes, pitchforks, winnowing-fans, sheaves, baskets, and the sacks of wheat stacked on the threshing-floor. He described their labors, how some, stripped to the waist, beat with their flails on the hard ground, while others, in a steady rhythm, carried the filled sacks to the granary, under the golden dust eddying in air.

He made a pretense of writing poems for them, adopting their simplicity. He wrote a litany for husbandmen to sing to Monsieur Saint Blaise, to the tune of *Te rogamus audi nos* :

> Holy Father, save our flocks
> From the colic, from the pox,
> From the hoven, tick, and rot ;
> Grant their fleece be ravelled not
> By the thorny bush and tree ;
> Hear us as we pray to thee.
>   Grant that on the fieldward way
> Wicked thieves may not waylay

Tender lamb and silly ewe ;
Guard them from the viper, too,
And the adder's knavery.
Hear us, as we pray to thee.

    Save us from the sun's excess,
From the winter's bitterness ;
Temper rain and temper shine
To the wheat and to the vine,
From the scab and mildew free ;
Hear us, as we pray to thee.

    Garde nos petits troupeaux,
Laines entières et peaux,
De la ronce dentelée,
De tac et de clavelée,
De morfonture et de tous :
Je te prie, écoute-nous.

    Garde qu'en allant aux champs,
Les larrons qui sont méchants
Ne dérobent fils ni mère :
Garde-les de la vipère,
Et d'aspics au ventre roux :
Je te prie, écoute-nous.

    Garde-nous de trop d'ardeurs,
Et d'excessives froideurs :
Donne-nous la bonne année,
Force blés, force vinée,
Sans fièvres, rogne, ni clous :
Je te prie, écoute-nous.

In his youth he had loved the hunt, and had kept his
own bird-dogs. He had described their strategy lovingly,
how they seem to have man's reason, sniffing the fields,
advancing toward the victim with tiny tense steps, then
standing immobile with paw uplifted and tail stiff. Now
the poet's gout forbade him such sport. He could still,
however, fish his streams. He confesses that he loved to
trouble the secret dwellings of the waters and pull forth
on quivering line the credulous fish. Such a trophy

made him happier than a prince could be, who struck down a panting stag, hunted a whole day through.

He was happier still in his garden, among his flowers. He had always loved them, and had delighted in listing them, recording their qualities, recalling the beautiful myths with which the Greeks had adorned the earth's adornments. When he describes a rustic spring, he decorates its borders profusely with the wild lily, the rose, the pink, the russet marigold, the fragrant wild thyme, the blue gladiolus, the tall foxglove, the Easter daisy, the gillyflower, the cockscomb, and the narcissus which lives but two days, and that April flower which is known by the name of the satyrs, and that other flower, the primula, which Juno created.

As much as the flowers, he loved the birds, and called on God to bless them. He watched the skylark, shaking the dew from his wings in the fields at dawn, and rising into the air with great leaps, singing madly the while. By night he listened to the nightingale, his rival, lamenting of love in his garden, on all the innumerable notes of sorrow.

He observed the busy little lives about him : the frogs, the wasps, the wild bees that hid their honey in the pitted pillars of the caves. He watched the big-bellied spider working in the dawn, attaching the first stays of her web, then running to and fro to form the perfect parallels of the cross-webbing. He watched the ants on his garden path. How pleasant it is to see their troop marching to the common task ! One carries a grain of wheat, and one a grain of barley, clasping it with the forelegs or dragging it painfully. They journey in single file along their elaborate roads, carrying the winter's food to their secret storehouses. Each has his

station and his duty ; their commonwealths are organized with laws, princes, and kings.

All the multitudinous activity of his fields he celebrated, with love.

However purely French was his Vendômois, the Nature that the poet saw was still clad in Greek robes. He
never lost his power to see the nymphs and fauns hiding
in the mottled shadows. They were as real to him as the
earth-colored peasants. His faith became a simple pan-
theism. All the universe was alive, and thus a part of
God ; and all the life of the world merged with a hidden
beauty, which took Greek forms to the rare perceiving
eye.

He suffered at every offense to beauty. His feudal
lord, the duc de Vendôme, who was at the same time
the famous King Henry of Navarre, lightly ordered that
great tracts of his woodland should be cut over and the
wood sold. King Henry did not know nor care that this
marketable timber was the very Forest of Gastine where
Ronsard, from boyhood to age, had wantoned with the
dryads. Nor did he care for the great poem which the
poet wrote in his affliction, calling down imprecations
on the master's head, and pleading in vain with the
hired assassin :

Hold, woodsman, hold awhile your lusty blow !
This is no lifeless thing that you bring low !
Why, that is blood upon the flying chips !
With blood of wounded Nymphs your axe-head drips !
Murderer, if we hang on gallows-tree
A thief for some poor gimcrack larceny,
What expert agony, by the torturer's knife,
Do you deserve, who take a Goddess' life !

Écoute, Bûcheron, arrête un peu le bras !
Ce ne sont pas des bois que tu jettes à bas :

Ne vois-tu pas le sang lequel dégoutte à force
Des Nymphes qui vivaient dessous la dure écorce?
Sacrilège meurtrier, si on pend un voleur
Pour piller un butin de bien peu de valeur,
Combien de feu, de fers, de morts et de détresses
Mérites-tu, méchant, pour tuer des Déesses?

Inconsolable, Ronsard bade farewell to the ancient oaks and the banished spirits. *Que l'homme est malheureux qui au monde se fie!*

He strained his eyes to see the loveliness which he could not now see long. He glutted his spirit with beauty. 'Don't you see the nymphs,' he wrote to a friend, 'in these painted and enamelled fields, plucking with dainty fingers the flowers, which should have been the spoil of the pretty bees, hovering from furrow to furrow, from garden to garden, with the butterflies, who in their little fluttering flights prudently amass the odors of the springtime flowers? Let this teach us not to defraud our years of all their usufruct, my friend. For here comes Death, old sour-faced Death, attended by her train of woes.'

Voici la Mort qui vient, la vieille rechignée,
D'une suite de maux toujours accompagnée.

In the observation of Nature and of all the earnest concerns of life, busy under its doom, he gained at last serenity. He forgot Paris and his long struggle for advantage; he took root again in his native soil. An old peasant pagan strain reappears in his work: love of earth's beauty, a sense of identity with Nature. This is a quality rare in French poetry.

He was surely happy. Far from the slights and forgetfulness of the courts, he had the affection of some time-tested friends, and the esteem of simple people about

him. They honored him still as the Prince of Poets ;
they did not know how changing fashions had injured
his courtly fame. They sang his songs, often ignorant
that he was the author. He learned with much satisfaction that as far away as Brittany, minstrels would recite
a lay of Tristan de Léonnois or an ode of that great poet
Ronsard. Much as he affected to scorn the vulgar mob,
he dreamt still of a national fame and of the applause
of posterity.

Long since he had taken as his device the proud words
of Horace :

> *Si fractus illabatur orbis*
> *Impavidum ferient ruinae.*

'Though the stricken world collapse, its ruins shall fall
upon me, standing dauntless.' Thus he imagined himself, dauntless in a stricken world. To us, he may seem,
rather, a pitiful, vain old man, the more pitiful in his
elderly happiness than in his youthful woes. There is
something very tender about happiness ; something
that moves to tears.

XIV

A Poet's End

'I SEE the winter's storms at hand,' wrote Ronsard to his friend Villeroy. 'It's high time to say farewell to poetry and love. I have lived so well that now, as I depart, I have no envy of life's pleasures. I have enjoyed them all, playing my part on life's stage. I have seen the day break, and evening fall, I've seen hail and thunderstorm, the rain and the clearing, I've seen peoples and kings; and for twenty years I have seen France in agony. I have seen wars, and wordy battles, and truce and peace, and compacts promised, unmade, and made again, then unmade and made once more. I have seen that all under the moon is chance, depending on Fortune's whim. Vainly is prudence the guide of men; invincible destiny chains her hands, holding her captive; and of all we sagely dispose, fortune otherwise disposes. I go now glutted with the world, as some guest goes surfeited from a wedding banquet, or from a royal feast, with never a frown if another crowds him from his place. I have run the flambeau-race; now I'm ready to pass the torch to another runner. There's no cause for anger; it's Nature's law, enjoined upon every creature at his birth.'

His spirit was serene, while gathering ills assailed his body. In August 1583 he excused himself from attending a provincial church council on the ground of daily fevers and pains of the bowels. His gout had become a constant, painful rheumatism. The body's distresses made him restless ; he distracted his mind by frequent removes from priory to priory, or from the country to Paris. In the winter of 1583-4 he visited Jean Galland, his μονοφιλούμενος, his solely loved, his second soul, in the friendly shelter of the Collège de Boncourt. Galland carried his guest from his carriage to bed. Later, Ronsard recovered enough to take little walks, leaning on Galland's ready arm. The wet Paris winter did him no good. When at Easter he communicated, he insisted on dragging himself on his knees from his seat to the altar.

He was held in Paris by delightful business. During his stay he published the definitive edition of his work, a noble and beautiful folio, with all Ronsard printed large, in two wide columns on an ample page. 'Like a Bible of the poetry of his time,' says Pierre Champion. No French poet had ever been printed so fine. As his author's rights, Ronsard demanded of his publisher sixty crowns, 'to buy wood to warm himself next winter with his friend Gallandius.' This was the only money he ever received directly for the sale of his works.

Immediately after Easter he had himself transported to Croixval, to see the coming in of the new season. With the sunshine and the flowers, and the green salads of his garden, some measure of health returned to him. He could sit tranquilly out of doors, watching the birds and the insects. He could write, and endlessly revise his old poems, and read. He returned, as we do in age, to the favorite writers of his youth. Especially to Vergil, 'the first captain of the Muses,' whom he had read as a page in windy Holyrood, whom he read again with a page's emotion in placid Croixval.

Occasionally he received a new book of poems from his Paris bookseller. He had no good to say of his young

rivals. 'Most of those who write in our time drag nerve-
less on the earth's floor, like caterpillars, which have not
yet the strength to climb to the tree-tops, and are content to feed on the base humors of the soil, without trying the food of the high branches, which they cannot
reach because of their witlessness. Others are too bombastic, swollen up almost as with a dropsy. They think
that nothing is excellent unless it is extravagant and
inflated, full of monstrous visions and snorting words,
which resemble rather thieves' slang or gypsy jargon
than the speech of an honest, educated citizen. If you
try to take their poems apart, you get nothing out of
them but wind, no more than from a pig's bladder full
of peas, which children bang about for a toy.'

His strictures might be set down to spite, or to the
natural artistic conservatism of his years, were it not
that all calm critics of today agree with him.

He seems to have had no personal grudge against
these unworthy poets. One of them was no doubt his
own Jamyn, who had now quitted his master's service
to pursue his own career in Paris. (Ronsard must put
up with an ignorant, exasperating secretary.) Even
toward Desportes, the supplanter, Ronsard showed no
jealousy, speaking of him rather with esteem.

In February of 1585 Ronsard revisited Paris. The
thickness of the Paris vapors renders its winters ca-
tarrhal, said the doctors, as they say still, in modern
terms. His rheumatism kept him fast in bed and denied
him the solace of sleep. He prayed to Mercury to cure
his insomnia, during the long winter nights.

For the return journey he had a coach specially built.
Private carriages, though rare and costly luxuries, gave
little comfort to the occupants. The clumsy springs
could not much ease the rocking and plunging of the

vehicle on roads almost untended since the Romans had
left. Mud and water lay deep in innumerable pot-holes ;
a moment's distraction of the driver was likely to mean
a broken axle, and even broken bones.

In June the arduous journey was made. Galland accompanied the poet to Croixval, and thence for a visit
to Saint-Cosme. On returning to Croixval, Ronsard
deeded to his friend his rights to the priories of Croixval, Saint-Gilles, and Saint-Guingalois, in near-by Châ-
teau-du-Loir.

Galland returned to his school duties from his summer vacation, and Ronsard remained in Croixval.

On October 22, Ronsard wrote to Galland that he
had been ill a fortnight ; he was very thin, very weak,
only an inert weight upon the earth, *iners terrae pondus*.
He feared that he would go with the falling leaves. But
better sooner than later ; and God's will be done. He
begged Galland to rejoin him soon ; the friend's presence would be the best medicine.

His suffering increased. His stomach pains prevented
him from sleeping. He summoned the curé of Ternay,
dressed and rose from bed, heard mass with great de-
voutness, communicated, and announced that he re-
pented of his sinful past, and hoped soon for a better
life in a better world. When he was undressed and put
to bed, he said : 'Here I am in bed, awaiting death, the
term and common passage of the best-lived life. When
it pleases God to call me, I am ready to go.'

He could not stay quiet. He insisted on being re-
moved the six miles to Saint-Gilles, to pass the Day of
All Saints. There Galland joined him, on October 30.
The two wept together, for Galland was beyond speech.
On All Souls' Day, the Day of the Dead, he demanded

to be carried back to Croixval. Pain and death's approach had not silenced the poet in him. He made for Galland an address to his own soul, an imitation of the delicious *animula blandula, vagula, hospes comesque corporis* which Emperor Hadrian wrote at Baiae, a few days before his death :

> *Âmelette Ronsardelette,*
> *Mignonnelette, doucelette,*
> *Très chère hôtesse de mon corps :*
> *Tu descends là-bas faiblelette,*
> *Pâle, maigrelette, seulette,*
> *Dans le froid royaume des morts :*
> *Toutefois simple, sans remords*
> *De meurtre, poison, ou rancune,*
> *Méprisant faveurs et trésors*
> *Tant enviés par la commune.*
> *Passant, j'ai dit, suis ta fortune,*
> *Ne trouble mon repos, je dors.*

It is a poem which our own bleak language, with its lack of affectionate toying diminutives, is powerless to render.

He prayed for sleep, for rest, even rest in death. Insomnia tortured him, though he drank the juice of the poppy and chewed its opiate leaves. No torture could prevent him from observing his own gradual dwindling, and turning it to poetic use. He wrote his epitaph :

> *Ronsard repose ici, qui hardi dès l'enfance*
> *Détourna d'Hélicon les Muses en la France,*
> *Suivant le son du luth et les traits d'Apollon :*
> *Mais peu valut sa Muse encontre l'aiguillon*
> *De la Mort, qui cruelle en ce tombeau l'enserre :*
> *Son âme soit à Dieu, son corps soit à la terre.*

And he dictated several sonnets, tragic and beautiful, the dreadful picture of his dissolution :

I am no more than bones, a skeleton
  Which the thin crust of flesh does not disguise.
  In my arms' gauntness I can recognize
Death's dispositions, grim to look upon.
Doctor Apollo and his doctor son
  Can cure me not, and all their trade is lies.
  Farewell, sweet sun ; the film is on my eyes ;
It's but a moment to oblivion.
What is the friend who sees me thus bestead,
  And comes to kiss me on my tortured bed,
  And does not weep, with heart and voice unsteady ?
Wipe me the eyes death's preparations blear.
  Adieu, dear friends ; adieu, companions dear ;
  I shall go first to make the mansion ready.

Je n'ai plus que les os, un squelette je semble,
  Décharné, dénervé, démusclé, dépulpé,
  Que le trait de la mort sans pardon a frappé ;
Je n'ose voir mes bras que de peur je ne tremble.
Apollon et son fils, deux grands maîtres ensemble,
  Ne me sauraient guérir, leur métier m'a trompé ;
  Adieu, plaisant Soleil, mon œil est étoupé,
Mon corps s'en va descendre où tout se désassemble.
Quel ami me voyant en ce point dépouillé
  Ne remporte au logis un œil triste et mouillé,
  Me consolant au lit et me baisant la face,
En essuyant mes yeux par la mort endormis ?
  Adieu, chers compagnons, adieu, mes chers amis,
  Je m'en vais le premier vous préparer la place.

In mid-December he was seized by a feverish desire to
see again his priory of Saint-Cosme. Out of all reason
he ordered that the remove should be made, and such
was the force of his will that his companions yielded.
His friend Davy du Perron tells of that cruel winter
journey : 'He had himself dressed, all crippled and
paralyzed as he was, and had himself carried to his
coach, like a log of wood, like a statue, without moving
or stirring, and without any other consciousness of life

than his feeling of pain. The weather was so bad that there was no reasonableness in starting off on a journey, if one were the healthiest man on earth. In fact he had to defer his trip, and wait till the bad weather was past. That was the catastrophe of the tragedy ; for he would not permit himself to be undressed, out of apprehension of the pain he would have to suffer in being dressed again ; so that he had to remain three days and nights thus clothed. On the fourth day, as he could no longer have the patience to wait further, he commanded that his coach should be made ready at two hours before dawn. And having set out through the country in the wind and rain, he did so little on this first stage that he spent the night only a league away. So that having spent five or six such days to cover the few leagues that remained, he arrived finally at Saint-Cosme on a Sunday, at about five in the afternoon.'

The effort had been too great for his racked body. For several days he lay half conscious in his priory, while the Loire flowed brown with its winter waters, while the bare willows swayed above the field where he had danced with Marie. On Thursday, the day after Christmas, he roused himself, and commanded that a monk should take down two sonnets from his dictation. The first was a great trumpet-call to his soul :

Quoi mon âme, dors-tu engourdie en ta masse ?
La trompette a sonné, serre bagage, et va
Le chemin déserté que Jésus-Christ trouva
Quand tout mouillé de sang racheta notre race. . . .

The second was a farewell to life and a welcome to death.

He bade the monk read what he had written ; and hearing some foolish errors repeated aloud, he fell into a deep discouragement.

The end was clearly near. On Friday, at a turn for the worse in his condition, the community was summoned. The chaplain of Saint-Cosme, a venerable priest, asked Ronsard in what resolution he wished to die. The poet answered, a little sharply : 'Have I not sufficiently made my will known here, and the purpose of my faith, so that one may judge how I would live and die ?'

The chaplain explained that he wished only to know if the sick man had any last wishes to express. Ronsard then spoke in an edifying way of his past errors and present repentance. He recognized that he had been a sinner, like all men, nay a greater sinner than most ; that he had let himself be gulled by the charms of sense, and had not sufficiently repressed and chastised them. He adjured his hearers to believe as he believed, not to live as he had lived. Then, noticing their tears, he begged them not to weep, at seeing him in his extremity, but to deplore their own condition, still being bound to languish after his departure. For the world was a perpetual agitation, torment, shipwreck, a sea and a confusion of sins, tears, and griefs, and the only haven from all these misfortunes and miseries was death. As for him, he had no further any desire nor any regret in life, he had tried all its false and pretended felicities, and had overlooked nothing that might have brought him the slightest shadow of content, but at the end he had found only the oracle of the sage : Vanity of vanities !

He asked that mass should be celebrated before him. He received the sacraments, and waited with great constancy and resolution for whatever disposition God might make.

He turned his face to the wall, and remained in a

torpor for about an hour. He then roused himself, and tried to speak. His words were so troubled that he asked a watching friend to nudge and check him if he should babble. These were the poet's last words : a summons to the critic to order his phrases. His final thought, properly, was given to art.

He let his head fall upon the pillow, and died.

His death was not such as he had prayed for, in his young manhood :

> I hail thee, happy, profitable Death,
> Sovereign physic for the pain of breath !
> When my time comes, Goddess, I ask of thee,
> Let me not languish long in malady,
> Tormented on a bed. Since thou art sure,
> Let me find suddenly my sepulture,
> Guarding God's honor, fighting for my king,
> My blood upon my own earth issuing.

Not for God's sake nor his king's, but tormented on a bed, he came at last to Death, whose image had obsessed him all his life. In a way, he had loved the thought of death, as much as he had loved roses and love and life. Death was only a change of form, he had insisted, and the change would surely be for the better. In the land beyond death, the woes of earth would be ended. Telephus would feel no more the wound he had received from Achilles, when Dionysus perfidiously tripped him ; and Achilles would feel no more the blows of Paris, nor would Hector feel anything at all, nor his brother Troilus. They would be happy in death, and Ronsard would be happy too. For his heaven showed Christ's cross over the great entry gate, but within the park was Elysium, was Greece. In his dreams, Paradise was filled with flitting nymphs and fauns ; it had the look of the Forest of Gastine.

The men of the Renaissance understood him. At a memorial service for Ronsard in the Collège de Boncourt chapel, Davy du Perron spoke the funeral oration (after a special requiem mass composed for the occasion by Mauduit). Said Du Perron : 'Now Pan is dead, and the oracles have ceased, and the Muses are abandoned !'

In the Christian church the clerics lamented their Christian Pan, as the goat-foot satyrs had lamented on the Aegean island. The speaker's comparison was uncommonly apt. Ronsard was the woodland god, the adorer of Nature. Hooves peeped out beneath his surplice. Pagan and Christian, base appetite and pure spirit, poet and self-seeking courtier, he was Pan, the union of animal and deity in man.

Ronsard was buried before the altar of his church of Saint-Cosme. His friends celebrated him lavishly in Latin, Greek, French, and Italian verse. Galland succeeded comfortably to his friend's priories. But no one took it on himself to mark the master's grave. Before many years its situation was forgotten. During the Revolution the property was sold for a farm, and the chapel became a barn. Horses stamped above the poet's bones. Some time in the nineteenth century the roof fell in, and the rains set about their long task of transformation. *La matière demeure, et la forme se perd.* But in 1932 that admirable organization, the *Sauvegarde de l'Art Français,* bought the crumbling remains of the priory. A search was made for the skeleton of Ronsard. It was found in the spot indicated by old records and identified beyond question. The second cervical vertebra still bears the tell-tale marks of arthritis.

The fame of Ronsard has suffered a fate curiously

similar to that of his bones. Soon after his death his reputation was submerged by that of newcomers. When his friends had died there were none to praise him, even to read him. Boileau, in his mid-seventeenth-century *Art Poétique,* spoke with brief, uncomprehending scorn of Ronsard's Muse, which in French spoke Greek and Latin. The posterity to which the poet had appealed so confidently seemed determined to defraud him. Only in the nineteenth century was he disinterred by Sainte-Beuve.

Now his fame stands secure. He was the greatest lyric poet of France before the coming of the nineteenth-century Romantics. With all his bathos, his pretension, his absurdity, his lack of profound philosophy, he was a poet. Only a poet could write such lines as these :

> *Ces longues nuits d'hiver, où la lune endormie*
> *Tourne si lentement son char tout à l'entour . . .*
>
> *L'absence, ni l'oubli, ni la course du jour . . .*
>
> *Les bois . . .*
> *Dont l'ombrage incertain lentement se remue.*
>
> *Je te salue, heureuse et profitable Mort,*
> *Des extrêmes douleurs médecin et confort.*

The wonderfulness of such lines is inexplicable. We can only say : 'These are touchstone lines. Whatever is like this is poetry. The men of the Renaissance were surely not far wrong when they termed the writer the Prince of Poets.'

He was their Prince, and the incarnation of their ideal. The Renaissance, the New Birth, was one of the recurring springtimes of history. Men had the sense of new things beginning, in art, faith, and life. In spite of the storms about them, and the mischief of their days, they felt that they were preparing the high summer to come.

I write these pages at the end of a northern winter. The snows still lie deep, and the brooks are roofed with ice. But as I write of Ronsard, my mind is full of the spring. He was the poet of the opening rose, of first love, of simple gayety and song, of the jocund wisdom of the Greeks, of Nature and her beauty. If, under all, was the terror of beauty's brevity and the knowledge of inevitable death, he kept the assurance of another spring to follow. This is a happy thought for our own winter.